ACCOUNTING THOUGHT AND PRACTICE THROUGH THE YEARS

Edited by Richard P. Brief

A Garland Series

LAW AND ACCOUNTING
Pre-1889 British Legal Cases

Jean Margo Reid

Garland Publishing, Inc.
New York and London
1986

For a complete list of Garland's publications in accounting,
please see the final pages of this volume.

Library of Congress Cataloging-in-Publication Data

Law and accounting.

(Accounting thought and practice through the years)
Includes index.
1. Accounting—Law and legislation—Great Britain—
Cases.   I. Reid, Jean Margo.   II. Series.
KD2042.A52L38   1986   346.41'063'0264   86-9949
ISBN 0-8240-7871-3   344.106630264

Design by Bonnie Goldsmith

The volumes in this series are printed on acid-free, 250-year-life paper.

Printed in the United States of America

Acknowledgments

I would like to thank Richard P. Brief for suggesting that these early legal cases might be a fruitful area of research. In addition, I thank Nayan V. Kisnadwala, who helped me obtain good copy of this material and who also took charge of producing the camera-ready manuscript.

Jean Margo Reid
New York
January 1986

CONTENTS

Introduction

INTRODUCTION

This book contains edited versions of thirty British legal cases involving accounting issues decided from 1849 to 1888. These cases are a valuable source of information about the development of accounting principles and practices in nineteenth-century Great Britain.

Lee has pointed out that "too little is known of accounting methods in the Victorian era. The generalisations that can be made rest mainly upon textbooks and manuals, most of which appeared after 1880."[1] The accounting literature of the period includes *The Accountant*, which began publication in 1874; Pixley's 1881 *Auditors: Their Duties and Responsibilities*, which appears to rely extensively on early judicial decisions; Dicksee's *Auditing* (1892) and *Accounting Theory* (1903); and other texts. While accounting historians have studied these texts as well as surviving accounting records,[2] company legislation, and the records of hearings before Parliament,[3] nineteenth-century case law in the pre-1889 period has received relatively little attention.[4]

Several steps were taken to identify all of the pre-1889 legal cases in which accounting issues arose. First, since no bibliography of cases with accounting content exists in legal indexes or elsewhere, relevant digests of British case law were reviewed. These include *Bacon's Abridgement* (1897, 1868), *Mews Digest* (1884, 1898), *The English and Empire Digest* (1975), *Jacob's and Fisher's Digest* (1883, 1886), *Harrison's Digest* (1846), and *Wares Law Reports Digest of Cases 1865–1880* (1882) and *Law Reports Digest of Cases 1880–1885* (1886). Since there were no listings for "profits" or "accounting and the law," topics under "company," "partnership," and "principal and agent" were searched. To illustrate the search problem, hundreds of cases were reviewed to determine whether, for example, a decision regarding director fraud involved accounting issues, since indexes of the period did not distinguish cases involving accounting fraud from fraud of other kinds.

Second, treatises on British company law were reviewed for case citations. They include Nathaniel Lindley's works on companies;[5] Sir

W. Hodge's work on railways;[6] J. Grant's treatise on banking law;[7] Samuel Williston's history of the law of business corporations;[8] F. B. Palmer's *Company Law*[9] and *Company Precedents*;[10] Sir H. B. Buckley's works on the company law;[11] and Halsbury's *The Laws of England*.[12] Finally, previously published articles on the subject were reviewed for citations to relevant cases.[13] Although many of the cases reprinted here have been mentioned by these writers, discussion has tended to focus on the 1889 case *Lee v. Neuchatel Asphalte Company* and later cases in the *Lee* series.[14]

This search resulted in the collection of fifty-one cases with accounting content. They spanned the fifty-year period from 1839 to 1888. Of these cases, twenty-one did not have sufficient interest to warrant inclusion in this volume.

Those who are unfamiliar with British law case reports of this time should note that these reports are not official court reports as they are in the United States. Instead, cases were reported under a competitive system where private companies hired reporters. Thus, one can frequently find the same case reported in *The Law Times*, the *Law Journal*, the *Law Reports*, and perhaps other reports. A cross-check of several cases showed that there were no substantial differences in these reports, although occasionally one reporter included more background information than another.

The thirty cases show that these court decisions involved a rich variety of accounting issues. In some cases courts upset private contractual stipulations regarding accounting and dividend matters. In others, management was held to have used incorrect principles in computing profits. Whether or not a contract or management decision was upset, the courts often discussed at some length the principles that management should apply in the preparation of balance sheets or income statements. It thus appears that the courts, in resolving issues of equity among participants in British companies, were applying normative accounting principles.[15]

The cases have been listed chronologically. They have been edited to exclude issues and discussion not relevant to accounting. In most instances, only the final appellate decision appears here. However, occasionally a lower court opinion was particularly interesting and is therefore included.

Information or discussion about contractual stipulations regarding accounting and dividend matters was retained. Such contracts, typically found in the agreement establishing the company, illustrate how accounting entered into agency relationships. Thus, in addition to typical contracts specifying that "correct" books be kept, or that annual balance sheets be prepared, one finds insurance company contracts that specify the establishment of reserves for risks [*Burnes v. Pennell* (1849)]. Banks were required to provide for bad and, upon occasion, doubtful debts and, in some cases, to dissolve in the event a certain portion of their capital were lost [see for example *Turquand v. Marshall* (1869)]. In an interesting commentary upon the importance of disclosure to shareholders, some banks' books were to be kept secret from the shareholders [see *Turquand* or *City of Glascow Bank v. Mackinnon* (1882)] and directors could inform shareholders of the probable losses they "deem expedient for the interest of the company . . ." [*Ex Parte Holme* (1852)]. Some contracts required that reserves for depreciation or amortization be established [*Davison v. Gillies* (1879), *Dent v. The London Tramways Company* (1881)], while others left such matters to the discretion of the directors [*Lambert v. The Neuchatel Asphalte Company* (1882)]. Some companies were required to distribute profits as soon as earnings reached a certain amount [*Stringer's Case* (1869)]. Others permitted directors to establish various types of reserves they deemed necessary, in their sole discretion, to establish before they distributed profits. In some cases, dividends were permitted to be paid only out of "clear profits actually accrued and reduced to possession" [*Turquand*] or "realized" profits [*In re Oxford Benefit Building and Investment Society* (1886)]. Less cautious companies permitted dividends to be paid on the basis of estimates of accounts [*Leeds Estate, Building and Investment Company v. Shepherd* (1887)]. Other contracts specified that funds received from particular sources, such as premiums on leases, were to be considered capital, not revenue capable of division [*In re Alexandra Palace Company* (1882)]; in other cases directors were given wide discretion to charge expenses to capital or revenue. In the 1887 *Leeds Estate, Building and Investment Company* case, the company was contractually required to annually audit its balance sheet; the auditor was to investigate and render an opinion regarding the validity of the balance sheet.

Court discussion on the propriety of particular accounting principles and practices gives insight, on the other hand, into normative accounting principles regulating accounting behavior during this time. Some examples may help illuminate the richness of the material contained here. The first case, the 1849 House of Lords case *Burnes v. Pennell*, is almost universally cited as the source of the rule that dividends must have profits as their source; in this case Lord Campbell declared that the declaration of dividends when there were no profits was fraudulent with respect to those who were led into a false belief in a company's prosperity. This case is almost universally ignored for its much more interesting discussion about accounting for risks. According to Lord Campbell:

> The complaint that the balance sheet contained no statement, and made no estimate of pending risks, is absurd. Such a statement could not be introduced into a balance sheet; . . . No estimate could be made of losses thereafter to occur, unless the directors had been endowed with the faculty of second sight, and could have discovered the shadows of coming shipwrecks and captures.

In *Ex parte Spackman*, also decided in 1849, Lord Chancellor Cottenham noted the difficulty of determining the principles regulating the insurance of human lives and acknowledged the difficulties to be even greater in this case, where a company insured the lives of cattle, although "the usual casualty which awaits cattle is . . . excluded." However, in *Rance's Case* (1870), a cash basis balance sheet that treated the funds an insurance company had received for risks as profits without making any corresponding provision for underwriting risks was called "extravagant" and "fraudulent and delusive."

Problems of accounting for risks in other types of companies also arose. In the case of a blockade-running company that traded cotton with the Confederacy during the United States Civil War, Vice Chancellor Malins held that the company's balance sheet, which included at face cotton stored in the Confederacy and debts due the company from the Confederacy, was delusive: "Knowing that the 62,000*l* [pounds] due from the Confederate States was not more certain than a chance at the hazard table, it was unjustifiable to treat it as an asset . . ." [*Stringer's Case* (1869)].

In banks the recognition of losses due to bad, or doubtful, accounts was an issue. In the earliest case the idea that bad debts ought to be recognized at the time the debtor became bankrupt or insolvent was proposed [*Ex parte Holme* (1852)]. But later, courts started to support the recognition of loss due to doubtful debts. When Judge Fry felt it necessary to justify an allowance for bad debt expense in *Lord Rokeby v. Elliot* (1878)[16] he did it as follows:

> I think that if the sale had not been for credit the price would have been

less, and therefore, to use a common expression, the thing is as broad as it is long. If the Defendant had had no bad debts he would have had to sell for less money. . . .

Other bank and loan company cases involved the recognition of income. One of the most interesting of these was *City of Glasgow Bank v. Mackinnon* (1882). The bank had lent £117,000 to an individual, secured by American railway securities, and had had to take over the securities on the debtor's default. For twelve years the bank "nursed" this nonpaying investment, advancing additional funds and accruing interest on all its advances, until the total investment of principle and interest was £905,000. Although Lord Deas considered this course of conduct "adventurous," three other judges were of the opinion that directors were entitled to accrue interest earned and deemed secured. Moreover, the court found that the directors were not bound to take into account unfavorable foreign currency exchange rate fluctuations over the course of a twelve-year period because they were considered "temporary."

A number of other accounting principles were also considered. Whether expenditures were capital in nature or ought to be charged to revenue was at issue in *Corry v. The Londonderry and Enniskillen Railway Company* (1860), with its holding that connected the resolution of this problem with the source of funds used to buy the item. Preliminary expenses came in for their share of attention. Lord Chancellor Hatherley, in *Turquand v. Marshall* (1869), found that preliminary expenses were not assets and should not be capitalized: "If the company had been wound-up the preliminary expenses could not have been provided for. Where was the fund? It had departed." Other courts also found it objectionable to capitalize preliminary expenses and spread their cost over several years, but held that directors could not be found guilty of preparing fraudulent balance sheets when they adopted the customary practices of auditors [*Bale v. Cleland* (1864)]. Thus, support is found in some of these early cases for the matching principle.

Several cases considered the issue of capitalizing interest accrued on capital during the nonincoming period of construction, including *Bloxam v. Metropolitan Railway Company* (1868), *Bardwell v. Sheffield Waterworks Company* (1872), and *In re Alexandra Palace Company* (1882), with different results. In *Bardwell* Vice Chancellor Malins held that such interest should be capitalized, because interest is a part of the cost or price of the works. In *Alexandra Palace* counsel for the defendant directors similarly argued that "The value of a building is not merely the sums actually expended on it, but the interest which those sums would have produced had they been bearing interest during the period of construction." Judge Fry was not impressed; he held this to be a mere "paper" transaction, lacking in substance.

Cases also shed light on judicially recognized objectives of accounting information. The judiciary recognized at an early date that financial statements of companies were representations to the public that affected the price of the shares and induced people to purchase them [*Ex parte Brockwell* (1857)]. Thus, foreshadowing the United States Securities Acts of nearly a century later, British courts in this period granted shareholders civil remedies in the event they purchased shares in reliance on accounting information deemed to be so incorrect that it was fraudulent.

The British legal cases reprinted here are not available in most libraries. They are a source of information on an important period in accounting history. Many issues discussed in these cases are perennial ones that continue to be debated. Their resolution in these cases frequently involved the application of accounting principles commonly believed to have originated fifty years later, and then in response to income tax laws or other legislation. Whether the British judiciary was formulating new principles in these decisions or applying those of accountants of the time, this material should be of value to all who are interested in the development of accounting thought.

NOTES

1. G. A. Lee, "The Concept of Profit in British Accounting, 1760–1900," *British History Review* (Spring 1975), p. 35.

2. See H. Pollins, "Aspects of Railway Accounting Before 1868," in A. C. Littleton and B. S. Yamey (eds.), *Studies in the History of Accounting* (Richard D. Irwin, 1956), pp. 332–335, and "Railway Auditing— A Report of 1867," *Accounting Research* (January 1957), pp. 14–22; S. Pollard, "Capital Accounting in the Industrial Revolution," in M. Chatfield (ed.), *Contemporary Studies in the Evolution of Accounting Thought* (Dickenson Publishing Company, 1968), pp. 113–134; and J. R. Edwards (ed.), *Studies of Company Records: 1830–1874* (Garland Publishing, 1984).

3. See H. C. Edey and P. Panitpakdi, "British Company Accounting and the Law 1844–1900," in A. C. Littleton and B. S. Yamey (eds.), *Studies in the History of Accounting* (1956), reprinted by Arno Press, 1978, pp. 356–379; L. W. Hein, *The British Companies Acts and The Practice of Accountancy 1844–1962* (Arno Press, 1978); and J. R. Edwards (ed.), *British Company Legislation and Company Accounts 1844–1976*, 2 vols. (Arno Press, 1980).

4. 1889 is chosen as the cutoff because in that year the Court of Appeal decided *Lee v. Neuchatel Asphalte Company* [L.R. 41 Ch.D. 1]. This case, and those decided after 1889, are well known.

5. *On the Law of Partnership, Including its Application to Joint-Stock and Other Companies*, 2 vols. (T.J.W. Johnson & Co., 1860); *A Treatise on the Law of Partnership, Including its Application to Companies*, Fourth Edition, 2 vols. (Callaghan & Co., 1881); *A Treatise on the Law of Partnership*, 2 vols., fifth edition (Callahan & Co., 1888); and *A Treatise on the Law of Companies, Considered as a Branch of the Law of Partnership*, Fifth Edition (Sweet and Maxwell, 1891).

6. *A Treatise on the Law of Railways, Railway Companies, and Railway Investments*, sixth edition (Henry Sweet, 1876).

7. *Grant's Treatise on the Law Relating to Bankers and Banking Companies*, fourth edition (Butterworths, 1882).

8. "History of the Law of Business Corporations Before 1800," *Harvard Law Review* (October 15, 1888), pp. 106–124; (November 15, 1888), pp. 159–166.

9. *Company Law: A Practical Handbook for Lawyers and Business Men*, second edition (Stevens and Sons, 1898).

10. *Company Precedents for Use in Relation to Companies Subject to the Companies (Consolidation) Act, 1908*, eleventh edition (Stevens and Sons, 1912).

11. *The Law and Practice under the Companies (Consolidation) Act, 1908, and the Limited Partnerships Act, 1907*, ninth edition (Stevens and Haynes, 1909).

12. Vol. 5 (Butterworth & Co., 1910).

13. See W. Strachan, "The Return of a Company's Capital to its Shareholders," *Law Quarterly Review* (July 1910), pp. 231–238; Prosper Reiter, *Profits, Dividends and Law* (1926), reprinted by Arno Press, 1976; W. A. Robson, "Legal Conceptions of Capital and Income," *London Essays in Economics* (1928), pp. 251–279; J. L. Weiner, "Theory of Anglo-American Dividend Law: The English Cases," *Columbia Law Review* (December 1928), pp. 1046–1060; R. S. Edwards, "A Note on the Law Relating to Company Dividends," *Economica* (May 1939), pp. 170–190; B. S. Yamey, "Aspects of the Law Relating to Company Dividends," *Modern Law Review* (April 1941), pp. 273–298; K. C. Keown and A. H. Mann, "Divisible Profits and Dividends of Limited Liability Companies," reprinted in K. C. Keown (ed.), *Readings in Australian Accountancy* (Butterworths, 1956); and R. P. Brief, "The Origin and Evolution of Nineteenth-Century Asset Accounting," *Business History Review* (Spring 1966), pp. 1–23.

14. Cases in this series include *Verner v. The General and Commercial Trust Ltd.*, 63 L.J. (Ch.D.) 456; *Bolton v. Natal Land Co.*, [1892] 2 Ch. 124; *Bosanquet v. St. John D'El Rey Mining Co.*, 77 L.T. 206 (1897); *In re National Bank of Wales*, [1899] 2 Ch. 629, affirmed *sub. nom. Dovey v. Cory*, [1901] A.C. 477, 85 L.T. 257; *Amonia Soda Co. v. Chamberlain*, [1918] 1 Ch. 266.

15. In fact, A. C. Littleton suggested this (*Accounting Evolution to 1900* [1933], reprinted by the University of Alabama Press, 1981), but he and others who have looked at nineteenth-century British legal cases for information about accounting principles of the time—for example, L. L. Briggs, "Asset Valuation in Dividend Decisions," *The Accounting Review* (September 1934), pp. 184–191—examined only a subset of the cases.

16. Not a bank.

BURNES v. PENNELL

9 English Reports 1181 (1849)
House of Lords

In the year 1839 some persons formed themselves into a joint stock company, called the Forth Marine Insurance Company, for the purpose of carrying on the business of marine insurance. It was not incorporated, but was represented by a registered officer. By the contract under which the Company was formed the capital stock was to be £100,000, divided into 4000 shares of £25 each : and the shareholders became bound to contribute the amount of their respective shares as follows,—viz. ten per cent. on the amount, or £10,000 in all, at the commencement of the business, and all the remaining £90,000, or £22 10s. of each share, were to be left in the hands of the shareholders themselves in the mean time, until the business of the company should require its capital to be paid up. They were to pay that sum at such periods, and by such instalments, as the directors for the time should appoint. The shareholders were to have the right to the profits, and be liable for the losses, and in relief to each other in proportion to their respective shares, and no person was to hold more than 100 shares.. . . .

The books were to be annually balanced on the 31st of May, and a balance-sheet made out, examined, docqueted, and signed by a quorum of the directors and manager, and laid on the table at the annual meetings in June, for the inspection of the shareholders, and the substance thereof was then to be read or stated by the chairman. It was declared to be in the power of each meeting of the shareholders. if they should think fit (to appoint a private committee, consisting of three of their number, holding at least twenty-five shares each of the company's stock, for auditing and reporting upon such yearly states at a future general meeting, to be called for the purpose. That there should be no division of profits at the end of the first year ; but that the clear interest and profits of every succeeding year, as these should appear at the time of each balance, after deducting fifty per cent. of the guarantie fund, should be divided rateably among the shareholders ; and that in striking the amount of the clear interest and profits for division, the directors should take into their consideration the extent of risks then pending, and deduct from the said interests and profits such a proportion thereof as they should deem it prudent and requisite to set aside on account of the then pending risks.. . . .

At the second annual general meeting, in June 1841, it appeared that the total amount of premiums for the preceding year amounted to £198,036 8s. 9d., and the amount of losses, averages, and other charges, to £111,962 12s. 7d., leaving £86,073 16s. 2d. to cover   , unsettled losses and pending risks. On the footing that this surplus was much more than sufficient to meet the probable future loss, the meeting, after setting aside £1500 as a guarantie fund, in terms of the deed of settlement, agreed that £1500 more, being fifteen per cent on the £10,000 of the stock which had been advanced, should be divided in name of profits. It was at the same meeting resolved, that the balance of the Company's business, to be reported at the meeting in June 1842, should be confined to the business transacted between 1st June and 31st December 1841. The object of this was to leave a space of five months, to exhaust, in some measure, the outstanding risks, so that a more certain estimate might be formed of the profit and loss.

During the course of the next year, it appeared that, in consequence of the storms, of unprecedented frequency and violence, which occurred in 1841 and 1842, and the many frauds perpetrated, there would be a loss on the Company's underwriting for the two first years. This was reported to the general meeting held in June 1842. Out of the £6000 which were estimated as the clear profits on the seven months' underwriting from 31st May to 31st December 1841, the meeting resolved to divide £700, being seven per cent. on the £10,000 of stock which had been advanced ; and a like sum of £700 was set aside as a guarantie fund.

The directors, on 26th July 1842, made a call for another instalment of ten per cent. on their subscribed capital, or of £2 10s. per share.

David M'Kenzie, who was a clerk of the appellant, Mr. Burnes, was a shareholder in the Company, to the amount of fifty shares thereof. He failed to pay the call which was made on him for the second instalment, : excepting a small sum of £7 1s. 8d., and he asked for indulgence as to the rest. This was conceded; but after some delay, the directors instructed the law-agent of the company, Mr. John Gilmour, to prosecute him for payment. Gilmour on the 5th November 1842, wrote to M'Kenzie, who on the 8th of the same month, stated, that he had communicated the demand to the appellant, whose clerk he was, and who was to be in Edinburgh on the 13th or 14th of that month, and would call on Gilmour as to the arrangement of the matter.

The appellant alleged that he saw Gilmour, who was a shareholder in the company and likewise its law agent, in order to obtain from him information as to the state of the Company's affairs; that Gilmour laid before him the balance-sheets and other documents, which professed to represent accurately the progress and success of the Company, and stated to the appellant that the affairs of the Company were flourishing, and that their stock was a valuable commodity; and that, mainly trusting to these representations, and relying upon the notorious fact, then pressed upon him, that large dividends had been made (but which he now averred to have been fraudulently made) the appellant was induced, in November 1842, to take a transfer to M'Kenzie's stock. . . .

2

Lord Campbell (July 16).—My Lords, on the 28th of July, 1843, the Forth Marine Insurance Company, established in the year 1839 as a Joint Stock Company, with transferrable shares, commenced an action against the appellant for calls, alleging that he had become a member of the company by purchasing and accepting the transfer of fifty shares, on the second day of December 1842. The calls sued for were, one ordered on the 19th of December 1842, of £20 per cent., and another ordered on the 21st of June 1843, of £15 per cent.

The appellant denied his liability as a shareholder; and on the 28th of May 1844, commenced an action of reduction against the company, ...

We now come then to the allegations respecting the acts of the directors themselves; and if the plaintiff has been deceived and defrauded by them, and induced by them to purchase the shares by their false representations, the interlocutor must be reversed. I do not think it necessary even that the representations should have been made personally to him. If the directors have made false representations for the purpose of fictitiously enhancing the price of shares for their own benefit, and the appellant has thereby been deceived, and induced to purchase shares greatly beyond their value, the transfer of the shares, although executed, ought to be set aside. But the transfer having been executed, a clear and strong case of fraud ought to be established, and it must be shewn that the purchaser   of these shares was induced to purchase them by the deceit of the director.

You will observe that the misconduct imputed to these directors, resolves itself into misconduct as between them and the shareholders. The directors are not charged with any design to raise the value of the shares in the market fictitiously, for the purpose of obtaining a high price for shares to be sold on behalf of the company, or which they themselves held individually. Nor is any connection alleged between the supposed misconduct of the directors, and the purchase of the shares by the appellant. Their acts of imputed misconduct begin years before he had purchased or entertained any intention of purchasing shares, and surely it cannot be contended that the purchaser of shares in a joint stock company, when sued for calls, may get rid of his liability by shewing that at some past period the directors have misconducted themselves. Assuming that the accounts rendered by these directors to the shareholders were erroneous or false, there is no allegation that they were ever brought to the notice of the appellant, except by Mr. Gilmour, or that he knew anything of their contents before November 1842, or that they were ever made public, or exhibited, except at a meeting of the shareholders. Suppose that an action should be brought by Mr. Burnes against the directors for a deceitful representation, whereby he was induced to purchase the shares at a fictitious value, what facts are alleged upon this record which could be used to support such an action? There are no allegations of that kind. Mr. Burnes himself attributes his unlucky purchase entirely to what passed between him and Mr. Gilmour, for which the directors are not answerable.

But looking to the accounts,·they really cannot be said to be false or fraudulent. It is not enough to bestow such epithets upon them, if, upon examination, they cannot be charged with falsehood. But the accounts rendered in June 1841 and June 1842, do not state what is false. There is in them no falsification of figures They gave a true statement of the premiums received, and the adjusted losses. In a balance sheet, liquidated items can alone appear, either on the debtor or creditor side. The complaint that the balance sheet contained no statement, and made no estimate of pending risks, is absurd. Such a statement could not be introduced into a balance sheet ; and if the business was prudently conducted, the greater the amount of pending risks, the more prosperous was the condition of the company. No estimate could be made of losses thereafter to occur, unless the directors had been endowed with the faculty of second sight, and could have discovered the shadows of coming shipwrecks and captures.

The grave part of the charge against the directors really resolves itself into the supposed fictitious dividends of £15 per cent., ordered in June 1841, and of £7 per cent., ordered in June 1842. I repeat what I threw out during the argument (and ·for which I had the high sanction of my noble and learned friend), that it is most nefarious conduct for the directors of a joint stock company, in order to raise the price of shares which they are to dispose of, to order a fictitious dividend to be paid out of the capital of the concern. Dividends are supposed to be paid out of profits only, and when directors order a dividend, to any given amount, without expressly saying so, they impliedly declare to the world that the company has made profits, which justify such a dividend. If no such profits have ·been made, and the dividend is to be paid out of the capital of the concern, a gross fraud has been practised, and the directors are not only civilly liable to those whom they have deceived and injured. but, in my opinion. they are guilty of a conspiracy for which they are liable to be prosecuted and punished. I am one of those who think Lord Cochrane was unjustly convicted of a conspiracy to raise, by false rumours, the price of the public securities for his own advantage, and to the injury of the King's subjects, who were deceived ; but no one has gravely doubted that the imputed offence was one of a kind which amounted in point of law to a misdemeanor. There can be no doubt therefore that a conspiracy by falsehood (as by a fictitious dividend) to raise fictitiously the market value of shares of a railway company, or any other joint stock company, that the Queen's subjects may be deceived and injured, and that at their expense a profit may be made by the conspirators, would be an indictable offence.

But setting aside the objection that here there is no sufficient allegation to connect the supposed fraud with the act of the appellant, in purchasing the shares, how can it be said that the dividend was paid out of capital. The capital of the company consisted of the £10,000, paid up out of the £100,000 of the capital subscribed. The £1500 set aside for payment of the £15 per cent. in June 1841, and the £700 for payment of £7 per cent. in June 1842, were taken from premiums which had been received to a vastly greater amount. It might be imprudent to order these dividends, but it does not follow that they were ordered fraudulently, and there is no allegation that they were ordered in contemplation of the sale of any shares, either for the benefit of the company. or for the benefit of any of the direc- ·tors. There is no surmise even that the dividends were connected with any traffic in the shares of the company. I may observe that in such a concern as this, there must be infinite diffi·ulty in fixing a fair dividend. In railroad companys, it must be comparatively easy, for there is no risk to calculate there, except (for which there ought to be a handsome reserve) that of killing a certain number of her Majesty's subjects.

The directors have only to take an account of receipts and outgoings, and, striking a balance according to the ordinary rules of arithmetic, to say how much is to be ascribed to each share. But the directors of a marine insurance company must look to the probabilities of war and peace, and take into consideration accounts of distant tempests, to which ships insured by them may have been exposed. If lives are insured, they must attend to the approach of the cholera, and the sanitary precautions adopted to meet it. This month there may be grounds for a good dividend, and the next month a call may be indispensible. . . .

. I believe
that his bargain was a very bad one, but he had only to blame his own want of
caution in entering into it. If he had made inquiries of the directors, or the
actuary, their authorized agent, to give information, he would probably have found
that heavy losses had lately arisen, which could not have been properly introduced
as items in any preceding balance sheet; but he was probably pleased with the
amount of premiums, and calculateu that these would all turn out to be pure
profit.

However this may be, I concur in the unanimous opinion of the Judges of the
First Division of the Court of Session, that he has not averred any facts which
eutitle him to be released from the engagement into which he deliberatcly entered
as a shareholder of this company.

Looking to the facts which the appellant avers, and taking those facts to be
true, I am of opinion they do not make out any case of fraud practised upon him,
and that he must be left to suffer from the effects of his own imprudence. For these
reasons I move that the interlocutor appealed from be affirmed, with costs. . . .

4

EX PARTE SPACKMAN

41 English Reports 1228 (1849)
Lord Chancellor - Court of Appeal

April 19. THE LORD CHANCELLOR [Cottenham]. This is an application made under the Joint Stock Companies Winding-up Act to dissolve the company, and to wind it up. Two questions have here arisen : the first, whether the company is of a description which subjects it to the operation of the Act ; and, secondly, whether the facts stated shew a case which makes it proper for, or incumbent upon, the Court to exercise its jurisdiction.

The company was established for a singular purpose, but one which very possibly may be of the highest utility. It is obviously of a nature which must have rendered it very difficult to bring it into a proper form, the object being the insurance of cattle. The principles which regulate the insurance of human lives are subject to considerable difficulty ; at first there were great difficulties in estimating the value of lives, and great errors and very erroneous calculations were made as to the effect which various habits, employments, situations, and casualties had upon the average duration of human life. Such calculations, with regard to cattle, are obviously more difficult. The usual casualty which awaits cattle is, I understand, excluded from the operations of this company ; but to all other casualties it remains open. With regard to these, it was found a very difficult matter for the company at once to bring its rates of insurance within that degree of certainty which was necessary to enable it to carry on business with success, and to realise the objects of its establishment. Thus it appears that, at first, the calculations were erroneous as to the chances of mortality, and the premiums far too low. It appears, besides, from the affidavits, that a disease of an epidemic character broke out, shortly after the establishment of the company, amongst cattle, by which considerable loss arose, and which involved the company in difficulties at its starting. The capital of the company was not all realised by calls, but remained outstanding on the liability of the parties who had engaged to furnish the capital as it was required ; in fact, they were the holders of the capital to the extent of the shares they had taken, until it was required by the company. The petition states all this, and then it states the difficulties which the company got into, and the losses which it had sustained, and compares the liabilities actually due with the capital existing. It not only does this, but also includes the liabilities to which the company might become subject ; but it is quite obvious that this ought not to have been taken into calculation, because the premiums hereafter to be paid may more than meet such contingent liabilities. The greater the amount of business done by the company, the greater would the amount of their liabilities appear : but then, in all probability, the profits would be increased in the same ratio. In respect of insurances against fire, if all the property insured were burnt, a company would be placed in great difficulties ; but that is not likely to be the case, and, generally speaking, the loss sustained by destruction of property which does take place is more than covered by the premiums upon property uninjured. I cannot, therefore, consider the liability this company is under by its contracts of insurance at all proper to be taken into account.

Have I, however, any right to look into the state of their accounts at all? The Act gives no such power. I cannot, therefore, enquire into the mode in which this company has carried on its business. The Act provides certain tests, which are to be taken as evidences of insolvency, and which, if coupled with other conditions, would prevent a company from going on ; but the Court cannot look into the affairs of companies in the manner here proposed. If such were the law, parties might come here and say that, in their opinion, any particular company had not money sufficient to carry on its business, and that its affairs ought to be wound up. Had this been contemplated, a very short Act would have been requisite, while a very difficult jurisdiction would have been thrown upon the Court. The Legislature, however, has made certain definite Acts the tests of insolvency ; and, in the case before me, insolvency has not been proved to exist at all. . . .

5

EX PARTE HOLME

22 L.J.Ch. 226 (1852)
Lord Chancellor - Court of Appeal

June 1.—The LORD CHANCELLOR.—The question in this case is, whether a person, who transferred his shares upwards of three years before the stopping of the company, can now be put on the list of contributories under the Winding-up Acts. In all these concerns in which there are necessarily floating balances and open accounts to a great extent, it is scarcely possible, from time to time, at any given moment, to ascertain what the actual losses are, and, therefore, generally speaking, when a man comes in as a purchaser of an interest in the concern, he takes it as he finds it, with a loss or a benefit, as the case may be; otherwise, there would be occasion, in the absence of any express provision to meet the exact case, in every instance to take an account (which after the event would be next to impossible) of the actual extent of the losses at the time of the particular transfer. Now in this case, there have been from twelve hundred to thirteen hundred transfers; and if the contention on the part of the appellant is right, there must be in each case an account taken such as I have mentioned. But this, I think, is quite clear, that on a question of this nature it cannot be said that the loss was incurred when the debt was incurred, that is, when the loan was made, because in the result the debt turns out to be desperate; that is quite out of the question. Then the question is, what is the exact moment when the loss accrued? This company went on in a course that must lead to ruin, taking paper securities, and when they found the debtor could not pay they took his renewed bills. It is impossible to specify the time when the respective losses accrued, because it would depend upon the fact when each particular debtor became insolvent. That difficulty is obviated in most cases by the circumstance that, having regard to the impossibility of ascertaining the actual state of the concern, a man buys a share in the concern just as it stands, and then no question arises. He may have a benefit, or he may have a loss by the actual insolvency of the company at the time he comes in. But this deed has a peculiar provision, that a member selling shall be absolved from future liabilities, but shall remain liable for losses already incurred. Now, that provision has introduced the question before me.
 . . . . but the question now before me is, whether there was any ascertained loss within that clause for which Mr. Holme was still liable. That I think must be determined upon the true construction of this deed. . . .

This deed provides, by clause 69, that the directors shall keep proper books of account, and that they shall enter into those books fair, explicit and true entries of all receipts, payments, transactions, &c., and of all profits, gains and losses, and "shall make or cause to be made out a full, true and explicit statement and balance sheet, exhibiting the debts and credits of the company, and the amount and nature of the capital and property thereof, and the then fair value of the same, estimated by the directors as nearly as may be, and to the best of their judgment; and the amount of the company's negotiable securities then in circulation, and the profits and losses of the company, and all other matters and things requisite for fully, truly and explicitly manifesting the state of the affairs of the company." Now, this clause admits of no doubt; nothing can be plainer or better framed. The company are to keep a true account of their transactions, their gains and losses, and are to exhibit the actual value of the property. If the directors had done their duty in this respect no question could have arisen. The 26th clause says, that the liability shall continue for past losses; but the deed also says, that the losses shall be shewn upon the face of the accounts; and, if the directors had done their duty, then it would have appeared what the losses were. In the previous clause, the 45th, which embodies the clause I have just read, there is this further direction: "At every half-yearly general meeting of the company the directors shall exhibit to the shareholders assembled such a balance sheet as they are required to prepare by the 69th article." That embodies, therefore, the 69th clause, and is, no doubt, cumulative. Besides giving such balance sheet, they are directed by the 45th clause to give "such a statement of the probable amount of the losses to be apprehended from the subsisting accounts or engagements of or with the company, and generally of the state and progress of the affairs of the company, up to the 30th of June and the 31st of December immediately preceding such meeting, as the directors shall deem expedient for the interest of the company to be made public." This is an additional duty thrown upon them, but it is discretionary. It is imperative upon them to make out an account shewing the actual loss, and they are to give such a statement of the probable losses and of the state of the concern as they may think it expedient to make public. Then, in the same clause, come these words: "And every such balance sheet shall be binding and conclusive on all the shareholders, their executors, administrators and assigns, unless some error shall be discovered therein respectively before the next half-yearly general meeting, and in that case such error only shall be rectified." By this clause, therefore, I consider that the balance sheet rendered by the directors was binding on all the partners in the concern, unless errors were discovered and rectified in the mode pointed out. Now, the parties forming this concern elected to have as little power over their affairs as was well possible; for by the 16th clause it was provided, "that no shareholder, not being a director or an auditor, his executors, &c., shall be entitled or allowed under any pretence whatever to inspect, or have in equity a discovery of, all or any of the books, accounts, documents or writings of the company, except such as may be produced for his inspection at any meeting of the company, and except the deed of settlement;" so that the body of shareholders must take the accounts just as they find them. . . .

Then the real question upon the whole of this deed is, whether upon the accounts made out by the directors, produced at the general meetings, acted upon and approved of by those meetings, and which in no one instance shew upon the face of them any losses which have not been provided for, this gentleman is liable ? Where am I to find any evidence of such losses ? It is sworn by Mr. Hedley, who assisted in preparing these accounts—I do not disbelieve him, but it has no weight with me—that from the first moment he knew the growing insolvency of the company, and assisted in concealing it ; but that concealment leads to the impossibility of charging Mr. Holme, because there is no evidence before me, on which I can act, to shew that at the time of his transfer there was any actual loss sustained. I am of opinion that, under the provisions of the deed, the losses for which it was intended an outgoing shareholder should continue liable, were intended to appear on the balance sheet, so as to lead to no difficulty. If the directions of the deed had been observed there would have been no difficulty, for I should only have had to open the accounts at the time of the transfer, and should have at once seen the amount of loss to which this gentleman was liable. But the balance sheets shew no loss, but gains and profits divided. I am clearly of opinion that this gentleman is not liable in respect of any loss, for none is shewn or can be shewn ; and therefore, without any reservation of any kind, I think he is not a contributory, and I dismiss this appeal, with costs.

EX PARTE BROCKWELL

26 L.J.Ch. 855 (1857)
Vice Chancellor - Chancery

A question was raised in this case, upon an adjourned summons from chambers, whether Mr. Brockwell ought to be placed upon the list of contributories to the Royal British Bank. It appeared that the company was formed in the year 1849, under a royal charter granted in pursuance of the provisions of the act 7 & 8 Vict. c. 113, for the regulation of joint-stock banks.

. . . . KINDERSLEY, V.C. — The question I have to determine is, whether Mr. Brockwell ought to be put upon the list of contributories. Mr. Brockwell contends that he is not liable, on the ground that he was induced, by the false and fraudulent representations of the company as to the condition of the bank, to take his shares. Is that defence available? Now, with respect to the legal question, how far a person who is led into taking shares in a joint-stock company on the faith of representations which turn out to have been entirely false and fraudulent is liable, let us consider how the matter would stand as between individuals. If a person by false representations induces another to enter into a contract with him, I apprehend it is beyond all question that the party who has made these false representations has no right to enforce that contract. I think that is a proposition too plain to require any citation of authorities in support of it. Any system of laws which did not embrace that principle would, as it appears to me, be not worthy of a civilized country. The person so deceived, that is, led into the contract by false representations, has a right to treat that contract as not binding upon him. . . .

The party deceived would have a right to say that the contract was a nullity. Now, applying these principles to the facts of the present case, how does the matter stand? The evidence appears to me to shew beyond all doubt that the annual or half-yearly reports of this joint-stock bank contained representations that were entirely false, and in that sense fraudulent. It appears to me that that applies most distinctly to the report that was made for the year ending the 31st of December 1854, which was the last report made before the time when Mr. Brockwell took his shares. . . .

Now, as I have stated, Mr. Esdaile sets out certain details with respect to the report that was issued for the period ending the 31st of December 1854; and these details may be stated without going through all the figures, because a mere statement of figures only puzzles, without distinctly explaining matters. The result of his statement is this . . . .

—the representation made by the balance-sheet that was issued, together with the report, for the period ending the 31st of December 1854, represents this: on the one side of the balance-sheet are the liabilities of the bank, and on the other side are the assets, and among the assets there is set down this item,—"Loans on convertible securities for short periods, advances on cash credit accounts, bills discounted, &c., 804,798*l*. 16*s*. 7*d*." That is represented as being an asset of the bank under the title which I have just read, and it is upon the faith and upon the assumption of that item, as well as all the other items appearing in this account, that the directors represent by the report and by the balance-sheet that there was a reserve fund on the 31st of December 1854 of 12,598*l*. 19*s*. 8*d*., and an unappropriated balance carried to the new account, making together 15,005*l*. 15*s*. 8*d*., that is, besides declaring a dividend of 6*l*. per cent. for the half-year upon the shares. Now, what does Mr. Esdaile state (that statement being corroborated by Mr. Anderson in full detail) with respect to the truth of that representation? He states this,—and really the statement is almost incredible, and yet it is perfectly true :— with regard to bad debts, past due bills, and overdrawn accounts and matters of that description, their course was that they never, from the beginning of the operations of the bank in 1849 down to the period to which I am now adverting, the 31st of December 1854, wrote off one single shilling of bad debts of any sort or kind whatever. They made no allowance whatever in respect of doubtful debts. That was a gross breach of duty, involving a gross misrepresentation; but not only did they do that, but in cases where the persons who owed them these debts had become bankrupt or insolvent, had taken the benefit of the Insolvent Debtors Act, nay, even where they had proved the debt in bankruptcy or insolvency and received a dividend, and only a dividend, upon the debt, they actually continued in the account of their assets down to 1854 and subsequently, the whole of these debts as at the full amount, as if they were still available assets. They did so even in cases where they had actually compromised with a debtor for a less sum than 20s. in the pound, and had released him from the debt. They continued the original debt at the full amount at which it had been originally contracted. One would think that fact sufficient to shew the glut of fraud that there is in this case,—the redundancy of fraud; but not only did they do that, but they actually continued to compute interest upon every one of these debts, as if it were a debt still due and yielding interest, and included all that in the 804,000l. ...

I may just observe also this, that it appears, taking the figures which Mr. Esdaile sets out (and, as I have observed, the figures as he states them are rather less than Mr. Anderson shews in detail), the matter would stand thus:— that of bad debts, overdrawn accounts, past due bills and matters of that sort, in short, debts owing in one shape or another, at the period to which I am referring, the 31st of December 1854, the actual bad debts, known to be bad, hopeless debts, amounted to 25,791l. and a fraction: and the doubtful debts (which doubtful debts of course only ought to have been taken at a certain estimated per-centage) were taken at their full amount, 94,193l.—the whole of the paid-up capital having been only 50,000l., even nominally. . . .

The conclusion I arrive at is, that Mr. Brockwell ought not to be put upon the list.

9

HENRY v. THE GREAT NORTHERN RAILWAY COMPANY

4 Kay & John. 1 (1857)
Vice Chancellor - Chancery

THE Plaintiffs were holders of preference stock in the *Great Northern Railway Company.* The Defendants were the Company and its Directors.

Dividends were duly paid in full upon the Plaintiffs' stock by half-yearly payments, up to the 30th of June, 1856, inclusive. But before another half-year's interest became due, it was discovered that at various times during the eight preceding years stock and shares of the Company, including preference stock similar to that held by the Plaintiffs, had been fraudulently created and issued by *Leopold Redpath,* a servant of the Company, by means of false entries in the books of the Company, and by fictitious transfers and otherwise, to the amount of £221,070, or thereabouts.

Under these circumstances, at the next half-yearly general meeting of the Company, held on the 12th of March, 1857, and which had been specially convened for the purpose, a report from the directors on the subject of *Redpath's* forgeries and frauds was read, together with a statement of the nett revenue of the Company, which shewed a balance of 243,923l. 5s. 8d. for the half year ending on the 31st of December, 1856 ; and it was resolved that no dividend should be declared, but that the meeting considered it desirable that the balance of 243,923l. 5s. 8d. should be applied to meet the losses caused by the frauds and forgeries referred to in the Directors' Report ; and that the directors should be, and they thereby were, requested and authorised to apply the said balance, when and in such manner as they might consider most beneficial for the Company, and to take such proceedings in Parliament and otherwise as they might deem most conducive to the interests of the Company. . . .

The net revenue of the Company for the half year ending the 30th of June, 1857, amounted to upwards of £200,000, and was more than sufficient to pay to the Plaintiffs and the other holders of the preference stock their several dividends, to be computed from the 30th of June, 1856, to the 30th of June, 1857.

The half-yearly ordinary general meeting of the Company being now about to be held on the 29th of August, 1857, the Plaintiffs filed their bill on behalf of themselves and all other holders of preference stock in the Company, charging that the Defendants intended at the meeting to declare a dividend out of the net profits of the Company made since the last dividend was declared, and to pay dividends to the holders of original ordinary stock in the Company, without regard to the claim of the holders of preference stock to be paid, as the Plaintiffs charged they were entitled to be paid, the full amount of the dividends payable in respect of such preference stock from the 30th of June, 1856, before any dividend or payment should be made in respect of the original ordinary stock, and praying that it might be declared that the holders of preference stock in the Company were entitled to be paid interest or dividends on the amount of preference stock held by them from the 30th of June, 1856, according to the amount of interest or dividends which the classes of preference stock respectively carried, before any payment in respect of dividends or otherwise should be made to any of the holders of ordinary stock; . . . .

VICE-CHANCELLOR SIR W. PAGE WOOD:—

The 3rd section of the Act of Parliament of 1857 has created a difficulty requiring much consideration. I was, therefore, anxious that the whole of this case should be most fully argued.

Whether the shares in question were preference shares, in such a sense as to entitle them to arrears, or not, in either event, except for the 3rd section of the Act, I should not have found any difficulty in the case; because it appears to me, that the purport and scheme of the Act are simply to carry into effect an arrangement, by which, out of the ordinary profits realised by the Company in a certain half year, and which would otherwise have been appropriated among the shareholders, a common calamity which has befallen the whole Company would be set right.

As regards that calamity, I entirely coincide in the view taken by the counsel who first advised the Company, that it is to be viewed as any other calamity—the fall of a tunnel, the effect of an inundation, or the like; and although, at first, it occurred to me that there might be some special case made for saying that the preference shareholders, as they are termed, ought to bear a proportion of the loss, regard being had to the forgery of their preference stock, which let in other persons to share in that stock, as well as to the difficulty by which they, in common with the other shareholders, were met in getting any dividend at all, independent of the Act, yet, upon further consideration—and even before hearing a reply—it did not appear to me that any such equity could attach to them. It appeared to me, that it was simply equivalent to a loss occasioned by the fraudulent conduct of a clerk, who might have absconded with a box containing the money that has been lost to the Company. Such a loss could be treated only as a common calamity, and could not, in the slightest degree, vary the position of the several proprietors of stock as between themselves. Like any other calamity, it would have to be met before profit could be realised; and any profit which would afterwards be realised would be applied, like any other profit, in payment of shareholders according to their priorities of dividend. . . .

It may not be the case with this, which is a successful Company, supported by wealthy men, who may have absorbed, to a great extent, the preferential shares; but in many, I may say, in the majority of Companies, strangers are brought in as holders of such shares when the original shareholders are nearly ruined. The original shareholders take the benefit of the capital so brought in, and stipulate to pay preferential dividends at

5 per cent. The majority clearly can have no right, as every one must see, to alter that bargain ; but what they cannot do directly, they may do with the greatest ease and without fraud by another course. To put the case beyond all question of fraud, suppose them to have half-yearly dividends, not making them for the occasion, but dividing half yearly, and repeating that division from year to year. Suppose, then, that they wish to speculate upon a larger amount of profit, by carrying on business to a larger extent with an increased number of carriages and locomotives. All this would be fair. Now suppose they were to say, 'let us make this outlay whenever there is only just enough to pay the preferential shareholders, and nothing to pay us ;' and suppose this to be done ;—the preferential shareholders would bear the whole burthen of paying for the whole of the rolling stock ; they would lose, to that extent, their dividends for that half year; and the next half year, if this construction be correct, they would have no claim whatever in respect of their loss. Presently, when the outlay had been made, and the business had increased in consequence, the Company might have a large fund coming in, and the ordinary shareholders would be entitled to divide it ; in other words, they would get, by force of this construction, a dividend—that is, a share of the profits—before the holders of the preference shares had received dividends, or a share of the profit amounting to the stipulated 5 per cent. per annum.

For these reasons, I am very strongly of opinion, that if you announce, that, by an Act of Parliament, certain shareholders are to have dividends amounting—some to $4\frac{1}{2}$ per cent., others to 5 per cent. per annum (that is to say, a share of the profits to that amount)—in preference to the payment of any dividend upon the ordinary shares of the Company, you must take care that the persons to whom you give this preference receive dividends to these amounts out of the profits of the Company (whenever accruing), before you take one sixpence for any dividend to the shareholders, whom I may term the ordinary shareholders of the.

concern. Having come to that conclusion as to the rights of the preference shareholders, independently of the Act of 1857, it appears to me, for the reasons I have already given, that no intention to the contrary is apparent on the face of that Act. There is no natural equity but what is the other way. The calamity which has befallen the Company does not affect the rights of the shareholders inter se, but is a common loss, to be paid for out of the general assets of the Company; and such being the loss, the profit is diminished accordingly. What remains of profit should be divided according to the stipulation made between the parties; . . . .

14

CORRY v. THE LONDONDERRY AND ENNISKILLEN RAILWAY COMPANY

29 Beav. 263 (1860)
Master of the Rolls - Chancery

This railway was constructed under the powers of an act passed in 1845, and the preference shares were created under the powers contained in subsequent acts passed in 1848, 1852, 1854 and 1856. · · ·

The undertaking was unsuccessful, and though some dividends were declared, the income was insufficient to pay the preference shares in full, and debts had been contracted by the company beyond the amount authorized to be borrowed by the acts of parliament to an extent, as the bill alleged, of about 30,000*l.*

In *March*, 1860, the company, under powers obtained for that purpose, granted a lease of the railway to another company for thirty-five years, renewable, at a certain rent of 26,000*l.* a year, subject to increase. This rent (subject to the question as to payment thereout of the debts) became divisible amongst the shareholders.

The bill was filed by *Corry* (a preference shareholder) on behalf of himself and all other preference half shareholders against the company, against the directors, and *Eckersley* and *Wright*, who represented the interests of the ordinary shareholders, and it prayed, in substance, a declaration that the income of the company, as the same should be received, ought to be applied, first, in payment of the working expenses of the railway and of the interest on the amount of the moneys authorized by the acts of parliament to be borrowed by the company. Secondly, in payment and satisfaction of the whole or a portion of the debts which had been incurred by the company beyond the amount which the directors were authorized by the acts of parliament to borrow. Thirdly in or towards payment to the preference shareholders, according to their priorities, of their dividends and arrears, and lastly in payment of the dividends to the ordinary shareholders. · · ·

The MASTER *of the* ROLLS.

This is a suit instituted for the purpose of determining what constitutes the profits of the company, and, secondly, how those profits ought to be applied....

The first question is, what constitutes profits, and whether the Defendants are entitled to pay any and what debts out of this sum before they divide it among the shareholders.

Upon this point I expressed my opinion during the argument, and I am confirmed in what I then stated by the further attention I have given to it. I am of opinion that all the debts of the company are first payable, other than those which, for want of a better expression, may be called funded debts; for instance, if the Defendants have raised money by mortgage, under the powers contained in their act, for the purpose of completing their line, this does not constitute such a debt as can be paid off out of the profits, before the profits are divided. But, on the other hand, any debts which have been incurred, and which are due from the directors or the company, either for steam engines, for rails, for completing stations, or the like, which ought to have been and would have been paid at the time, had the Defendants possessed the necessary funds for that purpose, those are so many deductions from the profits, which, in my opinion, are not ascertained till the whole of them are paid....

BALE v. CLELAND

4 F. & F. 117 (1864)
Civil Court

Guildford, Civil Court; coram Martin, B.

BALE *v.* CLELAND AND OTHERS.

THIS was an action by a shareholder in a joint stock
company, the Asphaltum Company, Limited, against the
directors and promoters, for representations contained in
the prospectus and report and balance sheet, and relating
to the supposed profits of the concern, and the declaration
of a dividend, which he alleged to have been not only
false but fraudulent, and by which, he alleged, that he was
induced to take 200 shares ; so that, therefore, he was
entitled to recover the amount he had paid for the shares.
The defendants were seven persons named Cleland, Chappell, Harrison, Wilson, Reynolds, Ford, and Ross.. . .

In January, 1859, the company was registered under the
Joint Stock Companies Act, 1856 (a).

(a) 19 & 20 Vict. c. 47. The
" Limited Liability Act," of which
sect. 9 provides, that if no regulations are prescribed in the memorandum of association for the regulation of the company, or so far as the
same do not extend to modify the
regulations contained in Schedule
(B.) of the act, those regulations
shall, so far as the same shall be
applicable, be deemed the regulations of the company. And that
section (63) provides, that the directors may, with the sanction of
the company in general meeting,
declare a dividend to be paid to the
shareholders in proportion to their
shares; but (64) no dividend shall
be payable except out of the profits arising from the business of
the company. And as to accounts,
it is provided that the directors
shall cause *true* accounts to be
kept of the stock in trade of the
company, and of the sums received
and *expended* by the company.
Such accounts to be kept in cash
book, journal and ledger. (70) Once
in the year at least they shall lay
before the shareholders a statement

It was projected by one Tripler, who was acquainted with the two principal defendants Cleland and Chappell, for the working certain strata or mines of asphaltum, for which he had obtained a concession from the Spanish Government in Cuba.

It was registered under the name of the Asphaltum Company, Limited, "to raise, and to import and sell in England, and other parts of Europe and America, a certain substance called asphaltum, and to manufacture it for sale," the nominal capital to be 100,000l., divided into 10,000 shares of 10l., the registered promoters being Tripler, Cleland, Chappell and several others, not including any of the other defendants.

The articles of association recited that the capital was subsequently altered to 100,000 shares of 1l. each. The defendant Ford had been out to Cuba to view the mines. The company was completely registered in January, 1859, and in 1860 all the defendants became directors. In November, 1860, Cleland ceased to be a director, and became auditor. The defendant Chappell, a solicitor, became secretary, both with seats at the board, and the defendants Reynolds and

of the income and expenditure for the past year. (71) The statement shall show, arranged under the most convenient heads, the amount of gross income and expenditure, distinguishing, &c. Every item of expenditure fairly chargeable against the year's income shall be brought into account, so that a just balance of profit and loss be laid before the meeting; and in cases where any item of expenditure, which may in fairness be distributed over several years, has been incurred in one year, the whole amount of such item shall be stated, with the addition of the reasons why only a portion of such expenditure is charged against the income of the year. (72) A balance sheet shall be made out in every year and laid before the general meeting, and shall contain a summary of property and liabilities arranged under the heads appearing in the form annexed to the table [one of which is "Profit and Loss," showing the disposable balance for payment of dividend, &c.] Probably preliminary expenses might under this be spread over several years; but it is essential that the accounts be *true*.

Harrison became directors. The others were so before September. In September, 1860, a prospectus was issued containing the representations set forth in the first count of the declaration. All the defendants except Harrison and Ross were then directors, and it was drawn up by Ford. It was not until November, 1860, that the plaintiff saw it. On 30th November, 1860, Cleland and Chappell ceased to be directors, and were appointed—the former auditor, the latter secretary—both with seats at the board; and at the same time Harrison and Ross were appointed directors, but did not act as such until a few days after the 4th December, 1860, the date of the plaintiff's first application for shares. There were two sets of shares issued, each to the amount of 50,000*l.*, the first being allotted to the directors.

The prospectus was as follows :—

" The Asphaltum Company (Limited).—The company is at present possessed of extensive works at Millwall, which have been for some time past in full operation. The oil and other products are highly appreciated, and command a ready sale, but as the existing plant is not capable of producing more than 7,000 gallons of oil per week, it will be necessary to increase the works in order to meet the daily increasing demand. [*The subjoined statement of the profits to be derived from the undertaking, deduced from the experience of actual workings, is based upon a calculation of the highest prices of labour and of raw material, and the lowest value of the manufactured articles :—*

" Statement of weekly expenditure and receipts in the working of 50 stills now in operation at the company's works, Millwall :—]

" OUTLAY.

75 tons of asphaltum, at £3 . . . . £225 0 0 (a)

[Then followed various other items, of which the total amount was] . . . £453 5 0

(a) This was untrue, the *actual* cost having been 5*l.* a ton (*vide* next page), and as to the statement here implied in a prospectus put into the plaintiff's hands in Nov. 1860 (*vide* next page) that *at that time* there were fifty mills at work, which were working up so many tons of asphalt a week, the supply had nearly ceased (*vide* p. 123), and there were only a few mills at work.

6,750 *gallons of oil, at* 2s.' 6d. . . .	.£843	15	0
750 *gallons of tar, at* 1d.	3	2	6
8 *tons of sulphate of iron, at* 60s. . .	24	0	0
5 *cwt.* ,, ,, pure, 16s. .	4	0	0
	£874	17	6
Outlay	453	5	0
Balance in favour	.£421	12	6

Equal to 21,924l. 10s. *per annum, or nearly* 22 *per cent. on the present entire capital of the company derived from the manufacture of oil, &c. at the Millwall works alone."*]

This prospectus was issued in September, 1860, and shown to the plaintiff at the end of November, 1860, before the 4th December, 1860, the date of his first application for shares.

In point of fact, as appeared from the evidence of the witnesses for the plaintiff, the company in 1860 had " extensive works at Millwall," and had fifty-three stills there, and they were " capable of producing 7,000 gallons of oil a week," and that supposing them supplied with the requisite raw material, and *all* to be kept at work, the result would be very much as set forth in the prospectus, and as an *estimate* it would be substantially fair.

But the case for the plaintiff, on this part of the case, assumed that the prospectus, at all events the passages in it within parentheses and italicised, represented that such had *in fact* been the actual results of actual working ; and, *in fact*, there has not been such results. And there were also positive misstatements in the prospectus: the fundamental fact as to profit—viz., the prime cost of the raw material being stated at 3l. instead of 5l. per ton, as the fact was.

In point of fact, there had been little asphalt actually obtained, except 200 tons already in stock when Tripler, the original projector, sold his interest in the mine; and which was paid for at the rate of 5l. a ton, not 3l. as stated in the prospectus.

And in point of fact, though there were fifty-three "stills," not much more than half had ever been at work at one time, and that only for a week or so at a time; and during September, October, November and December, often only ten of them at a time. And in December there were not more than five tons worked up in the course of a week.

In short, in December, 1860, the supply of asphalt had almost ceased, and what could be obtained was very inferior in quality and produced much less oil. Scarcely five tons a week were worked in December, and during that month and now hardly ten stills were at work, for want of asphalt to work.

While the original stock of asphalt, which was good, was working, down to September, 1860, the results were as stated in the prospectus. But after September, 1860, and down to December, 1862, the supply from the mines dropped off, both in quantity and quality; and at no time had the supply been such as to keep all the stills at work, nor much more than half of them, and that only for short periods. And in December, 1860, the works were in reality brought almost to a stand still.

In fact, therefore, there had never been such actual results derived from actual working as were represented in the prospectus; nor, even assuming the highest actual results obtained at any time to have been carried out over a year, would the results have been more than half what was represented.

On the 7th of November, 1860, there was an extra-ordinary general meeting held, at which all the defendants, except Reynolds and Harrison, were present (and they were soon afterwards, on the 30th of the same month, added to the direction), and it was resolved to raise 50,000l. more from the public, and shares to that amount were to be issued. An account of that meeting appeared in the newspapers, and some thousands of copies of it were printed and circulated by the defendants through the country. There was a speech of the defendant Chappell, which was extremely laudatory, stating that "their expectations had been more than realized," and that they could raise oil at 6*d*. a gallon and sell it at 3*s*. or 4*s*., and that they would be in a position to pay a dividend of 5 per cent. on the paid-up capital on the four months' working, which would be at the rate of 15 per cent. per annum.

The reprint of this speech was put in circulation through the country, and at Newcastle, where the plaintiff resided, after the 30th November, when Reynolds and Harrison were directors; and it was shown to the plaintiff prior to 4th December, but they did not act as directors until a few days after, and, when they were so, they sanctioned such statements.

One Mr. Howden was an acquaintance of the defendant Cleland, and in the latter part of the year 1860 spoke to him about the circulation of the prospectus among men of capital likely to take shares; and he received 10,000 copies for circulation, with a copy of a speech by the then chairman, the defendant Chappell, at the meeting of the company; and he went to Newcastle, where the plaintiff resided, and through one Roby, the company's agent there, showed him the prospectus and report of the meeting. In December 4, 1860, the plaintiff, through Roby, first applied for shares. He applied first for 1,000. In January, 1861, there was a meeting of the directors of this company at the European, at which were present Howden, Cleland, Chappell, Wilson, and, Howden believed, Ross and Reynolds. It was then said that the company was in a prosperous state, and the prospectus and report were discussed. Howden said he presumed the profit was calculated on actual facts, and was told that it was so. He had 20,000 shares for disposal, and he should have 1*s*. 6*d*. a share, out of which he was to pay country agents. He sold about 11,000 or 12,000 shares in the course of 1861. He went on to say, that in January,

1861, he went a journey to the north and went to New-castle-under-Lyne and other places. He had previously posted the prospectuses to those places to prepare people for his visits. In January, 1861, when he was at New-castle, he saw the plaintiff and also Roby, and he frequently saw the plaintiff.

Prior to the 4th December, 1860, Howden showed plaintiff a letter of Cleland before the order for the shares, dated the 30th of November, 1860 :—

" The company mentioned is one I have the highest opinion of. If it do not pay even by the end of next year from 20 to 25 per cent. it will be the result of mismanagement, as it possesses the materials for success in a measure exceeding any company I know. I am a considerable holder of shares myself, and take a very active part in promoting it."

Howden also showed the plaintiff a letter of Mr. Chappell to Roby in February, 1861, which ran thus :—

" Mr. Cleland has requested me to reply to you. * * * * The estimated relative proportion of expenses upon the production of 6,750 gallons of oil, with other products, is shown in the prospectus, and I believe is as nearly accurate as possible. At the present moment we are not working above half the quantities shown in the prospectus, owing to the fact that the demand was so great a few weeks since that we worked up nearly all our stock of the raw material, which did not come forward fast enough. We have, however, lately received supplies and advices of shipment of large quantities, so that in a week or two we shall again be working fully, and we are making preparations to increase our production to 10,000 gallons weekly. The raw material, which costs 3l. per ton, we sell a few tons of occasionally at 40l. No dividend has yet been declared, as the annual meeting does not take place until next month, but the accountants are now carefully examining the books preparatory to the meeting, with the view of reporting what dividend has been fairly earned. We expect that their report will show a dividend of 5 per cent. upon the four months' working up to the end of the year, and, if so, such dividend will be declared. Now is the time for parties to invest, while, owing to the state of the money market and the non-declaration of a dividend, the shares are in less demand. In my own opinion, there is little doubt, that, in the course of a very short time, the shares will go up to a considerable premium, and that those who delay their investments will come in by-and-by upon much less advantageous terms"(a).

(a) Query, whether this would make the letter evidence as against Cleland? At all events, these letters were only evidence as against these two defendants until others were shown to know of it.

At this time, February, 1861, the manager, M'Lean, had been sent out to Cuba, the defendant Ford having previously been there. On account of the falling off of the supply of asphalt, he found one of the mines full of water, and as to the other, or either, found the supply would be so inferior that he actually stopped the importation of it. He returned in May, 1861, and in June, 1861, made a report to the directors, to the effect that the price had fallen much more than was expected, and that asphalt could easily be raised at one of the mines at 10s. a ton, but not of such quality as the asphalt originally in stock, and which he thought could not have been raised from either of the mines. Tripler had gone away, and it was plain he had deceived the company, but Ford ha ' been out to Cuba, and knew the state of the works before the company set to work it.

In and about the preliminary expenses and experiments a sum of 9,460l., or, as the directors put it, 7,600l., had been expended, prior to and apart from the amount expended on the actual purchase of the mines and stock of asphalt on hand. The experiments ceased in 1859.

From January, 1860, to December 31, 1860, there was a year's actual working.

The books were made up to December 30, and in accordance with the Act (a) it was intended, on the 18th March, to send to the shareholders a statement of account and balance sheet up to the 30th December, 1860, accompanied by a notice for a general meeting of the shareholders seven days afterwards, that is, on the 26th March.

On the 15th March, 1860, a meeting to settle a statement of account and balance sheet for that purpose was held, attended by Cleland, Chappell and Wilson, and they acted as a committee in the matter.

The books kept were journal, cash book and ledger, and there were originally no false entries, though they were not kept quite in accordance with the provisions of the Joint Stock Companies Act (a), as regards the accounts to be kept.

There was a profit and loss account, in which the prime cost of the asphaltum, the new material, was truly stated at 5*l.* a ton, but there was no separate account of " preliminary expenses," and they were brought into the general account. From the books as thus kept and made up a balance sheet was prepared, which showed a deficiency on profit and loss of 2,052*l.*, and which was laid before the auditors, *i. e.* the defendant Cleland and one Evans, an accountant.

They both agreed that the whole of the preliminary expenses ought not to be brought into the account of profit and loss (*b*), and concurred in the following report

(*a*) 19 & 20 Vict. c. 47, s. 69. The directors shall cause true accounts to be kept:—of the stock in trade of the company ; of the sums of money received and expended by the company, and the matter in respect of which such receipt and expenditure takes place; of the credits and liabilities of the company. Such accounts shall be kept in a cash book, journal and ledger. 70. Once in the year the directors shall lay before the company, in general meeting, a statement of the income and expenditure for the year, made up to a date not more than three months before such meeting 71. The statement so made shall show, arranged under the most convenient heads, the amount of gross income, distinguishing the several sources from which it has been derived, and the amount of gross expenditure, &c. Every item of expenditure *fairly chargeable against the year's income* shall be brought into account, so that a just balance of profit and loss may be laid before the meeting; and in cases where any item of expenditure *which may in fairness be distributed over several years* has been incurred in any one year, the whole amount of such item shall be stated, with the addition of the reasons why only a portion of such expenditure is charged against the income of the year.

(*b*) A balance sheet shall be made out every year and laid before the general meeting of the company, and such balance sheet shall contain a summary of the property and liability of the company arranged under heads appearing in the form [" Profit and Loss," showing the disposable balance available for dividend]. 73. A printed copy of such balance sheet shall, seven days previously to such meeting, be delivered to or sent to the registered address of every shareholder.

to the directors, which, however, was not delivered until the 25th March, the day before the meeting.

The auditors' report was as follows :—

"London, March 25, 1861.

"Gentlemen,—We have examined the balance sheet issued by the directors, and find it to be sufficiently vouched, and that the books have been well kept, with the exception of the share ledger, which we should recommend to be written up upon a different principle. We are of opinion that the balance sheet which has been sent to you does not accord with the provisions of the Limited Liability Act, under which your company is constituted, and we have therefore prepared a balance sheet and a profit and loss account, which we would recommend for your adoption in place of the one already issued. The main differences between these accounts have arisen from the attempt to define exactly what portion of the expenditure of the company should be placed to preliminary expenses. No separate account of that nature has been raised upon the books of the company, and having regard to the peculiar circumstances of the business and to the difficulties necessarily experienced at its commencement in determining the best and most economical modes of manufacture, and also to the fact that many expenses attending experiments must have been incurred which it was impossible at the outset to distinguish from ordinary expenses, we have felt that any division must be, to a great extent, arbitrary, and that neither ourselves nor the directors were in a position to distinguish, with any exactitude, between preliminary and ordinary expenses ; all expenditure of the nature previously referred to, together with law charges, travelling expenses to Cuba, and other items, would be legitimately chargeable to preliminary expenses; and we would suggest that the meeting, after considering all the circumstances, should fix upon such sum as it may consider fairly chargeable to the account in question, and should vote that it be passed off to preliminary expenses, and that it be written off from that account at the rate of from 10 to 20 per cent. per annum.

"We are, Gentlemen, your obedient servants,

"L. H. Evans, } Auditors.
"W. Cleland, }

"To the Shareholders of the Asphaltum Company (Limited)."

In the meantime, between the 15th March and the 18th March, the balance sheet had to be sent round to the shareholders, seven days before the 26th.

Before the meeting of March, 1861, the secretary Gibson was directed to make out a balance sheet, and did so ; and laid it before a committee, comprising Cleland, Wilson and Chappell. It was preparatory to a shareholders' or general meeting. It showed a deficiency on the profit and loss account of 2,205*l*. The committee gave him instructions to make out another, as certain amounts, they said, ought to be charged differently. His balance sheet included preliminary expenses. They gave him instructions as to another balance sheet, saying that it was not fair to charge the whole of the expenses to the oil account, and asked him to alter the balance sheet; but he said that he believed it a fair statement of the affairs of the company, and that it was the result of the books. He was then instructed to make certain alterations, and to deduct from the cost of asphaltum on hand on the 31st of December, 1859, such a sum as would reduce the price from 5*l*. a ton to 2*l*. 10*s*. He afterwards was instructed to reduce it to 2*l*. 10*s*., and that made a difference of 852*l*., which was carried from profit and loss to the mine account. He was next desired to make other alterations. The alterations, altogether, brought the amount of difference to about 3,378*l*.—that is, this was the result of the alterations directed by the directors in the balance sheet, and the amount of the difference between the original balance sheet as prepared by him and theirs. He went on to state that he got another balance sheet made out upon their instructions, and was about the same as the one they printed, and the transfers of account mentioned were made in the books. He received instructions to alter the books from the committee; that is, the balance sheet was to be altered as I have stated, and the books were to be made to correspond with them. The balance sheet thus made out on these directions was the one sent round to the shareholders on the 18th March, 1860, and was submitted to the auditors, the defendant Cleland and one Evans, a witness for the plaintiff.

The balance sheet of the directors brought out a loss of

2,052*l.*, and made the general charges, including "preliminary expenses," 7,600*l.*

The balance sheet prepared by Evans, the co-auditor, brought out a loss " By balance of profit and loss account, including preliminary expenses, of 9,500*l.*"

On the 26th March, 1861, the general meeting of the shareholders was held, and both balance sheets were presented. There was a difference of opinion among the defendants as to whether there ought to be a dividend, and which of the modes of keeping the accounts was the proper one.

One of the defendants, Ford, was opposed to a dividend.

A shareholder proposed a dividend of 10 per cent. on the four months' working.

Before the meeting took place, certain of the defendants —Cleland, Chappell and Wilson—directed a clerk to make alterations in the books, not by way of alteration of the amounts of items, but by transfer of them to different accounts, the effect of which was to alter the loss of 2,052*l.* into a profit of 1,247*l.* And then a balance sheet in accordance with these altered books was made out.

On the 18th March this was sent round to the shareholders under the provisions of the Act (*a*).

The co-auditor Evans opposed it.

None of the defendants proposed it, or supported it, or voted for it.

But all were present and none of them opposed it, and it was carried.

Previously to the resolution for a dividend, a resolution

(*a*) A balance sheet shall be made out in every year and laid before the general meeting of the company, and shall contain a summary of the property and liabilities of the company arranged under the heads appearing in the form annexed to the statute, or as near thereto as circumstances shall admit [one of them is " Profit and Loss:" showing the disposable balance for payment of dividend]. 73. A printed copy of such balance sheet shall, seven days previously to the meeting, be sent to the shareholders.

had been proposed and carried, that the sum of 2,052l., then standing to the debit of profit and loss, be carried to the mines account, and that the preliminary expense account stand at 8,742l., the effect of which, coupled with the previous alterations in the books, would be to bring out a balance of 1,247l. on profit and loss account as profit; and after the meeting alterations were made in the books in accordance with this resolution.

The dividend of 10 per cent. was accordingly declared, but only paid upon the " preference shares," and in cases where it would come to sums not exceeding 10l.

On the 2nd April, the auditor Evans wrote to the directors the following letter, resigning his office on account of the proceedings adopted—all the defendants then being on the board except Cleland, co-auditor, and Chappell, solicitor, both with seats at the board :—

" 15, King Street, Cheapside, E.C., London, April 2, 1861.
" Gentlemen,—Since your ordinary general meeting I have reconsidered the matters upon which I then spoke. and also the position and past working of the company, and, having regard to the fact that its affairs may, in the event of its non-success, become the subjects of legal proceedings, I deem it my duty, as well on my own interest as in that of others, to protest against the resolution passed by the meeting for the payment of a dividend, and which has been stated in the daily papers (see " Daily News" and "Telegraph" of the 27th ult.) as at the rate of 10 per cent. per annum. According to the Act under which your company is constituted a dividend can only be legally paid out of profits. The following is the statement by which it is attempted to be shown that a profit has been made :—[He set it out.]

Balance, net profit, brought down . . . . £1,247 : 5s. 8d.

Any lengthened comment on this statement is unnecessary, inasmuch as the gross profit shown is produced almost entirely by an arbitrary transfer of part of the cost of your materials and labour ; while the stock has been valued at selling instead of at cost price, the repairs have been charged to plant and interest on loans to mines account. I would refer you to those clauses of Table (B.) of the Limited Liability Act, 1856, headed ' Dividends, Accounts, and Audit,' in which the powers and duties of directors and auditors in relation to the accounts and dividends are very clearly and very admirably stated. The question of the probable future success of your company is one altogether beside the present question, which is not whether you may make a net profit in future years, but whether you have done so in the past year. The cost of the oil made by you last year was the fuel, labour and materials consumed in producing it, and no considerations of errors, inexperience or badness of materials can countervail this fact, however much they may affect your views of the prospects of the company. I am informed that I was re-elected auditor to the company. I thank you for the confidence thus reposed, but, as I could not make your printed balance sheet (which has in effect passed by the meeting) a basis for future accounts, I must most respectfully, and with much regret, decline to accept the appointment.

" I am, Gentlemen, your obedient servant,

" LEWIS HENRY EVANS.

" To the Directors of the Asphaltum Company (Limited)."

The answer of Mr. Gibson, the secretary, was then read, dated the 19th of April. It simply acknowledged the letter, and accepted his resignation with regret.

The plaintiff's second application for shares was at that time before the defendants, and was acceded to, and 1,000 more shares allotted.

At the end of March, 1861, the declaration of the dividend was communicated to the shareholders, and among them to the plaintiff, who was then the holder of 1,000 shares.

Before the 18th March he was at the works, and was pleased with what he saw there, but he knew nothing of asphalt.

On the 15th April, 1861, he applied for 1,000 more shares.

In May they were allotted and issued. In December, 1861, he applied for and received 600 more; which were not mentioned in the declaration.

In 1862 he was sued for calls, and pleaded as to 600 that he was induced to and did become a holder by reason of the fraud of the directors, as to the rest he pleaded not indebted.

In the meantime, by reason of the failure of asphalt, the manufacture of oil from petroleum had been carried on at the works, and the plaintiff filed a bill in Chancery to restrain it.

In June, 1862, this suit was compromised, on the terms of the company taking back 1,000 shares, the last 600 and 400 of the second thousand.

Afterwards this action was brought, in which the declaration was confined to 2,000 shares.

The company was being wound up, and its books and papers were in the custody of the liquidators, whose attornies were also attornies for the defendants Cleland and Wilson.

Notice had been given to those attornies to produce the books and documents, and Spackman had received a *subpœna duces tecum* to produce them.. . .

The next witness called (before Gibson was called) was Evans, the accountant and co-auditor. He said a balance sheet was given to him to audit. The secretary, Gibson, told him that he disagreed— . . . .

The witness then went on to state that he refused to sign the balance sheet given to him as correct, and wrote to the secretary to that effect, and he prepared one which he deemed to be correct. He still believed it to be correct, and it brought out a loss. He now produced it, and it was read.

The witness then stated the result of his balance sheet, a loss of 9,547*l.*, including preliminary expenses.

The witness then stated that he gave the company a copy of this balance sheet, either on the day of the meeting or the day before it. He himself, he said, attended the meeting, and heard his balance sheet read to it, and it was passed as the balance sheet of the company. After that Mr. H. B. Sheridan, M.P., proposed a dividend, saying that in companies with which he was connected— insurance companies—it was customary to pay interest upon capital before a balance sheet of profit and loss could be struck, as years might elapse before a balance could be struck.

MARTIN, B.—What is the meaning of that as applied to a trading company? One can understand as to life insurance companies, it is all profit for some time until the persons insured begin to die off. It is otherwise in such companies as this. . . .

Hawkins then continued his cross-examination of the witness, pressing him particularly as to the passage in his report as to the difficulty in exactly allotting the heads of expense, and he said he had charged all the preliminary expense to "profit and loss," and he said his report was read. In the course of the cross-examination of the witness the balance sheet which had been called for in chief and not produced, was put into his hands. He was then pressed as to the resolution, before the resolution for a dividend, that the sum of 2,052*l.* then standing to the debit of profit and loss, be carried to the mines account, and that the preliminary expense account stand at 8,742*l.*, and was then asked whether, supposing that such a resolution was carried, it would not justify the directors in declaring a dividend, and he said it would not, as it would not make a profit.

MARTIN, B.—Of course not. How could the mere writing off a sum from one side to the other of an account make a profit if it did not exist?

Chambers.—But if fairly transferred it would.

Hawkins.—If charged against capital instead of profit and loss.

MARTIN, B.—But he says it is not so.

The witness.—If the whole 9,547*l.* were written off preliminary expenses it would not have made a profit.

Chambers.—We say that it is not a change of figures, but of facts.

MARTIN, B.—He says it is not a true representation of the facts.

Hawkins resumed his cross-examination of the witness, who said that he had tried to distinguish the preliminary expenses not chargeable against the trade account; but he admitted that he had recommended a lump sum.

MARTIN, B.—No doubt there may be difficulties as to bookkeeping, but the question is as to misstatements of matters of fact, of a profit actually made which was not made....

Lush then withdrew it, and continued his re-examination as to the manner in which the preliminary expenses were dealt with in the director's balance sheet, which spread over several years, on which

MARTIN, B., observed that he remembered the subject had been a good deal discussed as to railway companies some years ago, and there was a great objection to the course taken, but now it appeared that there was an agreement among auditors to spread such expenses over a number of years; that, indeed, was objected to, and it was the reason why the North-Western Railway Company were able to declare large dividends soon after they opened their line. But no doubt it was now done, and it would never do to impute it to the directors as a fraud that they had done what was usually done by auditors. . . .

The witness then stated, in answer to the objection, that the books did not show a profit in his opinion (*a*).

Gibson, the secretary, was called to prove the balance sheet he was instructed by Cleland, Wilson and Chappell to make out preparatory to the dividend meeting in March, 1861. It showed a deficiency on the profit and loss account of 2,052*l.*, including the whole of the preliminary expenses.

(*a*) The accountant was " an expert" as to accounts, and it would be difficult in any other way to prove the *result of accounts.* The books were in Court on motion to produce to the defendants and sub- *pœna duces tecum* to the liquidators. On the question of *fact* as to *actual* profit the manager was called; but the question of apparent profit would depend on *the accounts.* And that was most material.

A clerk in the office made it out and he settled it, and was then desired to alter it. The clerk also was called, who said he had made the alterations in the books which he had been instructed to make. The books he altered were the journal and the ledger.

Lush now called for the books referred to, which were produced from the custody of the liquidators of the company.

The witness pointed out the place where he made the alterations. An amount of 489*l.* was carried from "trade charges" into other accounts. Then 1,907*l.* was taken out of the "oil account" and transferred to "general charges" or "preliminary expenses," and 971*l.* was transferred from the "oil account" to the "mines account." Such alterations were made to affect the "profit and loss account;" and he prepared the printed balance sheet, issued by the board in accordance with these alterations, the effect of which upon the balance sheet was to alter a loss of 2,052*l.*, into a profit of 1,247*l.* The dividend meeting was the 26th of March, 1861, and the alterations he said were made before that meeting. This was the plaintiff's case

Chambers (for Cleland and Wilson), *Hawkins* (for Ford), and *Denman* (for Chappell), did not submit that there was no case as against them, and were about to address the jury, when

MARTIN, B., recommended them to confer together and make some mutual arrangement if possible to avoid their *all* addressing the jury.

They at once conferred with the plaintiff's counsel with a view to a settlement of the action.

In the result, upon terms agreed to (*a*),

Jury discharged by consent.

(*a*) A Judge's order for the whole amount claimed and costs.

MACDOUGALL v. JERSEY IMPERIAL HOTEL CO., LIMITED

2 Hem. & M. 528 (1864)
Vice Chancellor - Chancery

THIS was a Demurrer.

The Bill stated that the *Jersey Imperial Hotel Co.* (*Limited*), was a Joint Stock Co., limited by shares, registered under the Companies Act, 1862, on the 7th May, 1863, with a nominal capital of £40,000, in 4000 shares of £10 each; and, by the Articles of Association, power was given to the Company, by special resolution, founded on a recommendation of the Directors, to borrow on debenture, or mortgage, " or such other securities as they think fit," any sum not exceeding £20,000. . . .

The first ordinary general meeting of the Company was held on the 5th May, 1864, and thereat the following special resolutions were proposed :—

(1) That interest at £5 per cent. per annum be paid to the shareholders on the amounts paid up by them on their shares from the respective days of payment to the 5th May, 1864.

(2) That the Directors be authorised to borrow and take up on debentures, or mortgage of any of the property of the Company, or on such other securities as they may think fit, any sum or sums not exceeding £10,000, so soon as the roof shall have been put on the hotel now in course of construction.

The Plaintiffs opposed these resolutions, but they were both carried; and therefore the Plaintiffs handed in a written protest against the validity of these resolutions.

The Bill charged—

1. That the Company was not duly constituted, in as much as all the capital had not been subscribed; and that, therefore, the borrowing powers of the Company had not come into existence, and the second resolution was ultra vires.

2. That no profits whatever had been earned by the Company, and that the interest directed by the first resolution to be paid, would necessarily be paid out of the capital of the Company, or by borrowed money; and that such resolution was illegal. . . .

The Defendants demurred. . . .

VICE-CHANCELLOR SIR W. PAGE WOOD :—

I ought not to allow this demurrer.

Beyond all doubt there can be nothing more mischievous than that the Court should interfere with the internal administration of Companies of this sort; but the limit which the Court has laid down for its action is a very definite and intelligible one. The sole question is, whether the step about to be taken is within the competence of the shareholders as a body? and, if so, the matter must be left to their discretion. On this ground, I did not call upon Mr. Everitt on the point whether they were entitled to carry on business or not; the only relief which I feel it properly competent for me to give, is on the question of payment of interest; on all the rest of the case I did not hear a reply. I do not see why *The Westminster Palace Company's* case should not be followed. I see no reason why I should assume that there is fraud or impropriety attributable to the Directors, merely because, with a nominal capital of £10,000, they propose to commence business on a much smaller scale than they originally— to judge by the prospectus—intended. The Plaintiff knew that £10,000 was the "nominal capital," and that there were borrowing powers exercisable by the Directors; and I cannot hold that he has been misled. If the majority of shareholders think with him, he has his remedy in his own hands; if not, he is bound by their opinion.

As to the payment of interest, however, I am of a different opinion.

The Bill avers that there are no profits, and that interest has been paid, or is about to be paid, out of capital; that the shareholders have paid £4 per share, and are discharged to that extent, and that they are now about to take back sums equal to £5 per cent. of that very capital in the shape of interest.

On grounds of public policy, and on every principle, not only of honesty as regards the public generally, but of the interests of this Company itself, I feel bound to prevent this proceeding. This is not in accordance with the contract entered into with the Legislature on behalf of the public whereby it was determined that the share-holders should be liable to a certain defined amount, and no more, to the creditors of the Company; and not in accordance with the contract between the parties, whereby each shareholder was protected against creditors to the extent of the contributive liability of all the others.

Suppose the Company to agree to call up the whole £10 per share, and then to treat the sum thus raised as a fund out of which they were to draw interest at the rate of £5 per cent. as long as it lasted, the public would have lost the whole of their security. That might give rise to a very difficult question in case a creditor were proceeding to enforce his equity against a shareholder who had parted with his shares to an innocent holder, treating them as £4 paid up, when, in fact, in the eye of this Court, they would only have been paid to the extent of £3 : 16s.

Then consider the effect upon the shareholders, inter se. Suppose it to become necessary to pay further monies for the purpose of carrying into effect the pur-poses of the Company, and that the whole of the capital devoted to this purpose had been called up and handed back among the shareholders, might not a shareholder who had purchased his shares after this arrangement had been completed justly complain that a great part of the capital had been improperly employed? The Company may say, this is a species of administration, and is of great service in inducing persons to pay their calls readily : but the directors have other means for obtaining the payment of calls, and it is their duty to enforce such payment; and they can, if they please, charge £10 per cent. on the arrears, so that it is not necessary for them to adopt this mode of inducement, and I do not think that it is a right course for them to take.

I must, therefore, overrule this demurrer.

BINNEY v. THE INCE HALL COAL AND CANNEL COMPANY

35 L.J. Ch. 363 (1866)
Vice Chancellor - Chancery

KINDERSLEY, V.C. ⎰ BINNEY *v.* THE INCE
Jan. 29, 30; ⎱ HALL COAL AND CAN-
Feb. 12, 13. ⎰ NEL COMPANY.

The Ince Hall Coal and Cannel Company was formed in 1848, subject to the provisions of the act 7 & 8 Vict. c. 110, for the purpose of working certain collieries near Wigan. Its nominal capital consisted of 2,100 shares of 100*l.* each. . . .

The 17th article provided, " that no division of the profits of the company, or any part thereof, should be made amongst the shareholders, until provision had been made thereout for payment of interest in respect of certain debts (specifically mentioned), and also in respect of the debts for the time being owing from the company to the shareholders in respect of advances of capital as thereinbefore mentioned."

The other clauses of the deed material to the suit were contained in the 32nd and 142nd articles, and provided as follows:

32. "Any ordinary general meeting of the company may from time to time, after directing proper provision to be made for answering and satisfying the debts and liabilities of the company, or so much thereof as shall for the time being be payable or accrue due previous to the next annual general meeting, and also after directing such sum to be appropriated as such meeting shall think desirable as a reserve fund to provide for all or any of the ordinary or extraordinary expenses of the company, or to extend the operations of the company, determine the proportion of the clear gains and profits to be from time to time divided amongst the shareholders.". . .

At a general meeting of the company, held on the 20th of August, 1864, it was resolved: (1) "That a reserve fund be formed out of the gains and profits of the company for the purposes mentioned in the deed of settlement, and that for the purpose of commencing the formation of such reserve fund the directors be empowered to set apart a sum of 3,000*l.*

out of the gains and profits of the company." (2) "That the directors of the company be empowered out of the gains and profits of the company to apply a sum of 10,101*l.* towards the discharge ratably of the instalments of capital which have been paid by the several shareholders of the company." (3) "That a dividend be declared at the rate of 2*l.* per share upon the shares standing upon the register, to be payable out of the clear gains and profits of the company, for the period ending the 30th of June last."

Lancaster, whose rights under the deed of settlement had previously been the subject of controversy between himself and the directors, was present at the meeting, and protested against the application of the 10,101*l.* contemplated by the second of the above resolutions.

The plaintiff, as equitable mortgagee of Lancaster's shares, shortly afterwards instituted the present suit to restrain the company from carrying the resolution into effect, and praying that the said sum of 10,101*l.* might be declared to be clear gains and profits of the company, and, as such, applicable to the payment of dividends on the shares in the company; also that a receiver might be appointed of the dividends payable in respect of Lancaster's shares, without prejudice to the rights of the first mortgagee. . . .

The argument was then continued with reference to the distinction between gross profits and net profits, and the peculiar circumstances affecting the maintenance of capital in mining operations, in the course of which the Vice Chancellor admitted that his original view of the case was very much altered by the considerations submitted to him. Reference was made to the following definition of "profit" in *Adam Smith's Wealth of Nations*, note 7 : " By profit is meant that part of the produce obtained by the employment of capital in industrious undertakings, which remains to its employers after replacing the capital, or such portion of it as may have been wasted in the undertakings, and every other expense necessarily incurred in carrying them on." . . . .

KINDERSLEY, V.C. then gave judgment as follows.—The main object of this suit is to obtain an injunction to restrain the Ince Hall Coal and Cannel Company from applying the sum of 10,101*l.* towards the liquidation in part of the share-capital of the members. There are other collateral objects to which I will refer presently. . . .

Now, it appears to me, upon the whole view of the provisions in this deed, that the original intention of the parties was, that the contributed capital should be paid off at the termination of the company; but I cannot see how it would be inconsistent with such an intention to pay it off either wholly or in part during the continuance of the company. Certainly I find no express clause prohibiting such a course; nor is there any express obligation to divide as dividend the residue of actual profits, even after setting apart that reserve fund (which it is admitted beyond dispute that the company was authorized to do under the 32nd clause of their deed) to answer any extraordinary expenses that might be sustained through accident or emergency of any kind in carrying on the concern. It would be strange if they did not divide the residue of the profits, because it would, in fact, amount to putting by another reserve fund; but there is nothing in the deed to prevent their so doing.

But, then, no fund could properly be set apart, either for reserve or for division among the members of the company, unless it consisted of net profits strictly so called; and in the course of the argument upon this present case I think that we have arrived at a very clear perception of the principle upon which the directors and the company were bound to act in ascertaining such net profits. The first step would be to make good the capital by taking stock and putting a value upon all the assets of the company, of whatever nature, and deducting therefrom all the liabilities (including amongst those liabilities the amount of contributed capital), and the surplus, if any, then remaining of the gross receipts would be net profit. Now, assuming for the present that this sum, which the company have thought it necessary to keep back from division among its members and to apply, not as a reserve fund, but towards the liquidation of the share capital, represented part of the stock or capital of the concern, I do not see how it could be to the prejudice of Mr. Lancaster, in contradistinction to the other shareholders, to apply that money in reducing the capital, which was, in fact, a debt of the company. The only suggestion that I have heard tending that way was made by Mr. Osborne in reply, namely, that it is for the interest of all the shareholders to have sufficient working capital. No doubt it is. But it would be extremely detrimental to the shareholders if they were compelled to keep up a larger capital than they wanted to work with, or than they could safely employ; and I cannot find in this deed anything which precludes that general right of the company to determine by a majority what shall be their course of management in this respect. The anomalous position of Mr. Lancaster does not seem to me in the smallest degree to put him in a different situation from the other shareholders with regard to the advantage or disadvantage of applying a part of the capital (that is, of the money which has been kept back representing capital) in discharge of the share capital, because he is obliged to contribute his quota towards the annual payment of the interest on that share capital, and he will be liable ultimately to contribute his proportionate share towards the repayment of the principal at the dissolution of the company. It must be recollected that I am for the present taking the case not of money which might be divided as profit, but of money which represented capital, and which must be set apart before the profit could be ascertained.

But now comes the question, what is it that the company is intending to do? I cannot lay my finger on any evidence, nor has any been furnished which enables me to say that they were proposing merely to apply capital or what ought to be kept back as capital in discharge of the contributed share capital. . . .

therefore I shall direct an inquiry for the purpose of ascertaining what was the amount of net profit for the half year preceding the date of the resolution; and I think the inquiry should be prefaced by a declaration that the company are not authorized to apply any part of the net gains and profits (specifying the principle upon which those gains and profits are to be ascertained) towards the liquidation of any part of the share capital. . . .

BLOXAM v. METROPOLITAN RAILWAY COMPANY

L.R. 3 Ch. App. 337 (1868)
Lord Chancellor - Court of Appeal

Railway Company—Ultrà vires—Dividend out] of Capital—Auditor's Powers—Injunction—Bonà fide Shareholder.

A railway company whose original line was constructed and at work, obtained powers and money for the construction of an extension line, the shareholders in which were not to have more than 6 per cent. for the first three years, and afterwards were to have their shares amalgamated with the ordinary stock of the company.

The directors had in former half-years charged to capital one-half of the office expenses, and also a sum representing interest on debentures issued for lines in construction; they had also paid interest on the *Extension* share capital out of a sum of money paid by contractors as interest in respect of unfinished lines; and a dividend on the ordinary stock had been declared accordingly :—

Held, by *Wood,* V.C., on the application of a holder of shares in the *Extension* line, that the directors were wrong in all these charges, and that an interlocutory injunction must issue to restrain them from declaring a dividend calculated accordingly.

Held, by Lord *Chelmsford,* L.C., on appeal :—

That whether the half of the office expenses was or was not rightly charged to capital, no interlocutory injunction could be granted on that ground, inasmuch as the balance carried over to the next half-year on the revenue account was much larger than the sum so charged :

But that it was doubtful whether interest on debentures issued for lines in construction could be charged to capital :

That it was doubtful whether it was right to pay interest on the *Extension* capital out of the money received from the contractors :

That the questions were not concluded by the certificate of the auditors under 30 & 31 Vict. c. 127, s. 30:

That these were not merely matters of internal management, and that the Court would interfere in such cases if the directors were acting *ultrà vires*:

And that the questions were of such importance and doubt that the injunction must be continued till the hearing.

The Plaintiff had bought his shares a short time before the bill was filed, and to enable him to file the bill :—

Held, that he was not for that reason, or for the reason that these charges had been acquiesced in by the shareholders on former occasions, prevented from obtaining an interlocutory injunction.

BY an Act passed in 1854 (17 & 18 Vict. c. ccxxi.), the *Metropolitan Railway Company* was incorporated, and authorized to make a railway from *Paddington* to the *General Post Office*, with certain branches, and the Act provided, sect. 196, "That it shall not be lawful for the company out of any money by this Act or any other Act relating to the company authorized to be raised by calls in respect of shares, or by the exercise of any power of borrowing, to pay interest or dividend to any shareholder on the amount of the calls made in respect of the shares held by him in the capital by this Act authorized to be raised."

The *Companies Clauses Consolidation Act* (8 Vict. c. 16), was incorporated with this Act, by sect. 120 of which it is provided, that previously to every ordinary meeting the directors shall prepare a scheme shewing the profits, and proposing a dividend for the past half-year; and by sect. 121 it is declared that the company shall not make any dividend whereby their capital stock will be in any degree reduced.

By an Act (27 & 28 Vict. c. cccxv.) called the *Metropolitan Railway* (*Tower Hill Extension*) *Act*, 1864, powers were given to make an extension of the railway from *Moorgate Street* to *Tower Hill*, and by sections 26 and 28 the company was authorized to raise any further sums not exceeding in the whole £700,000 by the creation of new shares in their undertaking, and such shares were to be called *Extension* shares, and might be issued as a separate capital charged upon the profits of the *Extension* railway, or might be raised as new shares or new stock in the capital of the company; and the company were authorized by resolution to define the terms on which such *Extension* shares should be created, and might direct the application of the profits of the *Extension* railway, and might limit the amount of dividend, and provide for the ultimate amalgamation of the original capital and the *Extension* shares, and the company were empowered to borrow any sum not exceeding £233,000 under certain provisions and restrictions; and by sect. 32 all moneys which the company were authorized to raise by new shares or on mortgage, were to be applied only to the purposes of the said Act: the Act also contained a clause similar to sect. 196 of the Act of 1854.

By resolutions passed at a meeting of the company in February, 1865, under powers in the Act, the *Extension* shares were created in £10 shares in the company, and it was declared that the holders of *Extension* shares should not be entitled to receive any dividends out of the profits of the undertaking until December, 1866, and from that time should be entitled to dividends in common with the holders of existing ordinary stock, but limited in their case for the first three years to the rate of £6 per cent. per annum : that on the 1st of January, 1870, the *Extension* shares should be converted into stock, and amalgamated with the ordinary stock of the company.

The *Extension* shares, under this and other similar Acts for other extensions, were accordingly issued and taken up.

An agreement was made in 1866 between the company and Mr. *Kelk* and others, whereby Mr. *Kelk* agreed to construct the *Tower Hill Extension Railway* for £383,000, and £80,000 for stations, and the agreement contained the following clause :—

"The railway and station works, as before defined, and all consequent, contingent, and incidental works, are to be completed within, on, or before the 31st day of December, 1867 ; and in order to secure the punctual completion of the said railway and works, and in lieu of all penalties for the non-completion thereof within the prescribed period, the contractors shall, until the said railway be completed and opened for traffic, pay to the directors such sums of money as shall be equivalent to interest upon so much of the sum of £700,000 (being the share capital created in respect of the said railway) as shall from time to time be called and paid up at the respective times and the rates following (that is to say) :—For and on each of the four half-years ending respectively the 30th day of June and the 31st day of December, 1865, and the 30th day of June and the 31st day of December, 1866, at the rate of £5 per cent. per annum ; and for and on every subsequent half-year thereafter at the rate of £6 per cent. per annum ; and in case the said railway shall be completed and opened for traffic during any such subsequent half-year the contractors shall, on the completion and opening for traffic thereof, pay to the directors such sums of money as shall be equivalent to interest at the rate of £6 per cent. per annum upon the share capital so called and paid up as aforesaid for such a number of days as shall elapse between the last preceding half-year and such completion and opening for traffic. If in the opinion of the engineer there shall be any such delay in the delivery of possession of the land by the company as shall render it impracticable to complete and open the railway by the 31st day of December, 1867, such allowance in respect of interest shall be made by [*sic.*] the contractors as shall be equivalent to the interest payable by them for the period of the delay so occasioned."

On the 31st of July, 1867, the directors issued their report for the preceding half-year. The statement of accounts accompanying the report contained a capital account and revenue account.

The debtor side of the capital account consisted of the following items:—

	£.
"Consolidated Capital of £1,800,000 . .	1,799,909
£5 per Cent. Preference Capital, £300,000 .	300,000
Extension Share Capital of £1,900,000 . .	1,867,994
Debenture Capital of £1,333,333 . . .	1,255,283
Temporary Loans	60,000
	£5,283,186"

And amongst the items on the creditor side were: "Interest on loans, and proportion of debenture interest chargeable to capital, £8799;" "Office expenses, £3108, less one-half charged to revenue, £1554."

The debtor side of the revenue account shewed receipts from balance, traffic, rents, interest on balances, and transfer fees—total, £132,613.

The creditor side of the revenue account consisted of the following items:—

	£.
"Working Expenses	41,350
Compensations	1,750
Proportion of Office Expenses	1,554
Annuities	125
	44,779
Interest on £449,330 Debenture Capital . .	10,110
Dividend on £300,000 Preference Stock . .	7,500
Dividend on £1,800,000 Consolidated Stock, at	
7 per cent.	63,000
Balance carried to next account . . .	7,224
	£132,613"

It did not appear on the account how the interest on the *Extension* share capital of £1,900,000 was paid, but it seemed to have been paid out of the interest received from Mr. *Kell* under his contract, which also did not appear in the account.

The auditors certified the accounts in the usual form pursuant to 30 & 31 Vict. c. 127, s. 30.

The half-yearly meeting of the company was held on the 7th of August, and at that meeting Mr. *Parson*, the chairman of the company, in moving that the report and accounts be received and adopted, said that "the £449,330 stated in the accounts as debenture capital, on which interest was charged to revenue, was not the whole debenture capital, but was the whole raised in respect of those portions of the line which were productive of any return. The directors would endeavour in a short time to take care that the division of office and general expenses partly charged to capital and partly to revenue should be charged to revenue. The directors wished to do it, but the shareholders would see that, in an undertaking such as the *Metropolitan* was, its traffic growing with great rapidity, although comparatively small at the outset, they could not afford to pay large dividends and put every one of these charges to revenue. The expenses of the direction were, in a great measure, the result not of the old undertakings, but of the new ones. The dividend on the 6 per cent. *Extension* stock had been paid as usual, and the proprietors knew what that was. They had received from the contractor every half-year the amount necessary to pay that dividend, and should continue to do so until the line was opened. They put that fund aside, and meant to pay that dividend in January. They also wanted £855,000 for new works, and proposed to raise £600,000 in new redeemable shares."

In January, 1868, the directors issued warrants for dividends at 6 per cent. on the *Extension* capital, which were afterwards paid in cash to the holders. . . .

On the 25th of January, 1868, the Plaintiff filed the bill in this suit on behalf of himself and all other the shareholders of the *Metropolitan Railway Company*, ordinary, preference, and extension, except the Defendants, against the company and the directors, charging that the company had, for the purpose of increasing the sum represented as available for dividends, charged sums on the capital account which were properly payable out of revenue, and had for the same purpose included in the debtor side of the revenue account sums which ought properly to have appeared in the capital account, and had inserted on the debtor side of the revenue account sums paid as interest by Mr. *Kelk*, which sums were paid by him in consideration of sums paid or to be paid to him out of capital: that the company had raised nearly all the capital authorized to be raised for the *Tower Hill Extension*, but had no intention, unless they could obtain money from other sources, of constructing the works of that extension. And the Plaintiff prayed declarations that no dividend ought to have been declared as above mentioned, and for an injunction, and accounts, and consequent relief.

On the 28th of January, the Plaintiff moved for an injunction, the directors having in the meantime issued a report, and proposed a 7 per cent. dividend for the then past half-year, carrying over a balance of £6998 on revenue to the next account.

The accounts were prepared on the same principles as the former accounts, except that £57,000 appeared on the debtor side of the revenue account as "amount received from Mr. *Kelk*," and £57,000 on the creditor side as "dividend on £1,900,000 *Extension* capital at 6 per cent.". . . .

The Vice-Chancellor *Wood*, before whom the motion was made, granted an injunction (1), and the Defendants moved by way of appeal to discharge that order. . . .

(1) 1868. Jan. 31. Sir W. Page Wood, V.C.:— . . . .

Then, as to the merits of the case. The charge to capital of half the office expenses was indefensible. The officers of the company were not unaware of this, for the chairman at the meeting said that it was impossible to pay large dividends and put every one of these charges to revenue. That seemed to be the secret of all which had happened. The defence was that these expenses were chargeable not only on the working line, but on the incomplete lines. No doubt the directors were in a painful position between two classes of shareholders, one permanent, and the other temporary speculators, who abhorred anything like a diminution of dividends, and would agree to any amount of dividend. But this could not last for ever, and companies could not go on always paying dividends out of capital. The Legislature had attempted to provide against this by saying, in sect. 121 of the *Companies Clauses Consolidation Act*, that dividends should not be paid out of capital in any shape.

Then as to the question under *Kelk's* contract. He had contracted to do certain works, and until completion to pay so much as would produce a dividend to the shareholders during such time as the works should not be completed. But he of course stipulated that if there was any delay on the part of the company, then the engineer should certify to that effect, and the dividend would not be payable during that time. It appeared, however, that

Mr. *G. M. Giffard*, Q.C., with Sir *Roundell Palmer* :—

No one denies that this dividend has been earned, the only question is how the money is to be applied. Unless interest is paid on a line in construction, it is not, in fact, charged with all that it has cost, and if it is several years in construction the amount becomes very material. If the company borrowed money from time to time to make the line with, the company would have to pay the interest. The revenue of the old line is not to be taken to construct the new line. At all events, where such a practice is universal, and has been pursued for years, is the Court to interfere *brevi manu*, and say it shall not be done? The Court will not interfere with the internal management of a company unless the acts proposed are actually illegal: *Simpson v. Westminster Palace Hotel Company* (1). Would the Court entertain the question whether the line was in a bad state and the money ought to be spent in repairs and not in dividends? . . . .

these works had not been touched, and it was preposterous to suppose that Mr. *Kelk* would agree to pay this interest irrespective of the sum which he was to receive. He might recover these very sums if it appeared that the delay was on the part of the company. Still it was conceivable that, having regard to the state of the money market, a contractor might agree to pay such a penalty. It was also said that further information could be given, and that altogether this matter was too dubious to issue an injunction upon. The company ought, however, to have every opportunity of considering well, before they ventured to declare a dividend upon this. Of course Mr. *Kelk* would bring it into his account, and make it a charge, and it could not be considered income.

As to the charge of interest on the debentures, could there be a serious doubt about it? As to debentures to the amount of £449,330, interest was paid upon them out of revenue, but the directors said that they would not so charge the interest on the £900,000 debentures in respect of unfinished lines, and would charge it upon capital, and thus a dividend was declared as from profit, although all this interest must remain a charge upon the capital of the company. This remained unexplained at present, and His Honour could not see the principle upon which it was done.

As to the effect of the 30th section of the Act of 30 & 31 Vict. c. 127, it was not argued that the signature of the two auditors was conclusive upon any Court as to the accuracy of the accounts, and the section could not exclude the rights of the shareholders to see whether what was being done was not *ultrà vires* on the face of it. For instance, in this case it could not be held that the certificate of the auditors as to the office expenses excluded all investigation. It appeared to His Honour, therefore, that an injunction ought to be granted to stay the payment of the dividend, prefaced by a declaration that these expenses had been improperly charged.

Feb. 18. Lord Chelmsford, L.C. :—

This is not the occasion upon which I can be called upon to pronounce a definitive judgment upon the important questions raised
in this case, nor are there materials before me which would enable
me to form a satisfactory opinion upon them. All that I am called
upon to consider upon this appeal is, whether there are doubtful
questions of importance to be determined in the case, and if there
are, whether the proceedings of the company with reference to the
matters in dispute between the parties ought, or ought not, to be
suspended until the hearing. . . .

The questions which will ultimately have to be decided are
these :—

First : Whether the office expenses, and the fees of the directors
and auditors, are properly charged, one moiety upon capital and
the other moiety upon the revenue of the company.

Secondly : Whether the interest upon debentures ought to be
charged upon capital, instead of upon revenue.

Thirdly : Whether the dividend paid to the *Extension* shareholders under the agreement with the contractors, Messrs. *Kelk*,
can be justified.

Upon the first question, it is admitted that if it stood alone it
would not be a sufficient ground for the injunction; for whether it
is right or wrong to charge a moiety of the office expenses, and of
the directors' and auditors' fees, to capital, the amount so charged
is largely exceeded by the balance in the hands of the company,
and therefore no injury can happen to the shareholders which
requires the prompt intervention of the Court.

The second question, as to charging the interest of debentures
upon capital, is a large and general question, and one of the
greatest importance. The Vice-Chancellor has treated it as a
question upon which there could be no serious doubt, and he has
prefaced the injunction with the expression of an opinion that no
part of the interest on the debenture capital is properly chargeable to capital account. I should be very unwilling, without
necessity, to offer a single observation in opposition to an opinion
of Vice-Chancellor *Wood*, which is always entitled to so much
respect; but I am bound to say, without dissenting from that
opinion, that the question does not appear to me to be so entirely
free from doubt as His Honour supposed. There certainly is not
to be found in any of the Acts of Parliament any express prohi-

bition of the course adopted by the company. The prohibitions contained in the different provisions of the Acts which were referred to in the argument apply to share capital, and not to borrowed capital, with the exception of the 196th section of the Defendants' Act. That section does contain a prohibition against paying dividends out of borrowed capital; and the 120th and 121st sections of the *Companies Clauses Act*, taken together, seem to me to imply, if they do not express, that dividends can only be paid out of profits, and consequently not out of borrowed capital.

There has certainly been no direct payment of dividends out of capital in this case, but if the effect of paying the interest on debentures out of capital is to leave so much of the revenue to be applied to dividend, and the payment out of capital is improper, then it will be a question to be decided at the hearing whether it does not amount indirectly to the same thing as paying dividends at once out of capital, and if so, all the provisions of the Acts which prohibit such a course will be applicable to the present case.

But the question principally to be decided is this:—The Act of Parliament for making this *Extension Line* empowered the company to raise an additional capital, either to be issued as a separate capital charged upon the profits of the *Extension* railway, or as new shares or new stock in the capital of the company. Now, if the *Extension Line* had been carried on as a separate undertaking, it is quite clear that, until the line was finished and was making profit, the expenses of the undertaking must have been a charge upon the capital, whether arising from shares or derived from the borrowing powers of the company. But, under the provisions of the Act, it was resolved that the requisite capital for the *Extension Line* should be raised as portions of the general capital of the company by the creation of new shares, and consequently the *Extension Line* became part of the original undertaking. And then this question arises:—The *Metropolitan Railway Act*, 1864, authorizing this *Extension*, enacts "that all moneys which the company are, by the Act, authorized to raise by new shares or on mortgage shall be applied only to the purposes of the Act." Now, the *Extension Line* yielding no income, if the line were a separate undertaking, the interest of any debt incurred under the borrowing powers of the Act must have been charged upon capital; but the line having been made part of the general undertaking, which, as a whole, was yielding profit, the question which must ultimately be the subject of decision is, whether it can be considered to be a legitimate application of the moneys to be raised or borrowed for the purposes of the *Extension Act*, to charge the debenture debt, which belongs to the unexecuted portion of what is now an entire line, upon the capital of the undertaking, which, as a whole, is yielding revenue. The Vice-Chancellor may be right in saying that no part of this debenture debt is properly chargeable to capital, but I cannot treat it as a question upon which there can be no serious doubt.

The determination of this question bears upon all the objections which have been made to the interference of the Court; for the Defendants contend that, however improper may have been the conduct of the directors in this respect, what they have done is a matter entirely of internal arrangement, which, having been sanctioned by the shareholders, the Court will decline to disturb. But the matters of internal management which are beyond the province of the Court, were properly admitted to be such as are within the scope of the company's powers. If any acts are done which are *ultrà vires*, they must be subject to examination and control. If a company were generally to agree to violate the provisions of an Act of Parliament, they could not shelter themselves from scrutiny under the plea that they had a right to manage their affairs without external interference. If, therefore, the charging the interest on the debenture debt to the capital account was beyond the limits of the company's powers, the idea of its being matter of internal management has no foundation.

But (if I understand the argument) the Defendants' claim to protection from the interference of the Court, under the 30th section of 30 & 31 Vict. c. 127, goes much beyond this, and challenges for the certificate of the auditors a power to sanction charges which otherwise would be illegal. I cannot read the section in this sense. Suppose the interest upon debentures ought properly to be charged on revenue, and the auditors should either refuse to charge this interest upon the revenue of the half-year, or should charge it, and the directors should differ with them, and a general meeting of the shareholders should agree with the directors, can it be contended that in either of these cases the debentures could be made a charge upon capital contrary to law? Whatever may be the exact meaning of this section (which is not perfectly clear), it cannot, in my opinion, be intended to give the auditors power to transfer to capital any charge which properly belongs to revenue.

The third question, which must be determined at the hearing, relates to the dividend paid to the *Extension* shareholders from the moneys arising out of the agreement of the Messrs. *Kelk*, the contractors. It is said that these moneys are in lieu of penalties which would have been incurred by the non-completion of the works within the limited time, or, in other words, that they are the purchase-money paid by the contractors for the benefit of delay : if this is so, and the money is not afterwards to be refunded by the company, no objection could be made to the arrangement. But it is charged by the Plaintiff in his bill that the dividends so paid have been, or will be, repaid out of the revenues of the company. This is a fact to be ascertained upon the hearing, and it is obvious that this transaction will form another very material question in the case. . . .

I was pressed very strongly as to the extent of mischief which it was said would be produced by affirming the decree for an injunction, compared with the slight inconvenience which would be occasioned by dismissing it, and I regret that any persons should suffer from having the dividend withheld from them if it should ultimately be found that they are entitled to it. But it must be remembered that if I allow the dividend to be received, and the Court should, at the hearing, determine that it was improperly declared, it will never be recovered (even if recoverable) from those to whom it will be paid ; and in this sense the injury to the *Extension* shareholders may be not incorrectly described as irreparable.

I must, therefore, affirm the order and leave the costs to be costs in the cause, and as the declaration prefaced to the order has been made by a Judge of such great experience, I shall not interfere with it.

RISHTON v. GRISSELL

L.R. 5 Eq. 326 (1868)
Vice Chancellor - Chancery

Manager of Works—Agreement—Salary—Percentage of Profits of Business—
Principles on which Account should be taken.

The Defendant, in 1858, agreed that the Plaintiff should act as the manager
of his works, and should receive in each year 7½ per cent. of the profits of
the business, to be made up to £500 in any year in which the said share of
profits should be less than that sum. In the same year a valuation of the
buildings, stock, plant, and goodwill was made. In 1864 the Defendant
sold the buildings, stock, and business at an increase over the valuation of
£47,916.

In taking the accounts under the above agreement:—

Held, that the Defendant was not entitled to charge the profit and loss
account in every year with interest on his capital, nor with interest on old
debts, nor with £500 in respect of the Plaintiff's salary:

Held, further, that the Defendant was entitled to charge the profit and loss
account in every year with sums representing the depreciation arising from
the running out of the lease, and the waste of plant and machinery:

Held, also, that the Plaintiff was not entitled to treat as profit of the year
in which the property was sold, the excess of the amount realized by the
sale over the estimated value; but that the estimated value of stock first set
down must run through the whole account; the annual depreciations being
calculated on that constant quantity.

THIS was an adjournment from Chambers.

By an agreement in June, 1858, between the Defendant, *Henry
Grissell*, then the owner of the *Regent's Canal Ironworks*, and the
Plaintiff, *John Edward Makon Rishton*, it was agreed that the
Plaintiff should act as manager of the said works, and should
receive in each year 7½ per. cent. of the profits of the business, to
be made up to £500 in any year in which the said share of profits
should be less than that sum.

In that year the buildings, stock, machinery, plant, and other
assets of the business had been valued on the retirement of a
former partner, and stood in the books at about £22,000.

On the 4th of July, 1864, the Defendant agreed to sell his works
and business to the *Regent's Canal Ironworks Company, Limited*,
for the sum of £70,000, and upwards.

In April, 1865, this bill was filed for specific performance of the
agreement, and for an account; and by a decree dated the 19th of
July, 1867, inquiries and accounts were directed.

The Defendant had brought in various accounts under the decree; but it was found that they could not well be proceeded with until various questions affecting the principle on which they were to be taken were settled; and the parties being desirous of taking the Vice-Chancellor's opinion, the Chief Clerk now submitted the following preliminary questions:—

1. The Defendant had charged interest on his capital in the business.

2. In the profit and loss account he had charged interest on old debts due from the business.

3. In the same account he had charged the payments made to the Plaintiff on account of his guaranteed £500 per annum; and in the account for 1864 he had charged £554 paid to the Plaintiff in respect of his share of profits for the years 1859 and 1861.

4. In the same account he had charged for each year a percentage on the value of the leasehold premises in which the business was carried on in respect of the depreciation arising (as he considered it) from the leasehold term running out from year to year, also sums annually for depreciation of plant and machinery.

5. The Plaintiff claimed 7½ per cent. on £47,916, being the difference between what the items stood at in the books when the agreement was made with the Plaintiff in 1858, and the sum of £70,000 received of the *Ironworks Company.*

[The question as to the £554 was conceded by the Defendant's counsel.]

Mr. *Willcock,* Q.C., and Mr. *Hemming,* for the Plaintiff:— · · · ·
The fourth and fifth points go together. We say that whenever the true price of the property is actually ascertained (as here by the sale in 1864), we are entitled to bring into account the true value in place of any estimated value. The estimated depreciations were properly entered while the fact was doubtful, but when it turns out that there has been an increase of value instead of a depreciation, this should be brought to account as profit of the year when it is ascertained, without disturbing the accounts of former years. The evidence proves this to be the received way of keeping partnership accounts.

[The VICE-CHANCELLOR:—Is a lucky speculation in the sale of property part of commercial profit?]

Everything by which the stock is increased—everything which comes in by way of gain, from whatever source—should go into the books as profit. That is the commercial meaning of the word " profit.". . . .

Sir W. Page Wood, V.C.:—

The whole of this question is determined by attending to the circumstance that the Plaintiff was employed by the Defendant as manager. That was his exact position, neither more nor less. The Defendant agreed to give him 7½ per cent. of the profits in each year, with a guaranteed minimum of £500 a year. In other words, if the profits in any year did not amount to £500, they were to be taken at that amount.

An agreement of this sort is not a very wise arrangement on the part of an employer, because it gives to the person employed a right to overhaul the books and accounts of the partnership. But it gives the person employed no right or interest in the partnership concern ; only a percentage on yearly profit.

Now, taking this leasehold property, plant, and machinery—that will be a constant quantity, subject only to the modifications which may have taken place in each current year. If the plant and machinery were originally put down at £20,000, or at £50,000, it would not make the slightest difference to the person employed. He has no interest in it. At whatever price it is first put down, at that amount it must be put down, subject only to depreciation, in the following year ; and being put down as a constant quantity, it will strike itself out on both sides of the account, and be carried through the books at the same amount to the end of the partnership. If some new street were opened, the property might be sold at ten times the amount ; but with that the Plaintiff can have nothing to do ; he would have no profit upon the sale of the concern.

The proper course to take would be—that every article or item of expenditure laid out, not only in buying stock, but in the improvement of the premises, should be debited in the profit and loss account. Suppose the lease, plant, and machinery to be taken at a fixed sum of £20,000, and £5000 to be laid out in improvements, the profit and loss account must be debited with this new item of £5000, and credited with the depreciation arising from the running out of the lease, and the deterioration of the plant and machinery.

The Plaintiff has a right to a percentage upon the profits *de anno in annum*, but to nothing more. Otherwise he would have a right to have a sale, for he might refuse to rest upon the Defendant's estimate of the profits, and demand a sale. That cannot have been the intention of the parties, and the Court will not enforce the contract in that way. All that the Court has to do is to see that a *bona fide* estimate has been made, and not an estimate made merely at the arbitrary will of the employer.

Let us take the question of the running out of the lease. Suppose it to be known that, from adventitious circumstances, the value of the lease has risen largely at the end of the second year, the Plaintiff would not be entitled to put that increase into the profit and loss account. If it were originally valued at £20,000, he would be entitled to have the depreciation arising from the running out of the lease carried into the accounts, but a depreciation calculated on the £20,000, not on the increased value. Therefore, as to the fourth and fifth items, all the Court has to do is to see that the value of the lease, and the value of the machinery and plant, are uniformly charged in the accounts, and that the depreciations are calculated upon these constant quantities.

With respect to the three other items, I am in favour of the Plaintiff. I had at first a little doubt on one point, but on subsequent reflection I have none. The Plaintiff's engagement was that he was to be paid out of the yearly profits, and he was not to be called upon to advance a sixpence of capital. Then what is his right, as respects the employer's capital, with regard to the carrying on of the business? He has a right to expect that the employer will carry on the business with his own capital, but he has no right to inquire whether the employer has borrowed the capital, or how he has acquired it. He finds it is there; he is acquainted with the whole concern; he sees it at work; and he enters into the engagement I have described. He has a right, therefore, to expect that the employer will provide the necessary capital. I think the employer cannot claim a right to deduct £5 per cent. by way of interest upon capital before profits are estimated, on the ground that if he had put his money into another business he could have got that interest, although it may be that, according to writers on political economy, interest is to be first charged upon capital. Suppose a thing is bought for £100 and sold for £103, that may be a very bad trade bargain; still, poor as the gain is, it is profit, and the manager has a right to claim it, without any previous deduction for interest upon capital, unless there be some special stipulation to that effect.

The express point has been decided in this Court, that unless there be an express stipulation, or a particular course of practice shewn by the partnership books to the contrary, interest between partners is not allowed.

I confess I was at first struck with the argument that the employer might have to carry on business with borrowed capital, on which he would have to pay £5 per cent., and that the profit must be taken after that £5 per cent. has been deducted. But the manager, in this instance, does not know where the capital comes from, and has no right to inquire. Therefore it appears to me that neither as to the borrowed capital, nor as to the Defendant's own capital, has the Defendant any right to charge interest as against the Plaintiff in the estimate of profits.

The other question as to the £500 is much clearer. The Defendant is not entitled to deduct the £500 payment before the profits are estimated. The profits might amount to £750, then upon what principle can the Defendant deduct the £500? He says there might be a year in which there was no profit at all. But he has undertaken that the $7\frac{1}{2}$ per cent. shall always amount to at least £500, and he cannot deduct the £500 before he takes the percentage.

As to the first three items I concur with the Plaintiff's view, and as to the fourth and fifth with that of the Defendant.

The costs will be costs in the cause, and there will be a direction that the accounts be taken according to the Plaintiff's contention as to the first, second, and third items, and according to that of the Defendant as to the fourth and fifth.

TURQUAND v. MARSHALL

L.R. 6 Eq. 112 (1868)
Master of the Rolls - Chancery
20 L.T. 766 (1869)
Lord Chancellor - Court of Appeal

Chancery

THIS was a suit by *William Turquand*, official liquidator of the *Herefordshire Banking Company*, suing on behalf of the company; and it sought to render certain directors of the company liable for various acts and defaults in the management of the company's affairs.

The company was established in 1836, under the Act 7 Geo. 4, c. 46, with a nominal capital of £300,000, divided into 12,000 shares, of £25 each. The material provisions of the deed of settlement are set out below (1)

The company commenced business in 1836. Shares were allotted to the number of 4584: and on these calls amounting in the whole to £12 10s. per share were paid. In 1842 it was discovered that a large portion of the capital had been lost, and a meeting of the shareholders was called in accordance with the 108th clause of the articles to consider whether the company should be wound up. It was resolved that the company should not be wound up, but that the capital should be reduced by £2 10s. per share; and the shares were thenceforth treated as having only £10 paid upon them.

The company continued to carry on business down to June, 1863, when it suspended payment; and it was ordered to be wound up in November following.....

---

(1) By clause 88 the directors were required to cause all necessary and proper books of accounts to be provided and carefully kept, and to cause to be made in those books fair, explicit, and true entries of all receipts, payments, transactions, and dealings which should, from time to time, be made by or on behalf of the company, and of all profits, gains, and losses arising therefrom, and also an account of all dealings and investments which should be made with or out of the capital of the company, or of the money deposited with the company, and in the months of January and July in each year should settle, adjust, and balance the said books up to the last days of December and June previously, and make out a full, true, and explicit statement and balance sheet exhibiting the debts and credits

The first ground of complaint was that from 1846, down to the termination of the business of the company the directors annually presented to the shareholders false reports of the progress and proceedings of the company, and false balance sheets, and recommended the declaration of dividends upon repeated false statements that profits had been earned. The items in the balance sheets which were complained of were the following:—1. Shares in the company which, to the number of 2958, were from time to time purchased by the directors at prices below their nominal

of the said company, and the amount and nature of the capital and property thereof, and the then fair estimated value thereof, and the amount of the company's negotiable securities then in circulation, and the profits and losses of the company, and all other matters and things requisite for fully, truly, and explicitly manifesting the state of affairs of the company; but, nevertheless, no proprietor or shareholder who should not be a director or auditor, or one of the officers of the company specially appointed for that purpose, should be entitled to inspect or to have in equity a discovery of the books, accounts, documents, deeds, or writings of the company, except such as might or should be produced for that purpose at any general or special meeting of proprietors.

By clause 89, at every annual meeting of the proprietors the directors were to exhibit to the proprietors then assembled a true and accurate summary or balance sheet and report of the gains, profits, accumulations, and losses of the company, and of the state and progress of the affairs of the company up to the last day of December next preceding such meeting, and also such further accounts as the directors should deem expedient or for the interest of the company to be made public.

Clause 91: "At the annual general meeting to be held in the month of February in every year succeeding the the year 1838, during the continuance

of the said copartnership, the general directors for the time being shall declare such dividend out of the clear profits of the company then actually accrued and reduced into possession (including the interest and proceeds of capital laid out or invested in pursuance of the powers herein contained in that behalf) as they shall think fit."

Clause 92: "The board of general directors (if they shall so think fit) may retain all or any part of the profits of the said company which shall be made up to the 1st of January, 1837, and apply the same towards forming a fund to be called 'The Surplus Fund,' and may in each or any succeeding year during the continuance of the said company retain such portion of the net profits of the said company (after making deduction for bad and doubtful debts), and apply the same towards the said fund called 'The Surplus Fund,' as they the said board of directors shall think fit."

Clause 93: "The said fund called 'The Surplus Fund,' shall be added to and be deemed part of the capital of the said copartnership, and shall on the dissolution of the company belong to and be divided among the persons then entitled to the capital of the said company, in the same shares as they shall be entitled to such capital, but so that the money constituting the said 'Surplus Fund' be carried to a separate account in the books of the company; and the primary object of such surplus fund is value were included in the general item "current accounts" at the nominal paid-up value of £10 per share. 2. In the item "bills of exchange and cash in hand" were included over-due bills which were either worthless, or worth very much less than the sums for which they were drawn. 3. Debts to the company were treated as good which were either irrecoverable or probably bad. 4. An account was kept in the ledger called the "bad and doubtful debt account," on the debit side of which were entered some of the bad debts of the company, and certain charges, such as solicitors' bills, rents, &c.; while on the credit side were entered sums transferred from the profit and loss account; the difference between the price paid by the company for shares purchased by them and the nominal value of £10 per share, and dividends on such shares; the effect being to shew a balance on the credit side of the account, which was treated as an asset and included in the balance sheets under the item "current accounts." The result of this mode of dealing with the accounts was that in 1846 the assets were over stated by upwards of £13,000, and in each succeeding year by an increasing sum, until, in 1859, the over estimate exceeded the actual capital of the company. In order to make out these balance sheets trial balance sheets were first of all prepared from the accounts in the mode just stated, and if they shewed a balance sufficient to enable a dividend to be declared, they were presented

hereby declared to be, to meet and provide against unforeseen emergencies, losses, or extraordinary demands upon the company, and the same shall or may be applied by and at the direction of the board of general directors accordingly."

Clause 108: "If at any time the losses of the said company shall have exhausted the whole of the said fund called 'The Surplus Fund,' and also one-fourth part of the capital of the said company which shall have been actually paid up by the proprietors, without regard to the amount of the said subscribed capital, then the board of general directors of the said company for the time being shall, as soon as possible after the above-mentioned state of the company shall have been known to them, call a special general meeting of the proprietors or shareholders of the said company, and shall submit to such meeting a full statement of the affairs and concerns of the said company, and, if required, verify such statement by the production of the books and vouchers of the company, and in case it shall appear at such meeting that the losses of the said company shall have exhausted the said fund, and also one-fourth part of the then paid-up capital thereof as aforesaid, then the chairman at such meeting shall declare the said copartnership dissolved, and the same shall stand and be dissolved accordingly."

to the shareholders; but if not, alterations were made in the accounts so as to swell the apparent assets and shew in the balance sheets a sum out of which a dividend could be paid. Copies of these trial balance sheets were found among the company's papers. In consequence of these false statements a dividend of 8s. per share was paid in 1847; and a dividend of 10s. per share in each succeeding year down to and including 1863.

In addition to the false representations made by the balance sheets, it appeared that the directors had at the annual meetings and at other times, down to 1863, held out the bank to be a flourishing and prosperous institution. In particular, at the annual meeting in 1856, certain of the then directors, in reply to questions put by Mr. *Skey*, a shareholder, expressly stated that all bad debts had been written off, that the surplus fund was actually in hand to meet future bad debts, and that if the bank were then to be wound up the whole of the proprietors' capital was safe. By these statements Mr. *Skey*, who had previously had some intention of selling his shares, was induced not only to abandon such intention, but to purchase other shares in the company.

The next ground of complaint was the failure of the directors to dissolve the company under the 108th clause of the deed of settlement; the whole of the surplus fund and one-fourth of the paid-up capital having, to the knowledge of the directors, been lost in 1846. No part of such loss was ever recovered. . . .

The assets realized in the winding-up amounted to £55,285 14s. 4d.; the debts proved amounted to £92,497 3s. 8d., leaving a deficiency of £37,211 9s. 4d. to be provided by calls on the contributories. Of this sum £30,123 1s. had been raised. Mr. *Skey's* contribution alone amounted to £15,665.

The bill prayed: 1. For an inquiry as to the damages caused to the company and shareholders in consequence of the business of the company being continued after the surplus fund and one-fourth of the capital had been lost. 2. For an account of the dividends distributed by the directors since 1846, making allowance for so much (if any) of such dividends as should not appear to have been actually paid out of assets of the company. 3. For an inquiry as to the damages caused to the company and the shareholders by allowing directors and others to overdraw their accounts to an undue extent, and by allowing bad debts to remain so long outstanding as to become irrecoverable; by the publication of false reports and false balance sheets, and all other breaches of trust which might be shewn by the Plaintiff to have been committed by *Crowther, Smeeton, Powell, Edwards, Grayston,* and *Sowdon,* or any one or more of them. ...

[LORD ROMILLY, M.R. :—I cannot make a decree according to the second paragraph of the prayer of the bill. The shareholders cannot in this suit be heard to say that the dividends have been improperly paid; but if the payment has occasioned any loss to the company, the directors may be liable for that.] ....

Apr. 18. LORD ROMILLY, M.R. :—

This is a suit instituted by the official liquidator of the *Herefordshire Banking Company,* suing on behalf of the company, to make the Defendants liable for certain breaches of trust, and to compel them to repay to the shareholders the losses occasioned to them by reason of the misconduct of the directors. ...

The bank itself was formed in October, 1836, under the Act of 7 Geo. 4, c. 46. The nominal capital was £300,000, in 12,000 shares of £25 each. The deed of settlement bears date the 1st of October, 1836. It provides for the number of directors, and describes their powers; it directs how the minutes are to be kept; clause 53 I will read presently when I come to another part of the judgment. The 89th clause directs the delivery of a balance sheet to the shareholders, and clause 91 directs the dividends to be paid out of the clear profits of the company; clause 92 provides for the creation of a surplus fund; clause 94 provides for the holding of general meetings of the company; and clause 108 is in these words:—[His Lordship read it.] The company began to carry on business in 1836; 4584 shares were allotted, on each of which £12 10s. was paid up. The bank never seems to have carried on its business prosperously, and in 1842 a special meeting of shareholders was held for the purpose of considering their position, when by a resolution passed by them a reduction of 50s. per share was made from the capital of the company for the purpose of clearing off the bad debts of the concern. After this the business of the company was continued to be carried on until it stopped payment in June, 1863, and it was afterwards wound up under an order of this Court in November, 1863. ...

The charges against the directors are distinct, and must be separately considered. I shall first notice the complaints made of the misconduct of the directors in rendering false accounts, and in representing the concern to be in a very different position from that which it really held; and proof is given which, in my opinion, is very conclusive and distinct, that the accounts furnished and published to the shareholders were grossly inaccurate. Convincing proof is also given that the managing directors were well aware of this fact. I am also of opinion that the other directors, who may not have examined the books, must be taken to be liable for all the consequences which would properly flow from the fact if they had been acquainted with the contents of them. It was their duty to be so acquainted, and it was a duty which they had undertaken to perform by becoming directors; and therefore I am of opinion that they are also responsible for the falsity of the accounts. But I am of opinion that I cannot make this the subject of any decree in this Court; .... It may be difficult to speak temperately of conduct of such a character pursued by gentlemen holding such a position, but still the injury is confined to those who acted on these statements, and it does not affect the general body of the shareholders. It is on this principle that the falsification of accounts, and the paying of dividends out of capital, cannot, in my opinion, be made the foundation of a decree of this Court in the present stage of these proceedings, but can only constitute a ground for separate and distinct actions against the directors, in which the special damage and the amount of it would have to be made out in each case.

These observations appear to me to apply to every part of the Plaintiff's collection of charges against the directors, with two exceptions, which require more minute investigation. These are: first, the directors not having acted on the 108th clause in the deed of settlement which I have read; and, secondly, the loan of £8000 to Mr. *Higgins*.

First, as to the duty of the directors: under the 108th clause of the deed of settlement, which I have already read, this is imperative; it is not that the directors *may*, but that they *shall*, call a special general meeting of the proprietors. Of course, when the meeting is held, the shareholders may, if they please, enter into a fresh contract of partnership, or resolve to go on under the old contract; but the duty of the directors is plain and explicit. Two questions arise : First, did the event occur to meet which this section was provided? and, if it did, did the directors obey the directions contained in the clause and call the meeting? It is clear, on examining the books, that the first event did occur, and it is clear on the evidence that the directors did not call any meeting in pursuance of the directions contained in this clause. What is the excuse that is offered? The first is, that they did not know the state of the company, or the contents of the books. I have already dealt with this. I repeat, that the evidence shews that the managing directors did know the state of the books, and that all the others must be taken to have been fully acquainted with that which it was their duty to become acquainted with. . . .

I am, therefore, prepared to make a declaration that the directors for the time being, and the estates of those who are dead, are liable to make good such losses as may have been sustained by the shareholders by reason of the directors not having summoned a special meeting of the company when, subsequently to 1846, the losses of the company had exhausted the whole of the surplus fund, and also one-fourth part of the paid-up capital of the shareholders, ...

Equity Courts.

COURT OF APPEAL IN CHANCERY.

Reported by THOMAS BROOKSBANK and E. STEWART ROCHE, Esqrs., Barristers-at-Law.

Jan. 13, 15, 16. *and Feb.* 11.

(Before the LORD CHANCELLOR, (Hatherley).

TURQUAND *v.* MARSHALL.

The LORD CHANCELLOR (Hatherley).—It seems to me that in substance this case stands more on neglect and default than on anything else. I must treat the bill as proceeding on the neglect of the directors to comply with the 108th section of the company's deed, which directed them, when one-fourth of the fund should have been ascertained to have been exhausted, to call a meeting of the shareholders, and to put it to them whether they desired the company should proceed. It is alleged that there was a breach of that duty which was concealed from the shareholders by means of certain accounts, over and over again called "false," but which are not stated, except in one instance, to be false with the knowledge of the directors. Then it is said that this concealment was carried on until the company fell into that disastrous state that not only the whole of its capital and its surplus fund became exhausted, but these heavy debts, amounting to 37,000*l.*, accrued through the negligence and default of the directors. . . . In the 15th paragraph of the bill I find this charge: "The trial balance-sheet for the year 1846 has been discovered among the papers of the company, and from that it appears, as the fact is, that the first item of assets on the credit side of the balance-sheet for 1846, namely, the current account 83,163*l.* 15*s.* 9*d.* is made up by including in one aggregate sum, good, doubtful, and bad debts of the company, at their full amount without distinction. Amongst other sums forming part of the said item, is a sum of 3015*l.* 14*s.* 10*d.*, which is taken from the above mentioned account, called the 'bad and doubtful debt account', in the current account ledger of the company, and which sum is fraudulently treated as an asset"— that is the single instance in which the word occurs. "The second item in the said balance-sheet, namely, bills of exchange, &c., 42,051*l.*, 1*s.* 2*d.*, comprises past due bills to the amount of 8746*l.* 17*s.* 2*d.*, by far the largest portion of which were worthless, and must have been known to be so when the said balance sheet was prepared." That of course again would be a distinct charge. Now that single item is a little curious. After having said that 8746*l.* was put in as past due bills, by far the larger portion of which were worthless and must have been known to be so; Mr. Turquand gives "Past due bills at 8746*l.* less received, say 6000*l.*" being much more near three-fourths which were good, instead of being by far the greater part bad, as must have been known to be the case. That is an estimate only, but in every balance sheet the same degree of criticism is exercised on the different items, and I find past due bills are stated which, as the concern gets worse, become far less in proportion, recoverable; but while the concern was in a better state, I find, in one instance, 13,000*l.* past due bills, of which credit is given for 11,000*l.*, recovered. So that it is not clear by any means that this entry of past due bills, though no doubt improper, is of that gross character which it is represented to be by the frame of the bill. Having arrived at something like the objects of the bill, I think the Master of the Rolls has, in truth, reduced them to two main subjects, namely, the non-stoppage of the bank at the time when the loss accrued of the one-fourth of the capital, and the particular debt to Higgins, which I keep apart as a separate transaction in itself. I certainly concur with his Lordship's judgment in all that part of the case in which he rejected the claim to dividends and the interest upon them. It is a totally impossible demand to make in this court that persons who must have been taken to be receivers of that sum out of capital, should be able to sustain a special demand in respect of that which they had so received improperly, because it was represented as something which it was not, they nevertheless having the money in their pockets. Having disposed of that part of the case, it is reduced to this simple breach of engagement to the shareholders, in not stopping, under the 108th section, at the time they should have done; and the Master of the Rolls has considered it to be immaterial at what date that breach may have occurred, because, although it is alleged in the bill that this occurred in 1840, before Smeeton, whose executors are appellants, had become a director, and before Crowther, whose executors are also appellants, had become a director; it was a continuing breach of trust; every year that the directors were aware of the fact of the 108th section not having been so complied with, and having not complied with it, they are liable for all the losses that may have occurred to the shareholders in respect of such disobedience. It is very important to see what are the exact provisions of the deed, and what the transactions were in 1841 and 1842. The 108th section provides that when the losses shall have exhausted the whole of the surplus fund, and also the one-fourth of the actual paid-up capital, without regard to the amount, the directors "shall, as soon as possible after the above-mentioned state of the said company shall have become known to them, call a special general meeting of the proprietors or shareholders." . . . .

But a great deal more appears with reference to the meeting in 1842 and the anterior meetings, than the simple fact of the reduction of the capital which then took place to the extent of one-fifth, because it is plain when we come to consider the whole of the balance-sheets that it was known distinctly to the company at that time, and known beyond all possibility of doubt that when they stopped the one-fifth, the one-fourth of their capital was gone. When you have the facts before you that the shareholders knew everything that it was necessary for them to know, and exercised a judgment on that point, you cannot say after they agree to go on with the capital diminished to below the one-fourth to trade with, that the directors are liable under the 108th section, because they ought to have stopped the company immediately; and at the same meeting they vote a four per cent. dividend, therefore the shareholders agree to receive a dividend. It is the secret, 1 am afraid, of all these cases, that no shareholder will inquire, for fear that a dividend should not be forthcoming, and they take care after that time never again to inquire, and this will be found to be the key to the whole of this history. Now, I am bound to show that these matters stand in the light I have represented them. I shall state in the strongest manner against the directors the case that will arise on behalf of the shareholders. The directors have the sole control of the concern, and the sole management of the books. Nobody is to examine the books in any manner besides themselves, unless it be in the course prescribed in the deed, which does not wholly leave the shareholders defenceless, but exposes them to the impossibility of correcting on their own knowledge, and without a process which very few shareholders like to resort to, any misrepresentation or misstatement which may be made; because the shareholders are to have no access to the books, except such as may be produced at the general meeting. They have only this safeguard:—It is competent to any shareholder to move that there should be a committee of inquiry. Something of that kind seems to have taken place in the early part of the history of the concern, when, in 1836, it was found that although dividends had been paid, somehow or other it must have oozed out that matters were not so comfortable as they were represented to be, and accordingly there had been an examination determined upon into the affairs of the company. A very large general meeting took place on the 3rd June 1840, specially convened for the purpose of looking into the whole of the affairs of the company, and to receive a report made by a gentleman appointed to investigate. The auditors found that the preliminary account which was stated in January to amount to 8962l. was spent as follows:—2500l. in the purchase of a business at Hereford, which does not seem to have turned out very prosperously, certain sums in acquiring the goodwill of a house of business, and other sums applied to current expenses for different purposes. Then they go into an account of the net profits, and say in substance, "There was only one year in which an honest dividend could properly be paid; you have nevertheless had profits divided for a series of years." They then give an account of the bad debts which they say amount to 6517l., which, added to the capital taken to make up the yearly dividends, made a sum of 8629l., the then present loss of the company. Nothing can be more fair and open than the whole statement made by the auditors of every bad and doubtful debt upon full inquiry and examination. That being so, we come to the meeting in Feb. 1841. On the 5th Feb. a report was made, and the directors submitted to the shareholders a statement of the affairs of the bank. "They thought it right to inform such as were not present at the special general meeting held in June last for the purpose of receiving the auditors' report and on other affairs, that it was then resolved that the company's affairs and accounts be again investigated and examined for the purpose of testing the accuracy of the report then read, and they have now the satisfaction of informing the proprietors that the same has been certified to be correct in every respect."

Then they say they have appointed Mr. Hastings as manager, and continue: "The transactions of this company being now reduced to the establishment at Hereford, and the Leominster and Evesham branches, the directors have to call the attention of the shareholders to the circumstance of their being able materially to lessen the amount of expenditure; and by the business being less divided, the manager will have that superintendence and constant vigilance over the whole which is extremely desirable." They further say, "it will appear by these accounts that the directors are not in a situation to pay *bonâ fide* dividends." That is a very proper statement to make. "They have therefore passed the whole of the profits now realised, to a fund for reduction of the debts and preliminary expenses." That is quite right. They see that the preliminary expenses, instead of being an asset, are nothing at all. They have been paid, and they must be provided for. It forms no longer a part of the capital of the company, and they therefore wish to realise a fund for the reduction of the debts and preliminary expenses, and hope by so doing and pursuing the policy which has guided their management since the last meeting, ultimately to realise those expectations of profit which it is desirable they should obtain. We find even then a gentleman who does not like being paid no dividend proposes a dividend of 4 per cent. for the past half-year. There were three in favour of the proposition, but on the other side, ten. Then came the important meeting of the 2nd Feb. 1842. At that m..ting the report of the directors was read. It states:—"The directors have much pleasure in meeting the shareholders at the fifth annual meeting, and in submitting to them the usual balance-sheets and profit and loss statements, which are now laid upon the table for their inspection. The proprietors are reminded that a very considerable portion of the bank's capital has been expended in its formation, which, in a limited capital, may be considered excessive, and has tended much to paralyse the exertions of the directors." With respect to the preliminary expenses they give the goodwill of the business at 4000l., and a number of other items, the total being 9000l. It was 6000l. a little while ago; then it was 8000l., and now it is 9872l., or nearly 10,000l., of which only 4000l. was for the goodwill. Then they say, "After a careful estimate of the bad and doubtful debts (which have been reduced since last meeting 1768l. 13s. 7d.) they are found to be 3635l. 1s. 7d., making with the preliminary expenses a total of 13,407l. 2s. 6d." I observe that 13,407l. is within a few hundred pounds, one-fourth of the capital then paid up. They continue: "The directors ther re recommend to the proprietors to consent to a positive reduction of an amount equal to 2l. 10s. per share from the capital stock of the bank for the purpose of clearing off the bad debts and a portion of the preliminary expenses. The directors have to report that the profits upon the business of the bank for the past year, after deducting the current expenditure, amount to 1969l. 12s. 3d. They feel thus justified in recommending a dividend of 4 per cent. after the rate of 8s. per share, and they recommend the striking off the 2l. 10s. paid in the interval." The report concludes by congratulating the proprietary upon the very great progress the bank had made. Then comes this account, which represents the preliminary expenses of 9472l., and they propose that the 2l. 10s. which has been raised

65

should be applied in paying off part of the bad debts and part of the preliminary expenses. The very next year it appeared that although there was an attempt at reduction and a good deal of the 9000*l.* for preliminary expenses had been cleared off, there still remained 6000*l.* So it went on for several years until it was a good deal reduced, and the bank got into a somewhat better condition. The present shareholders must be taken to know all the original shareholders knew, and therefore must have been perfectly well aware while going on with these dividends at 4 per cent. that, in effect, if the company had been wound-up the preliminary expenses could not have been provided.for. Where was the fund? It had departed. Therefore, there being something considerably over one-fourth gone at that time it seems to me that from that moment these gentlemen must be taken to know what was done and cannot go back afterwards and fix those who have come in at a subsequent period, with a continuance of that which, with the knowledge and sanction of the shareholders had been already done. However, the case does not quite rest there as regards the position of these directors and their shareholders. The two great heads of what are called false charges in all the subsequent reports are these : the one, of the past due bills in respect of which it is said they were all credited with their full value, though it was well known the full value could not be recovered, and in the past debts were also included the past due bills. Further it was said there was another thing kept secret from the shareholders. There was credited into this account a series of transactions which Turquand, in the bill, appeared to treat as illegal on the part of the directors—an entire mistake—namely, the purchase of shares in the company by the company itself. That was perfectly legitimate according to the provisions of the deed. Whether it was wise and prudent is not for me to say; but there are two express provisions in the deed—one, that the company may deal with all things including the shares of the company, and another, that the investments to be made by the company of their capital, are to be, among other things, in shares of the company. This is a clear and express provision. Further than that, in the report of 1841 there is an express entry of 12,000*l.* paid in the purchase of shares. Again, I say, therefore the shareholders knew that the directors were doing what they were authorised by the deed to do. It would have been better undoubtedly if that had been brought out in each balance-sheet, but it was thought, I suppose, that the outside world would not like to know that the company was dealing with its own shares, as that would not give very great confidence in the bank. They knew there was that power, and had moreover the safeguard of the register, because it is sworn distinctly that the register was open to the shareholders. They knew, on the one hand, by the actual balance-sheet, that shares had been purchased to the extent of 12,000*l.* at that time, and ultimately to a much larger extent. 2900 shares, or more than half of the whole shares of the company, were afterwards bought by the company itself. That was a fact which the shareholders were perfectly capable of ascertaining for themselves whenever they pleased. As regards the past due bills, it is only just to say, on the part of some of the directors, although not

on the part of those who were actually engaged in making out the accounts, that it would not be so easy altogether to fix them with wilful default for not ascertaining whether the past due bills were recoverable or not, or for not ascertaining whether the debts were recoverable or not. There might be cases so palpable, such as bankruptcy or the like, as would make it impossible to put down a debt as an asset which could not by any possibility be recovered. You might fix the directors with this :— Wherever they have entered a debt in the list of bad debts, you may fix them with knowledge that they themselves treated it as a bad debt, and they ought not to have introduced it as an asset. The main feature of the case is as to whether or not under the 108th section of the deed the directors are now liable in respect of any loss accruing by reason of their not having stopped the concern at that time. Upon looking carefully through the evidence, it appears to me that with the fullest knowledge on the part of the shareholders, the shareholders persisted in being paid dividends when they knew from the accounts laid before them, that more than a fourth of the capital must have been exhausted, because the preliminary expenses must be deducted entirely from the assets. In that state of circumstances it is impossible to say that the parties have not agreed to waive the provision so made by the 108th section.. ••

It appears to me, therefore, that the bill really entirely fails, and it is not a bill in which it is possible for the court to give relief. I have passed over a great many points in the case as to the delinquencies of the directors and the impropriety of their conduct, but I have to consider that with reference to the remaining question of costs.... As to

what Crowther did we have one document signed '.." him, and it is a very unfortunate one.{ I mean that document as to which we have Taylor's story. though I should be inclined to give no more credit to Taylor than is absolutely necessary on the facts of the case. But there is that paper, which Taylor says he had signed for his security, because he would not venture to do what was proposed to be done without some authority. There is also a bit of paper which purports to be a transfer from the bad and doubtful debt account of a sum for the purpose of having sufficient to pay a dividend. The two pieces of paper appear to be signed, one by Crowther, and the other by the defendant, the other director. That was undoubtedly a very grave step to have taken. I do not see so much reason to complain of the non-statement of the purchase of shares, because I find in the earlier years—in 1841—that the purchase of the shares was stated, and the register was open. and it is not averred that the entries appear in that register of the purchase of those shares. I do not think so much of the transfer of the doubtful debts, though, of course, some allowance ought to be made for it. There is a transaction which, to my mind, is the worst of the whole, and that is the transaction in which that strange account is opened called the "Inoperative account," and it is summed up to about 15,000*l.* or 16,000*l.* altogether. Those accounts were dead and gone without any hope of anything coming of them, and yet that "Inoperative account" finds its way as an asset, though it is perhaps about as good an asset as the preliminary expenses; and it is done in a way in which the shareholders could have had no means of knowing whether it was rightly or wrongly entered. The Master of the Rolls has disposed of that part of the case. If Mr. Skey, upon those questions being answered as they were answered, had a right of action, that right he will retain, independently of anything here done, but the bill by the general shareholders will not stand upon that ground. Finding, then, Crowther apparently actively engaged in one of these very imprudent transactions —it is only justice to his memory to say he was ignorant of everything else that was going on—finding him in that position when these questions were asked by Skey, and assenting and consenting to the responses which were given (which he either did with knowledge of the facts, or, if not, he allowed them to be given in a solemn way without taking the trouble to ascertain the facts), I cannot say it is a case in which the court can properly mark its opinion of the conduct of the directors in the subject-matter before it, otherwise than by dismissing the bill without costs. The costs, therefore, of the appeal will be costs in the cause. There will be no costs in fact.

20 L.T. 553 (1869)
Vice Chancellor - Chancery
L.R. 4 Ch. App. 475 (1869)
Lord Justices - Court of Appeal

Chancery

V. C. MALINS' COURT.
Reported by G. T. EDWARDS, Esq., Barrister-at-Law.

March 13, 20, and 22.

Re THE MERCANTILE TRADING COMPANY.
STRINGER'S CASE.

This matter came on upon a summons and motion, under the 165th section of the Companies Act 1862, in the winding-up of this company ; the object being to make the managing director liable in respect of a dividend of 25*l.* per cent. received by him as a shareholder in the company, and also in respect of a certain commission, the case being a representative one.

The company was established on the 12th June 1863 and registered under the Companies Act 1862, the objects, as stated by the articles of association, being the purchase of goods and ships to trade with America by sale and barter, and the carrying and transporting such goods to this country and to certain ports. The object was, in fact, to employ these vessels to run the block de established by the Federal against the Conf derate States, and to supply the Confederate Government with such articles as they required, bringing back cotton in return. . . .

The articles of association of the company were framed upon table A. of the Companies Act 1862, which provided that no dividend should be paid out of capital, nor from any fund except out of actual profits in hand. The provisions contained in the articles, and other facts relating to the formation and working of the company, are referred to by the Vice-Chancellor in his judgment. . . .

The VICE-CHANCELLOR.—This case raises a point of the highest importance under the Winding-up Acts, with respect to this company, established with the specified object of purchasing goods and ships to trade between this country and America; but in reality to run the blockade formed by the Federal against the Confederate States. No doubt, if goods had been successfully transported both ways, the profit would have been enormous, whatever the consequences arising from the infringement of the neutrality between two belligerents might be. The professed capital was 150,000*l.*, 112,000*l.* only being subscribed, and the result was that the whole was lost, the debts amounting to 80,000*l.*, against which there are said to be some assets; but there is little possibility of the debts being paid. The undertaking was a most hazardous one, and four out of six ships were lost before the dividend in question was declared, exposing the parties concerned to a total loss. This was from the very commencement, and the loss of life and property in consequence of the war was such that it must have ended within a reasonable time, and not until then could it be ascertained whether there had been a profit or not. It is not surprising that in such a state of things the provision in the articles as to the division of profits, was not in the ordinary form ; but table A of the Act being incorporated, not only is there, therefore, the general provision against declaring a dividend out of capital, but the 4th clause of the articles provides for remuneration to the directors by a commission on net profits; the 5th (which is most material) provides that the directors shall declare a dividend on the subscribed capital of the company as soon as the existing profits of the company in hand shall be sufficient for a dividend of 5*l.* per cent. This meant nothing more than that a dividend should not be declared out of capital, but only out of profits actually in hand. That was introduced in consequence of the nature of the business; and the articles are so short that they might have been learned by heart, and it was the duty of everyone concerned to know them. What was done? The company, commencing in June 1863, a material date, on the 20th Feb. 1864 make up their accounts, a most unusual period, and unintelligible, except upon the fact of overwhelming profits; whereas on this most hazardous undertaking each person took a liability of 1000*l.* The ships were uninsured, probably because no underwriter would take the risk. Four out of six were lost by capture or foundering before Feb. 1864, and another, not actually belonging to the company, but in which they had an interest, was taken by the French. The balance-sheet was then made up, showing for the eight months a profit of 42,816*l.*, 15*s.* 2*d.* By an arrangement with the Confederate Government, if a loss occurred, they were to bear two-thirds, the company one-third, and this balance-sheet charges the company therefore with one-third, and credits them with two-thirds, and places as assets 62,000*l.* due from the Confederate Government, and 17,000*l.* for the value of cotton in the Confederate States. The result was that the 62,000*l.* realised 15,000*l.* only, being a loss of 47,000*l.*, and the cotton was totally destroyed either by the Federals or the Confederates to prevent its being taken by the Federals. On other items there was a loss of 10,000*l.* and other large sums, so that instead of a profit of 42,800*l.*, there was a loss of 22,000*l.*, admitted, although I have no doubt it was in fact as much as 50,000l. Was it just under such circumstances to declare a dividend, which was only to be declared out of profits in hand? The balance at the Agra Bank was 667l. 10s. 8d., and 21l. 12s. 6d. cash at the office, and therefore there was 6698l. 3s. 2d. to pay a dividend of 25 per cent. on 112,000l.!—that is, 28,000l. That was not actually declared till the 17th May, not on a new state of things, but made up to the 29th Feb. At that time there was an overdrawn account at the Agra Bank of 5000l., and there being nothing to pay the dividend of 28,000l. the Agra Bank was induced to lend 16,020l. 5s. on the 25th May, and 2000l. being paid in from some other source, a dividend account was opened, and the remaining 5320l., borrowed of the bank to make up the 28,000l., and there was a sum of 20,000l. odd against the company. Mr. Jackson, in his able argument, said, what I hope may be overstated, that companies scarcely ever pay out of profits. But reckoning, as prudent men, that realising profits must depend on the success of the Confederated States, how it happened that mercantile men could be found so to act, passes credibility. That they took a too sanguine view, is the mildest term applicable to it, and it is inconceivable that the Agra Bank, a joint-stock company, with the interests of innumerable families committed to them, should have lent 21,000l. at such a time, to furnish a delusive dividend which never could have been paid, had it not been for the facilities afforded by the bank; which, as is not surprising, came to an unfortunate end. Knowing that the 62,000l. due from the Confederate States was not more certain than a chance at the hazard table, it was unjustifiable to treat it as an asset; and although Mr. Jackson contended that it was justified because the cotton purchased at 6d. would realise 2s. 6d. if it got home, nothing should have been done until the "if" became "no if," and if so no dividend would have been declared. There was never a profit but a loss day by day, and money being borrowed under such circumstances, on every principle of honour and honesty, that money should be returned, although I am not able to make that order on the present occasion. It was a diminution, and therefore a return of capital, and I cannot conceive how any gentleman, actuated by honourable motives, can retain this money. Had a bill been filed I should have decreed a return without hesitation, but I cannot do it on this summary proceeding. . . .

I am justified in the conclusion I have arrived at, by the fact that although the same question has arisen in very numerous cases where a dividend has been improperly declared, yet this is the first time that there has been an application for a return. I am unable in this shape to do what is asked, and therefore the summons must be dismissed; but by reason of the nature of the case, and the moral obligation to make the return, without costs.

Court of Appeal

Company—Winding-up—Order upon a Contributory or Director to repay a Dividend improperly declared—Companies Act, 1862, ss. 101, 165—What amounts to an improper and delusive Dividend—" Profits in Hand."

The Court has summary power, under the 101st and 165th sections of the *Companies Act*, 1862, to order a contributory or director to repay a dividend declared and paid under a delusive and fraudulent balance sheet.

In re Royal Hotel Company of Great Yarmouth (1) disapproved of.

But the balance sheet of a company engaged in a hazardous trade will not be considered delusive and fraudulent merely because an estimated value was put upon assets of the company which were then in jeopardy and were subsequently lost, or because the company was obliged to borrow money to pay the dividend, provided the facts fairly appeared on the balance sheet and the balance fairly represented profits.

A company was formed under the *Companies Act*, 1862, for running the blockade during the civil war in *America*. The articles provided that dividends should not be paid except out of profits, and that the directors should declare a dividend as often as the profits in hand were sufficient to pay £5 per cent. on the capital, subject to the resolutions of a general meeting. In 1864, a dividend was declared and sanctioned at a general meeting, and subsequently paid, upon a balance sheet in which a debt due from the *Confederate* government, and cotton in the *Confederate States*, and also ships engaged in running the blockade, were estimated at the full nominal value. All these assets were lost, and the company was wound up:—

Held, that as the estimate was made *bonâ fide*, and the facts appeared truly in the balance sheet, the balance sheet was not delusive, and the dividend must be considered to have been made out of profits, although the company had actually to borrow the money to pay it.

The order of *Malins*, V.C., affirmed, but on different grounds.

THIS was an appeal from an order of Vice-Chancellor *Malins*, made in the winding up of the *Mercantile Trading Company, Limited*. . . .

Sir C. J. Selwyn, L.J.:— . . . .

There remains, however, the question upon the merits of this case, and that question may be shortly stated thus:—Whether the dividend of £25 per cent. which was declared and paid by the directors in this case is to be considered, as the learned Vice-Chancellor has considered it, so wholly delusive and improper, or, in substance, such a return of capital, as to justify the Court in any jurisdiction in making Mr. *Stringer* pay the amount of £25 per cent. on the nominal value of the shares standing in his name. Now, I quite agree with the argument which has been addressed to us on behalf of the official liquidator to this extent, that the Act which confers on these companies the privilege of limited liability imposes upon them at the same time certain conditions which they are bound to observe, and which may be considered as the price of that privilege; and if it is made to appear that for the purposes of fraud, or for any other improper motive, a company has declared and paid a wholly delusive and improper dividend, and has thereby in effect taken away from its creditors a portion of the capital which was available for the debts of those creditors, I entertain no doubt that the Court would have full jurisdiction, and would exercise it by ordering the repayment of the money so improperly paid. But in the present case we have to consider whether this dividend was, in truth, a dividend declared under such circumstances. I think that (having regard to the amount of the balance) we may dismiss from our consideration some of the minor items upon which considerable discussion has arisen. The substantial question in the case depends upon the consideration of three items in this account. Those are, first, the ships which were actually lost; secondly, the debt due from the *Confederate* government; and, thirdly, the cotton which was in the *Confederate States* at the time when the balance sheet was made out. It is very material to observe in this case that no fraud on the shareholders can be, or is attempted to be, alleged in argument, because in this case a full and fair dividend was declared, and was paid, or intended to be paid, to all the shareholders equally without any preference or priority. Neither was there any fraud upon the public intended or practised, nor even upon that part of the public who might be expected to become purchasers of the shares, because it is admitted that the shares of this company were not sold at all, but were held from the beginning to the end by the same persons. Neither is it, I think, possible to say with justice that any attempt has been made in this case to commit any fraud upon the creditors, for though it appears at the time when this balance sheet was made out that a very large debt was owing from the company to the *Agra and Masterman's Bank,* and that a very large debt is still owing to that bank from the company now being wound up, it does not appear (with the exception of one claim recently made by a creditor at *New York*) that there are now any other debts existing at all against this company. The singularity of this case is, that the balance sheet discloses on its very face, when it first begins to deal with the profit and loss, the names of the four ships which had been lost. So, also, with respect to the debt due from the *Confederate* government. The experience which we have unfortunately had in this Court of this sort of statement put forth by companies shews how very easy and how very common it is to dissemble in their balance sheets, and instead of setting forth the real truth of the transactions with respect to their assets, debts, and liabilities, we find that where there is an asset of a doubtful character it is mixed up with others that are good in such a manner as to render the one undistinguishable from the others. Here the debt owing from the *Confederate* government is plainly stated as being a debt owing from that government. It stands by itself, and is not attempted to be dissembled or cloaked in any way. In like manner, with respect to the third item, the cotton in the *Confederate States,* nothing would have been easier than to mix up the cotton in the *Confederate States* with the larger amount of cotton which appears to have been either on the way or actually in *England;* but so far from that being the case, an amount of cotton to the extent of £17,000 is plainly stated upon the face of this balance sheet as being cotton in the *Confederate States* as distinguished from cotton in *England* or on the way. Then this balance sheet containing these plain and fair statements is actually produced to the principal creditors of the company, who had very large dealings with the company, who had several accounts with the company, who had advanced them money generally and upon special undertakings and securities, and who had the fullest knowledge of all the transactions of this company. It was produced to those creditors for the purpose of inducing them to advance a still larger sum; and what renders this matter still more singular is, that it was in order to induce them to lend this sum for the express purpose of paying this dividend; so that this application, which is substantially an application made at the instance of the *Agra and Masterman's Bank*, is an application which asks the Court to treat as delusive and improper that dividend which was, in fact, made and paid with the money advanced by the *Agra and Masterman's Bank*, and advanced by them with full knowledge, or with the means of knowledge, of all the transactions of the company, and which was money advanced for the very purpose of paying this dividend, for it appears that a new account was opened with the bank, intituled "The Dividend Account."

The question with respect to the dividend is mainly rested upon the provisions in Table A. in the *Companies Act*, 1862, with respect to the payment of dividends, and the 5th article of this company, which qualifies and adds to the rule laid down in Table A. The expression in Table A. is in the negative form, "That no dividends shall be payable except out of the profits arising from the business of the company." The 1st clause of the articles provides "that all the articles of Table A. shall be deemed to be incorporated with and to apply to these articles and the said company as near as may be and circumstances will permit, except as hereinafter modified or altered." Then the 5th clause says, "That the directors shall declare a dividend on the subscribed capital of the company as soon and as often as the profits of the company in hand are sufficient for payment of a dividend of £5 per cent. on such capital, subject to the resolutions of a general meeting." I agree again with the argument which was adduced by the official liquidator to this extent, that if it could be shewn that this dividend was declared in fraud either of the negative provisions of Table A. (which is incorporated with the articles of this company) or in fraud or violation of the provisions of their own articles, so far as they relate to the creditors, namely, the 5th article, it would be then a matter which this Court would be competent to set aside, and all moneys paid in respect of such dividend ought to be returned. But the first question we have to determine is, whether the conclusion at which the learned Vice-Chancellor arrived with respect to this matter is correct, which I think is shortly summed up by him in his judgment, in these words: "It was obvious to all the world that the consumption of life and property in the war was such that it must necessarily come to an end within a reasonable time, be it one, two, or three years, and the company, according to my judgment, could only then for the first time ascertain whether its operations had been profitable or unprofitable." Now if the learned Vice-Chancellor is correct in that view of the case, it puts an end to any further consideration of the question with respect to future profits or profits in hand; because it is obvious that according to that view of the case there could be neither profits nor profits in hand until the termination of the war, and until all the operations had been concluded, because he says until that time it could not be ascertained whether the operations of the company had been profitable or unprofitable. I think, in order to test the soundness of that conclusion, we may take, for instance, the figures which appear in Mr. *Stringer's* affidavit, and assume that by reason of the successful voyage of some of these ships the two sums mentioned of £32,000 and £24,000, making in all £56,000, had been actually realized and received in respect of profit upon adventures and cargoes actually landed and sold, and suppose that no ship had been lost at all, still the whole of the ships belonging to this company would be subject to the very hazardous adventure in which they were engaged; they had cost more than £100,000, and they were liable to destruction at any time, and, according to the Vice-Chancellor's view, until the war was determined and the safety of those ships was ascertained, it could not be ascertained whether the transactions of the company had been profitable or unprofitable. Therefore, in that view of the case, even if the company had had this sum of £56,000 in their hands in respect of realized profits, inasmuch as they would be subject to the possible loss of the value of the ships, no dividend could be paid by the company. Having regard to the provisions of Table A. and clause 5 of the articles, which contains no negative words at all, in my judgment the company would have been perfectly justified at that time, in the case I have assumed, in declaring a dividend out of the profits so received, provided that they had put a fair—and no more than a fair—value upon the ships and the assets which they actually had. Taking it one step further, and assuming the case that several of the ships had been lost, that the company was bound to put down, as they did put down, their proportion of that loss as being a loss upon this balance sheet, the other two-thirds of the loss were to be covered by the responsibility and guarantee of the *Confederate* government, and according to the view of the learned Vice-Chancellor, inasmuch as until the end of the war the value of that guarantee could not be ascertained, no dividend could be declared. I confess I am unable to agree with that view. I think that under those circumstances the company was fully justified in putting a value on the ships and on the *Confederate* debt; and inasmuch as it is clear that, having regard to the extremely hazardous nature of the operations in which the ships were engaged, no insurance of them could be effected, the valuation of the ships became a matter of mere estimate; and inasmuch as with respect to the value of the obligation on the part of the *Confederate* government, there could be no fixed principle on which it could be valued—for it depended upon the views which different persons might take, and we know well what different views were taken by very eminent persons with respect to the probable conclusion of that great struggle—I think the company was justified in doing that which, in truth, is done in almost every business, namely, taking the facts as they actually stood, and forming an estimate of their assets as they actually existed, and then drawing a balance so as to ascertain the result in the shape of profit or of loss. If, indeed, it could be shewn that that estimate had been made in any fraudulent way with any intention or purpose of deceiving any one, or that, in point of fact, anyone was deceived by it, very different considerations would arise. I have already shewn that no fraud was intended or attempted against either the shareholders, or the public, or the creditors of the company. If we were to lay down as a rule that there must be actually cash. in hand, or at the bankers of the company, to the full amount of the dividend declared, we should be laying down a rule which, in my judgment, would be inconsistent with what I understand and believe to be the custom of all companies of this description, and also inconsistent with mercantile usage, and we should be laying down a rule which would open the door to and encourage a very great amount of litigation, because there are very few dividends indeed which would not be open to more or less question if such a rule as that were laid down. I think that in the absence of any fraudulent intent as against the shareholders, or as against the creditors or the public, the Court ought not to be astute in searching out minute errors in calculation, in an account honestly made out and openly declared; especially as in the present case, where the account was submitted to, and the dividend consequent upon it was ratified, by the general meeting so long ago as 1864, long before the winding up of this company, and more especially where, as here, that account is now attempted, after that lapse of time, to be impeached substantially at the instance of persons to whom all the items of the account were fully and fairly made known, who themselves were the principal actors in, and mainly assisted in the payment of the very dividend they now seek to impeach.

I think, therefore, for these reasons, that the claim originally made against Mr. *Stringer* fails upon the merits, and that the application which was made in the Court below ought to have been then, and must be now, refused with costs, and I think also that the present appeal must be dismissed with costs. That, therefore, will be the terms of our order; but, in accordance with our usual practice, we shall leave to the decision of the Vice-Chancellor any question which may arise as between the official liquidator and those whom he represents with reference to the costs so ordered to be paid by the official liquidator.

Sir G. M. Giffard, L.J. :— . . . .

Now, with regard to this case, the first important matter that we have to consider is the effect of these articles of association, and I quite agree that if the effect of these articles was that you could have no division of dividends until all the transactions were wound up, that you could have no legal dividend except out of what is termed profits in hand, there might be a great deal to be said in this case; but if we look at the articles of association as compared with Table A., it is clearly manifest that the articles of association amount to nothing of the kind. [His Lordship then referred to the provisions in Table A., and in the articles of association, which have been before mentioned, and continued:—] I have no hesitation in saying—especially if you compare the word "may" in Table A., and the word "shall" in the 5th clause, and consider that there are negative words in Table A., and that there are none in this clause—that this clause was intended simply to have this effect, and no other, viz., that when the directors had in their hands profits they should not be able to set them aside for a contingency fund, and that they should then, at all events, be compellable to make a dividend. It did not prevent their making a dividend; but I agree, it must be out of profits, although those profits were not profits in hand.

Then, when we come to the facts themselves—I will not again go through them, for they have been considered at very considerable length, not only in argument, but also by my learned brother—it was not argued or suggested, nor could it be argued or suggested, that it was intended that this thing, though in terms a dividend, should cover what was not really a dividend transaction. The mode in which the matter was done was fair enough. The books were put into the hands of an accountant, calculations were made, and a certain conclusion was arrived at. True it is, no doubt, that these proceedings were full of risk; but although, on the one hand, there might be a great loss everyone knows that whenever there was a success the profits were something very enormous, and upon the balance sheets as taken from the books it did appear that there was a profit of £42,000, and it was proposed out of that to divide somewhere about £28,000, the profits, I agree, not being profits in hand. The fault that is found with that is, that the estimate was an erroneous estimate; that too sanguine a view was taken of the prospects of success; and that there ought to have been a very much less sum put upon the face of this balance sheet as assets than really was put there. But I do not think that anyone can say it was not at this date possible for honest persons carrying on this trade, entertaining the view which they did entertain as to their prospects, honestly to make out such a balance sheet as this, and honestly to believe that those were profits fairly divisible between them. As I have said before, this was not done in any underhand manner; the whole thing was patent and open; it was known, or capable of being known, by every shareholder, and if the directors of the *Agra and Masterman's Bank* did not know anything about it, they neglected their duty, and behaved most shamefully to their own shareholders whose money they lent; for the balance sheet was put in their hands, and they had accounts of every description, and they must have known perfectly well that it was neither more or less than a blockade-running company ; the very nature of the accounts shewed it; and so far from there being any concealment, the balance sheet itself was put into the hands of the auditors, and no person who knew what the business of the company was could look through that balance sheet without seeing at once that the full value was put upon the *Confederate* government debt, and that the four ships had been lost, and without knowing at once that if things turned out adversely that which was profit might, from subsequent events, become a great loss. Again, this dividend was declared in May, 1864, and was actually paid in June, 1864, and I cannot forget that it was actually paid by the *Agra and Masterman's Bank*, who not only advanced the money, knowing the affairs of the company, but who paid the dividends through the medium of cheques drawn upon them by the shareholders. I think it would be a gross injustice if at this distance of time, when a dividend has been made and paid in this way so long ago as the year 1864, because things turn out adversely afterwards, and the company is wound up in 1867 at the instance of a creditor, such a dividend should be repaid. I quite agree when there has been what can be termed fairly a misappropriation of assets as against a creditor, that creditor has a right in the winding-up to have those assets recouped ; but I cannot think that such a dividend as this was in any sense a misappropriation as against either the *Agra and Masterman's Bank* or any other creditors, or that it was in any sense delusive, or in any sense a fraudulent transaction, or that it was any other transaction than this, viz., that mercantile men who were engaged in adventures which might result in very great or even total loss, and which might also result in very great profit, took a sanguine view of what the value of the assets was, looking at what at that date was the actual profit made, and acted upon that *bonâ fide*, not intending to defraud in any way any person whatever.

Therefore, I am of opinion that this appeal must be dismissed with costs.

RANCE'S CASE

L.R. 6 Ch. App. 104 (1870)
Lord Justices - Court of Appeal

In re COUNTY MARINE INSURANCE COMPANY.

RANCE'S CASE.

Company—Voluntary Winding-up—Repayment by Director—Bonus improperly declared—Delusive Balance-sheet—Profits—Companies Act, 1862, *ss.* 138, 165.

The Court has summary power in a voluntary winding-up, on the application of the liquidator, to make an order under the 138th and 165th sections of the *Companies Act,* 1862, calling upon a director to repay a dividend of bonus declared and paid to him under a delusive balance-sheet.

In such a case where a bonus was declared and credited to a director against arrears of calls then due from him, it was held a payment within the section.

Where directors, after proper investigation of the financial position of the company, declare, and the shareholders agree to, a dividend or bonus, the Court will not lightly interfere with the payment of such dividend or bonus, on the ground that the estimates on which it was founded have turned out to be erroneous. But where the directors declare a dividend or bonus without proper investigation or professional assistance, and it is afterwards called in question, the burden lies on them to shew that it was fairly paid out of profits; and if they are unable to do so, the Court will order them to refund what they have received.

The directors of a *Marine Insurance Company* declared a bonus of 10s. per share, which was agreed to at a general meeting and paid. The directors prepared no profit-and-loss account, but only an account of the receipts and payments of the company, which made no allowance for the risks to which the company was liable. The company having resolved to wind up voluntarily :—

Held (reversing the decision of the Master of the Rolls), that an order ought to be made on a director to repay the bonus paid to him.

THIS was an appeal from a decision of the Master of the Rolls, made in the winding-up of the *County Marine Insurance Company, Limited.*

The company was registered under the *Companies Act,* 1862, on the 13th of November, 1866. The capital consisted of 25,000 shares of £4 each, of which £2 were to be paid on allotment. The principal articles of association, which were referred to in the argument, were as follows :—

Art. 111. The directors shall cause to be kept, in and according to the mercantile manner and system, full and true accounts of the paid-up capital for the time being of the company, and the receipt and expenditure of all moneys received and expended by the company, and generally of all its affairs, transactions, and engagements, and of the profit or loss resulting therefrom, and of all such things as shall be requisite to exhibit the true financial condition of the company.

Art. 112. At the first ordinary general meeting of every year the directors shall lay before the company a report comprising a balance-sheet, shewing, as accurately as circumstances will permit, the financial position of the company up to a date to be therein mentioned, and which shall be as near the day of meeting as can conveniently be fixed.

Art. 123. The expenditure of the company shall be charged to capital or revenue as the directors shall from time to time determine, and whenever the directors shall think it desirable that any part of the assets shall be divided or distributed between the members by way of dividend or bonus, they may recommend payment thereof accordingly, and with the consent of a general meeting cause the same to be paid.. . .

On the 8th of October, 1867, a general meeting of the *County Marine Company* was held. The notice stated that the meeting was held to receive the report of the directors, to pass the accounts from the commencement of business to the 30th of June, 1867, for the declaration of a dividend or bonus, and for the election of directors and auditors. A preliminary balance-sheet was laid before the shareholders in the following form :—

80

PRELIMINARY BALANCE-SHEET FROM THE COMMENCEMENT OF THE COMPANY
TO JUNE 30, 1867.

Dr.

	£	s.	d.	£	s.	d.
Capital of the company, of which there are subscribed 1985 shares. Received on ditto ..	..			1288	18	5
To Premiums received :						
Underwriting department	915	9	0			
Less brokerage, &c.	132	1	1			
				783	7	11
To Premiums received :						
Mariners' lives	2437	18	8			
Less allowances	32	16	5			
				2405	2	3
To Sundry creditors	..			69	14	7
				£4547	3	2

	£	s.	d.	£	s.	d.
Preliminary Expenses		..		144	0	0
Claims and Returns (Marine)		..		147	0	3
Re-insurances (Marine)		..		124	^	10
Rent	23	15	0			
Stationery and Books	54	8	4			
Salaries and Directors' Fees	753	6	8			
Postage, Offices, &c.	42	1	9			
Liverpool Agency	50	0	0			
				923	11	9
Investments:						
Cash and Stamps in hand	9	2	6			
On Deposit..	1000	0	0			
Furniture	48	16	6			
In hands of Agents, Brokers, and others..	1527	3	11			
Sundry Debtors	56	14	10			
Balance at Bankers	566	4	7			
				3208	2	4
				£4547	3	2

. . . .

A resolution was passed by the meeting for dividing a bonus, as
recommended by the report. No profit and loss account was presented to the meeting, nor had any been prepared by the directors.
Nor did it appear that any formal resolution had been passed by
the board of directors to recommend the bonus.

In pursuance of this resolution the directors divided a sum of
£1072 10s. among the shareholders, which was credited to their
account in the proportion of 10s. to each share. At that time Mr.
J. Rance was a director of the company, and held 250 shares, on
which he had paid £125, leaving £375 due from him in respect of
the allotment money. Against this he was credited with £125 in
the books of the company, as the amount of his share of the bonus.

. . . .

In the month of May, 1869, resolutions were passed for a voluntary winding-up of the *County Marine Company.* The liquidator
took out a summons against Mr. *Rance,* calling upon him, as one of
the directors of the company, to refund the sum of £125, being the
bonus received by him in October, 1867, on the ground that the
bonus was paid out of the capital, and not out of the profits of the
company, and that the declaration of it was beyond the power of
the directors. . . .

On the other hand the managing director, Mr. *C. Walford*, made an affidavit, in which he said : " Although at the time of making up the preliminary balance-sheet to the 30th of June, 1867, no profit and loss account was actually made out, yet the figures were carefully gone into and considered, and the assets and liabilities of the company carefully estimated; and with regard to the latter I say that I and the underwriter of the said company made what we considered to be a fair provision for all losses likely to arise, as well on marine as mariners' life and marine casualty policies, and that there was then, after making such provision, quite sufficient assets to declare a bonus of 10s. per share."

He then set out what he considered would have been a fair profit and loss account up to the 30th of June, 1867, shewing a balance profit of £1072 12s. 2d., and he explained that in making out such account it was according to the custom of other companies that the debits for preliminary expenses, fixtures, and for the goodwill of the *Accidental Death Company*, should be spread over a period of five years, and the debit for stationery over a period of three years; and that it was fair and proper on the other hand that the company should be credited, not only with the sum of £1000 paid by the *Accidental Death Company*, but also with the sum of £500 then due from that company, inasmuch as there was no reason to suppose at that time that the company would be insolvent. In this account the probable claims on marine policies were estimated at £170 13s., and on mariners' life policies at £650.

The Master of the Rolls was of opinion that, although the declaration of the bonus was not justified by the state of the company, yet there was no proof that the directors had not acted *bonâ fide*, and accordingly dismissed the summons (1). From this decision the liquidator appealed.

(1) 1870. Nov. 4.

Lord Romilly, M.R. :—

This is a summons taken out by the liquidator to compel Mr. *Rance*, who was a director and shareholder of the company, to refund the sum of £125, being the bonus received by him in October, 1867, and which he took part in declaring. . . .

Although it may not be always of easy application, the principle which governs cases of this description is very clearly established by all the cases. When an improper payment has been made, if it be a mere error of judgment, it cannot be recovered; if it be a fraudulent payment, then it can. These words however, "*bonâ*

SIR W. M. JAMES, L.J.:—

This is an application by way of appeal from an order of the Master of the Rolls, and it asks that the Respondent, who was a director of the *County Marine Insurance Company, Limited,* should

fide; payment" and "fraudulent payment," are found in use to be somewhat vague terms, and it becomes necessary therefore in the present case that I should state in what sense I use the words, and then I must proceed to examine the facts of the case for the purpose of ascertaining within which of these two descriptions this transaction ought properly to be classed.

By a fraudulent payment, which for this purpose includes the declaration of the bonus which creates the payment, I mean one where the person who makes it, or who is concerned in making it, is at the time aware of the impropriety of making it, but does so in order to obtain a benefit for himself. All other payments must be treated as *bonâ fide.* . . .

I have looked into this as carefully as I can, and after careful investigation of the matter as far as I am able to judge, I think the declaration of the bonus was an improper proceeding, and that there did not exist at that time a probability of any profit, but that there was a probability of a considerable loss if the company had then been wound up. But of this I am quite clear, that it was not an easy matter to discover, as, in fact, it rarely is in these insurance cases, and that it required a very careful investigation of the matter by competent persons to come to an accurate conclusion. In these cases of insurance, where the duration of the insurance has to be taken into account, and the probable risk varies very much, it is extremely difficult to ascertain what the exact state of the company is, and I think it might be reasonably disputed by competent persons that the company was then in the state which the liquidator represents it as being. This is the strange part of the case, that there is not throughout this case the slightest trace of the directors having made the payment or declared the bonus knowing that it was improper or that they entertained any suspicion of such being the case: nor is there the slightest suspicion that any individual benefit was obtained by any one of them in the matter. And in this case the competent advisers who conducted the affairs of the company recommended them, and did so after advice and after carefully examining the state of the company—in which opinion they still concur. It is also to be observed that they did not get the £500 from the *Accidental Death Company.* The impropriety of the bonus is not, as appears to me, an obvious result of the account laid before the meeting, nor does any one at the meeting appear to have pointed out or suspected that it was not a fit and proper proceeding. To compel the repayment of money paid or credited under such circumstances would, in my opinion, lead to very serious and, as I believe, disastrous results. A transaction which at the time seemed to be perfectly fair and proper, might from the light to be derived from subsequent events, be shewn to have been a most rash and inexpedient proceeding; but if the directors who ordered it, and the shareholders who sanctioned it, and who are afterwards called upon to make good the injury they sustained, were of opinion upon the facts stated before them that it ought properly to be made, then, in my opinion, it cannot afterwards be disturbed. If it were not so, it would not be possible for any company to be safely or usefully conducted. . . .

pay a sum of £125, the amount of a bonus paid or credited to him in the month of October, 1870. . . .

Now, with regard to the propriety or impropriety of the transaction, it appears to me to be one of the most startling and improper proceedings that ever came under my notice. The company was a company formed for marine and other insurances. Subsequently the directors took in life assurances, but they seem to have begun with marine insurances. The company had been in existence for only eight months when a bonus of 10s. per share was declared, a bonus which, of course, could only be lawfully made out of moneys which had been earned, or believed to have been earned, in the way of profit. Independently of one particular item which I have severed from the rest, as it has been severed in the course of the argument, the business of the marine insurance proper was this: They had received for premiums £783 7s. 11d., and out of that they had expended· in re-insurances £124 8s. 10d. There had been marine claims actually ripening into demands amounting to £147. Then they had spent in preliminary expenses £144, which they say might have been spread over a certain number of years. They had spent in stationery and books £54 8s. 4d., which they seek to divide in the same way. Besides those, there were actual current expenses which could by no possibility be spread over any period in that way—such as rent, £23 15s.; salaries and directors' fees, £753 6s. 8d.; postage, office, and travelling expenses, £42 1s. 9d.; fixtures, &c., for office at *Liverpool*, £50—so that, in truth, there was nearly £800 which had been actually expended in annual expenses, and their gross premiums to cover the risks which were coming on in future were only the sums which I have stated. But then it is said that they had made a bargain with another insurance office to take off their hands a number of policies. The policies had been going on for some time, and, of course, the annual premiums would not be the proper compensation for the risks to be incurred. The two companies, in one of which Mr. *Walford*, who speaks to these transactions, was the managing director, and in the other was connected with the management, therefore agreed that £2000 was the proper compensation to be given to the one company for taking over the onerous policies of the other; in other words, that the premiums were not worth the risk by the sum of £2000. And it was further agreed that the £2000 should be paid in this way, namely, £1000 to be paid at once, £500 at Christmas, and £500 to be set against the goodwill, as it was called, of this transferred business. It appears also, that upon this transaction they received premiums amounting to £405 2s. 3d. Then they say, that out of the profits of that transaction they were justified in making a division by way of bonus of £1000. How was this done? Was there any attempt to make a balance-sheet or any profit-and-loss account in such a way as any mercantile body, and certainly any insurance company, ought to have done? To take the money which the company had received to answer risks, and to treat it as money capable of being divided as profits, without making any estimate of what the risks were in respect of which the money was paid, seems to me to be the most extravagant proceeding that I ever heard of. The directors simply had before them the cash balance of the receipts and payments, and, without making the slightest provision in that account for anything whatever, they proceed out of that balance to declare this bonus. I quite agree that it would have been different if there had been, as there ought to have been in the ordinary course of business, a balance-sheet *bonâ fide* made out with proper assistance, so as to ascertain the true state of the company. If the directors had followed the directions of the 112th article of their own deed, and if at the first ordinary general meeting they had laid before the company a report comprising a balance-sheet shewing, as accurately as circumstances would permit, the financial position of the company up to that date—if that had been done, I am of opinion that it would not be right for this Court to sit as a Court of Appeal to decide upon such a state of facts so made out. If the directors, by placing unfounded reliance upon the representations of their servants or actuaries, had arrived at the conclusion that they had made a divisible profit, this Court ought not, I say, to sit as a Court of Appeal from that conclusion, although it might afterwards be satisfactorily proved that there were very great errors in the accounts which would not have occurred if they had been made out with greater strictness or with more scrutinising care. But no such account at all was made out. A mere cash account or balance-sheet in such a company as this, presented in order to determine whether there had been a profit made, and for the purpose of declaring a bonus thereon, is, to my mind, within the meaning of *Stringer's Case* (1), a fraudulent and delusive balance-

(1) Law Rep. 4 Ch. 475.

sheet. It purported to shew something, as was said in that case, which any man who applied his mind to the subject would say afforded no clue whatever to the profit which had been made. They might as well have put before the meeting a sheet out of a newspaper. An attempt is made by the managing director to justify it in this way: The respondent himself has not ventured to pledge his oath to the fact that he ever applied his mind to the question whether there was any profit or loss made, or that he believed there was such a profit as to justify the payment of that bonus. But Mr. *Walford*, the managing director, says this:— [His Lordship then read the paragraph from the affidavit of Mr. *Walford* set forth above, and continued:—]

Whatever estimate was made was in Mr. *Walford's* own mind, and was never before the directors at all, but, notwithstanding this, Mr. *Walford* contends that he was fully warranted in recommending the bonus, because the transaction with the *Accidental Death Insurance Company* was so profitable. He says they received £415 in premiums, and £1000 in cash, and they were to receive £500 more, and that they afterwards, in December, sold that business to the *Colonial Insurance Corporation*, and had not to pay so much to them as they had received from the first company. It is pretended in the account that they had received £2000, but £500 was paid for the goodwill, which would of course pass with the policies transferred to the new company. Now it is clear that this was a transaction which was only begun, and which had not ripened into any profit, at the time when this bonus was declared, and before I could have given the sanction of this Court to a division on the notion that they had made a good bargain in buying a business, I should have liked to know what the estimates were—how it was that £2000 as between the two companies, was considered as the proper sum to be paid, and yet that £1000 was considered the proper sum to be paid by some other company a few months afterwards. If the company, as is stated, sold the property in December, and thereby made a profit of £1000, that was a profit which was realised at the time the bargain was made, but I cannot allow it to be said that they were justified in dividing as profits made up to the 30th of June the result of a very favourable bargain that was made in the December following. Therefore it appears to me that the Respondent is not entitled to bring that into account, and that in truth no provision was made in the estimates for the risks they were running on the different policies. Reliance is also placed on the fact that by great good fortune the policies resulted in scarcely any substantial claim being made against them in the next year, and it is contended that they had a right to consider all that as profit made in the year during which the premiums were paid. This contention also seems to me to be perfectly idle. • • •

SIR G. MELLISH, L.J.:— • • • •

Then that brings me to consider the case upon the merits, and those merits unquestionably raise a very important issue. I must say that I differ from the judgment pronounced by the Master of the Rolls; but I think the difference of opinion between us has arisen mainly from the circumstance that the Master of the Rolls has not, as it appears to me, given sufficient weight to the fact that no profit-and-loss account up to a particular day was ever made out at all, and that the directors did not profess to be dividing a profit which had been earned up to a particular day. For that purpose it is important to look at the notice convening the meeting, and to the report of the directors, and the resolutions passed at that meeting. If those are looked at, it will appear that the directors never stated to the shareholders that they had made a profit, and that they did not profess to be dividing a profit. Now, this is the notice:—[His Lordship read the notice.] At the meeting the preliminary balance-sheet (which is simply a balance-sheet of alleged receipts and payments, mixing the receipts on capital account and the payments on capital account with the receipts on revenue account and the payments on revenue account, and making no allowance of any sort or kind in respect of the further or future risks) was the only account that was laid before them. This balance-sheet was laid before the secretary, together with the following report:—[His Lordship read the report.] In this report there is no statement that they had made a profit of 10s. per share up to the 30th of June, and it really cannot be implied. It professes, on the face of it, to be a return of capital. It does not profess to be a declaration of bonus upon profit made.

In my opinion, such a declaration of bonus without any profit or loss account having been made out is a *mala fide* proceeding on the part of the directors within the 165th section. I quite agree that if directors or a proper actuary had made out a profit and loss account the Court ought to assume, very strongly indeed, that it was a correct account, and ought not without very strong reasons shewing that it was done *mala fide*, to set it aside, or declare a dividend made upon it improper. But, if directors choose to declare a bonus or a dividend without making out any account at all, and if shareholders choose to vote that dividend or bonus, knowing that they have got no account before them, knowing that the directors do not even profess to have made a profit out of which that bonus or dividend can be declared, I cannot help thinking that under those circumstances it lies on the parties who contend that such bonus or dividend was properly declared, to shew that it was made out of profits.

That being the view which I take generally of the case, I have now to consider whether it has been made out on the part of the directors that this bonus was really made out of profits. Here is an insurance company which had carried on business on a very small scale for a period of seven months, when this balance-sheet was made out. During that time the actual working expenses had very considerably exceeded the whole amount of the premiums received. Then they attempt a justification on account of this particular transaction with the *Accidental Insurance Company*. It appears to me that they cannot avail themselves of that. In the first place, no profit had really been made. They had, it is true, agreed to have paid to them a sum of £2000; but of that amount £500 was in fact to be returned for the goodwill, so that practically they were to receive £1500, and of that sum £500 was not to be paid until December. That £500 ought not to be brought into this account as a profit earned previous to the end of June. So that makes the balance-sheet £1000 wrong. Then, again, if this sum had been agreed to be paid in respect of risks, it must be taken *primâ facie* that the risks would be fully equivalent to the sum that was to be paid. It turned out afterwards, no doubt, that in respect of those particular risks very fortunately no loss occurred at all, and they were ultimately, after this bonus was declared, able for £1000 paid to another company to get those risks taken off their hands. But that was merely a subsequent bit of good luck. They had also other subsequent bits of bad luck. On the marine insurance they lost to the extent of upwards of £500, which they say was a great deal more than they had anticipated. How can you divide a profit on one part of a transaction which turned out fortunately, and then say as to the losses on the other part which turned out greater than were anticipated, you will not make any estimate at all? It appears to me that they had really substantially derived no profit at all up to that time. I do not think that Mr. *Walford's* affidavit is satisfactory in which he makes an estimate *ex post facto* of the probable losses, especially when he estimates those probable losses at very much less than what they ultimately turned out to be. And I think he is wrong in including in the account the sum which was to be paid for the goodwill, and in treating the sum of £500, which was not to be paid until the end of December, as a profit of the past year. Upon the principles I have mentioned, I think it incumbent on the director against whom this application is made, to shew that this bonus was really made out of profits under the circumstances under which it was made, namely, without any examination of the accounts at all. I think he has not made that out, and consequently that the order of the Master of the Rolls must be discharged, and that the order asked for ought to be made with costs in the Court below.

MILLS v. NORTHERN RAILWAY OF BUENOS AYRES COMPANY

L.R. 5 Ch.App. 621 (1870)
Lord Chancellor - Court of Appeal

Company—Ultrà vires—Injunction—Locus standi of Plaintiff—Simple Contract Creditor — Equitable Shareholder — Averments of Illegality — Recouping Revenue out of Capital.

THIS was an appeal from an order of Vice-Chancellor *Stuart,* granting an interlocutory injunction against the *Northern Railway of Buenos Ayres Company, Limited,* under the following circumstances :—

The company was established in July, 1862, and registered under the *Companies Act,* 1862. . . .

The original capital of the company consisted of £250,000, divided into 1500 guaranteed preference shares of £10 each, 600 deferred preference shares of £10 each, and 4000 ordinary shares of £10 each. By the articles of association it was provided that the company, with the sanction of a general meeting, might increase the capital of the company by the issue of new shares ; and power was given to the directors to borrow any sum or sums not exceeding £150,000, on debentures or other securities. . . .

On the 30th of April, 1870, the directors issued a report, in which they stated that they had a balance in hand of net profits of £32,681 3s. 2d. ; that the charge for interest upon the company's loan capital, &c., was £5838 6s. 2d., leaving, after lending to the capital account £10,350 17s. 4d. for special expenditure, £16,491 19s. 8d. available for distribution. The directors recommended that this sum should be applied in payment of the arrears of dividend due to the guaranteed preference shareholders for the eighteen months ending the 30th of June, 1867.

The directors explained, in a subsequent paragraph of their report, that the payment of the arrears out of accumulations of revenue would occupy a considerable time, and that in order to accelerate the desired result a certain amount must be funded ; and that as legal difficulties prevented this until the revenue was sufficient to enable the company to declare equivalent dividends, and as expenditure was being incurred in new works and additional plant, which might be legally charged to capital, it was recommended, under the advice of counsel, that the amount expended last year under the above-mentioned heads, as well as that to be expended in the present year and 1871, estimated at about £10,000, should be treated as a payment on capital account, which would be afterwards discharged out of a sum of £20,000, which they purposed to raise by issue of debentures at £6 per cent. The report also recommended the conversion of the tramway from the customhouse to the principal station into a railway adapted for locomotive engines.

This report was adopted at the general meeting of the company held on the 16th of May, 1870, and the sum of £16,401 19s. 8d. was distributed according to the proposal contained therein.

The bill (par. 39) contained the following charge:—"The effect of the proposal contained in the report is, that sums which have been paid out of revenue, and ascribed in the accounts of the company to revenue account, are now to be treated as payments on account of capital account, and considered as having been borrowed for the purpose of capital from the revenue, so as to create an apparent or fictitious fund for the payment of shareholders. The money for this purpose is proposed to be raised by means of the issue of debenture stock, and the effect of the proposal is to increase the liabilities of the company by the issue of debenture stock, for the purpose of borrowing money, in order to distribute the same among the shareholders under the guise of revenue.". . . .

LORD HATHERLEY, L.C. :—

The Vice-Chancellor appears to have formed his judgment in this case, partly at least, upon the view which he took that one of the Plaintiffs, Mr. *Mills*, was a shareholder in the company, and therefore had a right to interfere. But, so far as the case rests on the simple fact of the Plaintiffs being creditors of the company, it seems to me hardly capable of argument. Work is done for a limited company; no engagement is taken from them by way of security; no debenture or mortgage is granted by them; but the work is done simply on the credit of the company. The only remedy for a creditor in that case is to obtain his judgment and to take out execution; or it may be that he may have a power, if the case warrants it, of applying to wind up the company. But it is wholly unprecedented for a mere creditor to say, " Certain transactions are taking place within the company, and dividends are being paid to shareholders which they are not entitled to receive, and therefore I am entitled to come here and examine the company's deed, to see whether or not they are doing what is *ultrà vires*, and to interfere in order that, as by a bill *quia timet*, I may keep the assets in a proper state of security for the payment of my debt whensoever the time arrives for its payment."

The case must have occurred, of course, many years ago, before joint stock companies were so abundant, but certainly within the last twenty or thirty years the money due to creditors must have been many millions, and the number of creditors must have been many thousands; yet I have never before heard—and I asked in vain for any such precedent—of any attempt on the part of a creditor to file a bill of this description against a company, claiming the interference of this Court on the ground that he, having no interest in the company, except the mere fact of being a creditor, is about to be defrauded by reason of their making away with their assets. It would be a fearful authority for this Court to assume, for it would be called on to interfere with the concerns of almost every company in the kingdom against which a creditor might suppose that he had demands, which he had not established in a court of justice, but which he was about to proceed to establish. If there is this power in any case, of course it would apply not only to the raising of money by debentures and to paying shareholders, but it would extend to an interference in every possible way with the dealings of the company. . . .

Then comes the only other question arising as to the proper application of the money. The bill sets out a report which has been made to the shareholders, by which it appears that the balance in hand of net profits amounted to £32,681 3s. 2d. The charge for interest upon the company's loan capital, &c., for 1869, and for some old claims of previous years, was £5838 6s. 2d., leaving, after lending to the capital account £10,350 17s. 4d. for special expenditure, £16,491 19s. 8d. available for distribution. Then they proceed to say that they propose paying that over to the guaranteed shareholders. Those guaranteed shareholders had a right to carry on their surplus debt, beyond what they were paid *de anno in annum*, to following years, the consequence of which was that arrears of debt had accrued upon the income due to the guaranteed preference shareholders, and therefore the company intended to reduce that debt, which then amounted to about £25,000, by raising money under their borrowing powers. Then they say, "When we have raised the money under our borrowing powers" (and they are keeping considerably within the limit of their borrowing powers) " we shall apply that capital so to be raised in paying off £10,000 of this guaranteed debt, because we find that we have really to our credit in respect of capital £10,000 as against this arrear of interest, this £10,000 having been taken from revenue account formerly, and applied to purposes which were really and in fact capital purposes." That is what they state. The only averment in the bill with respect to the illegality of this proceeding is the following, and there is nothing stronger in the affidavit: "The effect of the proposal contained in the report is, that sums which have been paid out of revenue, and ascribed in the accounts of the company to revenue, are now to be treated as payments on account of capital account, and considered as having been borrowed for the purpose of capital from the revenue, so as to create an apparent or fictitious fund for the payment of shareholders." The only words that would at all point to anything wrong are the words "apparent or fictitious." But the substance of the averment does not point to anything of the kind, because the substance is only this, that some sums which formerly were carried to revenue account are now going to be treated as capital. There is no averment that they ought not to be so treated. We are left to find out whether it was wrong or not as well as we can by looking into the accounts; and from them it appears that, as to certain locomotive engines and certain other stock, they were formerly charged to revenue; and it seems, as far as I can collect—for the accounts are not very clear—that these are now to be carried to capital. No doubt many great frauds have been practised by companies both upon themselves and sometimes, unfortunately, upon the public, by carrying to capital account things which ought to go to revenue account, and thereby leaving an imaginary profit, which is not a profit at all. But the bill avers nothing of this kind distinctly and definitely, and the affidavit does not go beyond it. The affidavit verifies a quantity of reports, out of which I am to pick the items as I best may, to ascertain whether they should or should not have been charged to capital or revenue account. If I saw anything grossly extravagant or fraudulent in them—such as the working expenses of the year, or the wages of the men, carried to capital account, in order

93

to make things look pleasant, as it is called—I should have to pause, and consider how it might be proper for this Court to deal with transactions of that kind. But the only thing pointed out to me is the purchase of new locomotives. I do not know exactly on what principle railway companies proceed in their accounts with respect to their locomotives, whether the whole value should be credited, or whether a deduction should be made annually for the stock wearing out, or whether the value of the stock should be taken, which would be the more regular course, at the end of every year. But, certainly, that new rolling stock is in a sense capital as long as it lasts, and that its value on each succeeding stock-taking is capital, there is no doubt whatsoever. Then, why am I to assume that in doing this the directors are acting fraudulently? In the answer it is sworn that things which were properly capital had been paid for out of revenue. If that is the case, I have no hesitation in saying that the circumstance that they had been paying what ought to be charged to capital out of revenue does not prevent their right or their duty to the persons who are looking for their payment out of revenue, to credit back to revenue those things which have been carried for the time to capital account. Mr. *Dickinson* started a very curious theory, which, I apprehend, never found its way into any mercantile arrangement—that there never can be any available income, or any profit, as long as there is any debt remaining unpaid. If that be so, I suppose there is hardly a railway company in the kingdom which could pay any dividends at all to their shareholders. I fancy there are very few indeed which have not debentures out in some shape or other; and if all those are to be paid before a single sixpence could be paid in dividend, of course the companies would be in a very different position from what they suppose themselves to be in. The whole scheme of railway arrangements, as I have understood them, has always been this, that the companies are authorized to raise part of their capital by shares, and to raise further capital by means of borrowing to the amount of one-third of the whole share capital. They expend that money in executing the works, and the works having been executed, the capital of the company remains in the shape of the station-houses, the permanent way, the ware-houses, and everything else which requires expenditure of capital.

The shareholders, especially those who are guaranteed preference shareholders, are not to be told that all these things are to be paid for before they are to have any dividend out of the income.

Therefore the whole of the averment, as I read it here, is really this, that the directors have said in their report that they are going to carry back to revenue what they borrowed from it for the purposes of capital, and when they have carried that back to revenue then they are going to make a dividend. I do not see anything *ultrà vires* in what is either there alleged or suggested. Therefore, even if we assume the Plaintiffs to be shareholders, as to which more argument and more investigation might be required if it were necessary to determine that question, the Plaintiffs have shewn nothing *ultrà vires*; and, counting them as creditors, the case is utterly unfounded as regards both principle and authority. I think, therefore, that the motion for an injunction ought to have been refused with costs; and I make an order to that effect.

SALISBURY v. METROPOLITAN RAILWAY COMPANY (1)

20 L.T. 72 (1869)
Vice Chancellor - Chancery

Payment of dividend out of capital—Moneys payable by contractor by way of penalty.

Sect. 22 of the Metropolitan Railway Act 1868 provided that all moneys paid to the company or directors by way of penalty for the non-completion of certain extensions, should be carried to the revenue account of the extensions, and deemed to be income of the company applicable to interest and dividend on extension capital:

By an agreement between the company and Messrs. K. their contractors, Messrs. K. were to pay certain penalties in the event of their not completing certain extensions by a given time; but if, in the opinion of the engineer, the delay should be attributable to the company, then there should be a rebate equivalent to the interest payable by the contractors for the period of delay so occasioned by the company:

Messrs. K. having paid 43,000l. by way of penalty, the directors declared a dividend out of the moneys so made, but at the same time repaid to Messrs. K. the exact sum by way of rebate, having admitted that the delay was attributable to the company:

Held, that the 43,000l. was not a payment by way of penalty within the meaning of sect. 22, and an injunction granted restraining the payment of any dividend out of it.

This was a motion on behalf of the plaintiff (suing on behalf of himself and all the other shareholders except the defendants) for an interlocutory injunction to restrain the defendants from declaring or paying any dividend, directly or indirectly, out of the sum of 43,000l., or any other moneys which they had received or should receive from Messrs Kelk and Co., under the terms of their contract in the bill set out in the bill of complaint.

The plaintiff was the holder of 200 shares in the company, purchased on the 23rd Dec. 1868.

In 1865 the directors of the Metropolitan Railway entered into a contract with Messrs. Kelk and Co., the contractors, by which Kelk and Co. undertook to construct and complete the Eastern or Tower-hill Extension by the 31st Dec. 1867 for 383,000l., and 80,000l. additional for stations.

By this agreement it was provided that, " In order to secure the punctual completion of the said railways and works, &c., and in lieu of all the penalties for the non-completion thereof within the prescribed period, the contractors, shall, until the said railway shall be completed and open for traffic, pay to the directors such sums of money as shall be equivalent to interest upon so much of the sum of 700,000l., being the share capital created in respect of the said railway, as shall from time to time be called and paid up, at the respective times and rates following—that is to say, for and on each of the four half-years ending respectively the 30th June and the 31st Dec. 1865, and the 30th June and the 31st Dec. 1866, at the rate of 5l. per cent per annum, and for and on every

subsequent half-year thereafter at the rate of 6l. per cent. per annum; and in case the said railways shall be completed and open for traffic during any such subsequent half-year, the contractors shall, on the completion and opening for traffic thereof, pay to the directors such sums of money as shall be equivalent to interest at the rate of 6l. per cent. per annum upon the share capital so called and paid up as aforesaid for such a number of days as shall elapse between the last preceding half-year and such completion and opening for traffic. If, in the opinion of the engineer, there shall be any such delay in delivery of possession of the land by the company as shall render it impracticable to complete and open the railway by the 31st Dec. 1867, such allowance in respect of interest shall be made to the contractors as shall be equivalent to the interest payable by them for the period of the delay so occasioned."

The plaintiff then amended his bill, stating that Messrs. Kelk, professing to act under the provisions of their contract, had paid to the directors the sum of 43,000l. as and for the dividend for the half-year ending Dec, 31, 1868, on the extension stock, and that the directors, professing to act under these provisions, repaid to Messrs. Kelk the like sum out of the capital moneys of the company. This sum of 43,000l. was about to be distributed by the directors as the dividend on the extension stock for the last half-year, and the present motion was directed against the distribution.

The bill charged that there never was any real intention on the part of the directors that the Eastern extension should be completed by the 31st Dec. 1867, and that the provisions of the agreement were a mere scheme for transmuting capital into dividend through the medium of Kelk and Co. contrary to the express provisions of the Metropolitan Railway Act 1851, s. 196, and the Companies Clauses Act 1845 therewith incorporated; and further, that in pursuance of this scheme, the directors had from the first creation of the Eastern Extension shares, paid all the dividends thereon, directly or indirectly, out of the capital of the company.

In Jan. 1868 Bloxam filed his bill, and obtained from Sir William Page Wood, then Vice-Chancellor, an injunction restraining the company from declaring or paying any dividend except so far as the profits or income of the company might be applicable to such dividend : (17 L. T. Rep. N. S. 637). This decision was affirmed by Chelmsford, L. C. : (18 L. T. Rep. N. S. 41.)

In the Session of 1868 the directors obtained the passing of the Metropolitan Railway Act. Sect. 22 of the Act was as follows :

And whereas the company were authorised to raise the money for the construction of the Notting-hill and Brompton Extension and the Tower-hill Extension (hereinafter called " the Extensions ") as a separate capital, and to execute and keep such extensions as separate undertakings, and to provide that the liabilities thereof shall not be chargeable on the original undertaking until the same extensions should be open for public traffic ; and whereas in settling the conditions under which the capital for the extensions should be created, it was intended that the interests of the then existing shareholders should be protected by arrangements which would prevent the new capital from becoming chargeable on revenue until the extensions should be opened for traffic, and moneys have been applied out of capital with that object; and whereas the company have not, as they ought to have done, kept the several capitals separate and distinct until the time fixed by the said conditions—viz., the 1st Jan. 1870—for their ultimate amalgamation with the original undertaking, but have regarded and kept them, both as respects the moneys authorised to be raised by shares and on mortgage, as one general or consolidated capital; and whereas it is expedient to reduce the expenditure on capital account by annual appropriation out of the profits of the undertaking in the manner in this Act mentioned; and whereas, notwithstanding that all matters done have from time to time been submitted to and sanctioned by general meetings of the company, litigation has arisen with reference to the arrangements and payments made by the company in respect of the extensions, and inasmuch as the progress and completion of the undertaking may be delayed, and the company greatly embarrassed, and the interest of the shareholders endangered if such litigation continue or be revived, it is expedient that such provision be made with reference to the charge and application of the extension capital as hereinafter expressed. Be it therefore enacted that until the time of amalgamation, the following provisions shall have effect for the regulation of the past and future capital account of the company in respect of the extensions (that is to say):—For the purposes of the raising and expenditure of extension capital, the extensions shall be deemed to be and to have been one undertaking. Until the time of amalgamation the extensions shall be deemed an undertaking separate and distinct from the original undertaking of the company as now open for public traffic, and until the time of amalgamation all payments, including interest on borrowed money made in respect of the extensions, shall be charged upon the separate undertaking and paid out of money raised for the purposes thereof; and this provision shall have a retrospective operation. All moneys paid to the company or directors by the contractors by way of penalty or otherwise for the non-completions of the extensions, or arising under their contracts or engagements, and all net receipts from traffic and other sources of income arising in respect of the extensions, and not otherwise specifically appropriated, shall be carried to the revenue account of the extensions, and shall be deemed to be income and profits of the company applicable to interest and dividends on extension capital. . . .

The VICE-CHANCELLOR, ... What, then, is the question before me? I take it to be admitted for the purposes of this motion, and to that extent only, that the money paid by Messrs. Kelk has been furnished out of moneys paid to them beforehand out of the funds of the company. By their contract Messrs. Kelk are, on the one hand, liable to the company for any default in the completion of the works, while on the other hand they are entitled to a rebate where the default is to be attributed to the neglect of the company itself. It now appears that they have nominally made a payment in respect of the delay, and have received before the payment, or after the payment, the exact sum back again, the company having admitted that the delay, in truth, was on their part, and not on that of the contractors. I now come to the Act of 1868, which says (sect. 22) that, "All moneys paid to the company or directors by the contractors, by way of penalty or otherwise for the non-completion of the extensions, or arising under their contracts or engagements, shall be carried to the revenue account of the extensions, and shall be deemed to be income and profits of the company applicable to interest and dividends on extension capital." In my opinion this section is not intended to include that which is a mere sham payment, or a device for the purpose of making that appear to have been paid which has not really been paid. I do not hesitate to say, even at this interlocutory stage, that this money has been paid by Messrs. Kelk out of money found for them for the purpose, or to be repaid to them out of money afterwards to be paid by the company, and is not money "paid to the company or directors by the contractors by way of penalty, or otherwise, for the non-completion of the extensions, or arising under their contracts or engagements;" in truth, no money has been so paid, and no money has so arisen, so far as the 43,000l. is concerned. I have no hesitation, therefore, in saying that the injunction must go to restrain the payment of any dividend out of the 43,000l. or any other moneys the directors shall have received, or shall receive, from Messrs. Kelk under the provisions of their contract, and which have been repaid, or are to be repaid, to Messrs. Kelk by the company.

SALISBURY v. METROPOLITAN RAILWAY COMPANY (2)

22 L.T. 839 (1870)
Vice Chancellor - Chancery

Wednesday, June 29.

SALISBURY *v.* METROPOLITAN RAILWAY COMPANY.

Railway company—Surplus lands—Real and conjectural value of—Payment of dividend out of conjectural value—Liability of directors.

Where the directors of a company paid a dividend out of the capital moneys of the company, they were held to be personally liable for the amount so paid.

A company were possessed of surplus lands of the alleged value of 1,200,000l., which sum, if invested at 5 per cent., would procure an annual income of 60,000l. The net rental of such lands was about 28,000l. The directors paid a dividend, not according to the actual income received from the surplus lands, but according to the conjectural one of 60,000l. On bill filed by a deferred shareholder who had not participated in such dividend:

Held, that the payment of such dividend was ultra vires, and that the directors were personally liable to make good the sums so paid, without prejudice to any right they might have to recover the same from the shareholders.

This suit was instituted in Nov. 1869, by the plaintiff against the Metropolitan Railway Company and John Henchman, the secretary of the company, to restrain the directors from paying any dividend on the ordinary extension stocks or shares of the company (other than the new ordinary 5l. shares, 1868), and from distributing by way of dividend any of the capital moneys of the company until a certain sum mentioned in the bill should be repaid to the company or otherwise carried over to the capital account of the company.

The plaintiff was the registered holder of 100 new ordinary 5l. shares 1868, on which he was not entitled to receive any dividend until the expiration of the half year ending December 1869, from which time the holders of new ordinary 5l. shares 1868 were to be entitled to dividends *pari passu* with the holders of ordinary stock in the company.

In making the railway, the company had been obliged to purchase surplus lands which the directors alleged to be of the value of 1,200,000l. which if realised, and the proceeds invested at the rate of 5 per cent. per annum, would produce an income of 60,000l., whereas the net rental of the surplus lands was only 28,260l. 2s. 4d. The directors had distributed by way of dividend, not the actual income received from the surplus lands, but the conjectural one of 60,000l. They had, in fact, in the accounts for the half year ending the 30th June 1869 credited the revenue of the company in respect of the surplus lands with the sum of 39,000l. instead of the real income of 14,128l. 1s. 2d., by which means they had carried to the credit of the revenue of the company a sum of 15,871l. 18s. 10d. in excess of the actual revenue of the company. . . .

Sir *Roundell Palmer,* Q.C., *H. F. Bristowe,* Q.C., and *H. Fellows,* were for the defendants, and contended that the accounts having been audited and certified, and adopted by the proprietors, could not now be altered; that the money having been certified by the auditors to be available for the purposes of dividends, the directors were not liable to repay them; that the payment of dividends consequent upon the certificate of the auditors was final and binding, and that although an injunction might be granted as to future dividends, it was not applicable to a dividend already declared. . . .

The VICE-CHANCELLOR said: It appears to me in this case that the plaintiff is entitled to the relief which he asks. The case stands thus. The company having two bodies of shareholders—the one a body of shareholders actually in receipt of dividends, the other a body whose receipt of dividends was deferred for a certain number of years—were restrained by their Act of Parliament from applying capital, except to a certain limited extent, which does not affect this case at all, in payment of dividends. The company did attempt to apply capital in one or two modes by devices which did not succeed, and it appears to me they have now tried a third plain and palpable device for violating the Act of Parliament, that is to say, for paying dividends out of capital. The way in which they put it is this. We have a great quantity of surplus land. If we were to sell it now we could probably sell it for 1,200,000l. That is its value. But if we keep it we are satisfied from what we know we shall some years hence get a good deal more than 1,200,000l., and it is to our interest to keep it for the benefit of the capital. That being so, we are depriving the income of the benefit which the income would receive, if we sold it, converted it into money, and invested it at 5 per cent. We will consider the fictitious income of the surplus property at 60,000l. It is agreed that the income is only 30,000l. The difference between the actual income and the potential income is a thing that the income is losing for the purpose of future benefit of the capital. That is certainly a very novel way of distinguishing between income and capital. Sir Roundell Palmer puts it in another and more feasible way, which is not the way it is put by the defendants in their answer. He treated it as an asset of a partnership. I have no doubt, in valuing partnership assets an increase or decrease in the value of an article is treated, and properly treated, as part of the profit or loss at the end of the year. It is the duty of a partnership to ascertain in any way it can the value of the assets ; and any diminution in the selling value is a loss. and any increase in the selling value is a profit, and is dealt with accordingly. In this case, if that were so, there is a tremendous loss of balance to be made good before a single farthing could be applicable for the payment of dividend, because this property cost so many millions. It is admitted that the land cost, I think, two and a-half millions in round numbers; then if that contingent increase in value—or the actual increase if it is year by year, from 1,200,000*l.* if they choose to consider it so, is to be taken into consideration as profit, the difference between two-and-a-half millions and 1,200,000*l.*, which is a mere matter of estimate, ought to be taken into account, and no dividend ought to be paid till the same has been made good. In truth, it is a mere speculation, it is a mere fictitious mode of treating the property by talking about the possible future value of things. This court never authorises persons who are in a fiduciary position to indulge in a sanguine speculation as to the future, or at all events to divide it as available dividend, because of the sanguine speculations of some people who are trustees. I am of opinion, therefore, it is quite clear that what has been done is a direct, plain, and wilful violation of the Act of Parliament. I cannot conceive it possible that these gentlemen could ever have taken any legal advice whatever; they may have taken the auditors' advice which may be treated as a suggestion. . . .

99

BARDWELL v. SHEFFIELD WATERWORKS COMPANY

L.R. 14 Eq.517 (1872)
Vice Chancellor - Chancery

Special Case—Income and Capital—Interest on unproductive Capital—Statutory Jurisdiction—Sir G. Turner's Act (13 & 14 Vict. c. 35, s. 1)—*Practice—Representative Parties to Special Case.*

THIS was a special case under *Sir G. Turner's Act* (13 & 14 Vict. c. 35), between *Frederick Bardwell*, on behalf of himself and all other the ordinary shareholders in the *Company of Proprietors of the Sheffield Waterworks*, except such as were Defendants thereto, as Plaintiffs, and the *Company of Proprietors of the Sheffield Waterworks*, and certain persons named, and *John Russell*, for and on behalf of himself and all other the holders of B, C, and D preference shares in the said company, as Defendants.

The special case stated that by the *Sheffield Waterworks Act,* 1853, the company had power to raise, for the construction of reservoirs and other works, £450,000, and to borrow or raise by preference shares £110,000; and that the whole £450,000 had been raised by ordinary shares, and £11,200 of the £110,000 by preference shares; and that two reservoirs had been completed before 1864, in which year one of them, the *Dale Dike Reservoir*, gave way and caused an inundation which subjected the company to heavy losses and liabilities; to provide for which the *Sheffield Waterworks Act*, 1864, was passed.

Under that Act the company was empowered to raise £400,000 in addition to all other money which they had power to raise, which was to be applied, first, in payment of liabilities arising out of the inundation; secondly, in the purchase-money for land taken under the Act; and thirdly, for other purposes of the Act, and, subject thereto, for the general purposes of the company. ...

It was then stated that a dividend had always, except in 1864 and 1865 (when, in consequence of the inundation, there was none), been declared for the half-year ending the 30th of June, and paid on the 1st of November following, and that three reservoirs were in course of construction during the whole of the year ending the 31st of December, 1871, and were not used, and could not be used, for the supply of water within the district of the company, and produced no income to the company.

The special case then, after stating that money produced by the ordinary share capital had been employed in the construction of the reservoirs, continued as follows:—

"The said three reservoirs are, and all other the works by the company's Acts authorized to be made will be, such as would, in the ordinary course of business, be constructed out of capital, and would be entrusted to contractors who would contract to construct the same in consideration of stated sums to be paid by the company at deferred periods, and on the ascertainment of which the contractor, in the ordinary course of business, might and would charge the company with the full amount of the interest on the outlay from time to time incurred by him in the execution of the works, so that on the instalments due to him under the contract being paid to him by the company, as they in their ordinary course would be paid out of the company's capital, the interest on capital during construction would in effect be defrayed out of capital. . . .

The facts were then stated, shewing that the amount of capital applied to works as yet unproductive amounted in the year 1871 to £190,941 3s. 5d., and it was explained that it was for the interest of the parties represented by the Plaintiff that the interest on the unproductive capital should be provided out of capital, and that the parties represented by the Defendant *John Russell* were interested in maintaining the opposite contention.

The questions submitted for the Court were: Whether by law the company and the directors, in declaring and paying dividends on ordinary shares, were at liberty and ought to charge against and defray out of capital all or any and what part of the interest and dividends accrued since the 31st of December, 1871, and thereafter to accrue due on or in respect of the capital from time to time raised by borrowing or the creation of preference shares or stock, and expended in the construction of the reservoirs and works, or the acquisition of land, till the works should come into operation? There was another question, as to whether the same principle could be made to apply to the year 1871, and a further one as to the costs of the special case. . . .

Sir R. Malins, V.C. :—

I do not think there can be any reasonable doubt as to this matter. The difficulty has arisen out of the disastrous bursting of the reservoir in 1864, which gave occasion for a great expenditure of capital in the restoration of the old works and the construction of new ones. It does not appear whether a contractor would have undertaken the performance of the works on the ordinary system; but they have occupied three years, and large sums of money have been expended upon them, which have been provided by the exercise of borrowing powers and the issue of preference shares. The question is whether the sum paid for interest on the sums borrowed and the dividends on the preference shares during the time in which the capital remained unproductive are to be attributed to income or capital. I think it is clear that if the works had been performed by a contractor in the usual way, he would either have arranged his prices so as to include in the profits the interest on the capital and plant employed by him, or would have added interest on capital to the amount of his estimates. Therefore in either case the interest on the capital employed would be found in the price paid for the work.

In the present case the company, having performed the work, have been compelled to pay interest on the unproductive capital, and I think the interest so paid formed part of the capital employed in the work. I think that *Bloxam* v. *Metropolitan Railway Company* has no application; but I find that in that case Lord *Chelmsford* expressed a doubt as to the soundness of the principle which had been laid down by the Vice-Chancellor, and I concur in the doubt he expressed. I understand also that the railway company obtained an Act of Parliament to sanction the practice which led to that suit.

The first two questions will therefore be answered in the affirmative, and the costs of all parties will be borne by the capital account.

LORD ROKEBY v. ELLIOT

9 L.R. Ch. 685 (1878)
Chancery

Mining — Winning — Working—Expenses—Profits—Allowances—Bad Debts.

By a deed of grant and license the licensee was empowered to work and win the coal mines under certain lands, and, out of the profits to arise by the sale of the coals, to reimburse himself all expenses of the winning thereof; and after full payment of such expenses of winning the coal mines the licensee was to pay the licensor a sum of money in respect of the coals raised as therein mentioned.

The licensee reached the coal mines by a driftway from an adjoining colliery, and worked the coal :—

Held, that the coal was won, according to the meaning of the deed, on the day when it could be worked through the driftway, and that no expenses subsequently incurred could be included in the expenses of winning:

Held, that the expense of the driftway was to be paid out of the profits, though it had been used for the purposes of the adjoining colliery:

Held, that in estimating the profits out of which the expenses of winning were to be reimbursed, all the expenses of working and selling the coal, including bad debts, must be allowed . . . .

The suit now came to a hearing, and much evidence was adduced as to the meaning of the word " winning," and as to the expenses incurred. The principal questions argued were as to the time when the coal was won, and the allowances to be made to the Defendant for the cost of winning; and as to the manner in which the profits were to be ascertained, so as to determine when the Defendant was reimbursed the costs of winning. . . .

FRY, J., ...

The second question which arises is this. What is the meaning of " the profits to arise by sale of the coals which shall be wrought or gotten out of" these coal mines, and out of which the costs of winning are to be satisfied?

Now, here again two views have been presented. The Plaintiff says the profits to arise by the sale are the gross returns from the coal. The Defendant says they are not the gross returns, but the gross returns after deducting all working expenses, in which he says should be included not merely the wages of the workmen and the expenditure on stores, but just allowances in respect of bad debts, the interest on the capital expended by the persons doing the work, and an allowance for wear and tear and depreciation. It appears that the word " profits" may be used in both ways, and I have to consider what is the natural and probable meaning of it in this case. Now, I think there is something absurd in paying a man his winning expenses out of profits, but not allowing him to deduct his working expenses from his gross profits. You would be apparently indemnifying him in respect of one expense when you at the same time would be depriving him of that advantage by charging him with another expense. It is true, as has been urged by Mr. *Cookson*, that perhaps the referees might take that into account in estimating the amount of *quasi* royalty to be put on the coal raised, but I do not think that that is a satisfactory answer. I think the profits out of which the expenditure of the licensee is to be made good are what I may call a clear fund—a fund which is reasonably applicable to the winning expenses after satisfaction of everything in the nature of working expenses. Therefore I propose to declare in substance that the profits, according to the true construction of the deed, are the gross returns, less the working expenses, and that in such working expenses are to be included just allowances in respect of interest on capital expended, in respect of bad debts, and in respect of wear and tear of machinery. Perhaps I might say with regard to bad debts that I think it is reasonable to allow them; for, in the first place, I think the sale must be considered to have been a sale according to the ordinary mode of selling coal, which, no doubt, is to some extent on credit. In the next place, I think that if the sale had not been for credit the price would have been less, and therefore, to use a common expression, the thing is as broad as it is long. If the Defendant had had no bad debts he would have had to sell for less money, and if he sold so as to incur bad debts, he got nominally more money, although perhaps in the result he did not get above the same amount. . . .

His Lordship then directed the accounts to be taken accordingly, reserving further consideration; when the questions as to fixing the amount to be paid to the Plaintiff would if necessary be argued and decided.

DAVISON v. GILLIES

16 L.R. Ch. 344, @ 347n. (1879)
Master of the Rolls - Chancery

THIS was a motion by the Plaintiff *William Davison*, suing on behalf of himself and all other shareholders of the *London Tramways Company, Limited*, and the company, for an injunction to restrain the Defendants, the directors of the company, from applying any part of the assets of the company which represented capital, or ought to be retained to represent capital, in the payment of dividends on the shares in the company, and from submitting to the shareholders any resolution to confirm or permit the payment of dividends out of capital, or summoning any meeting for the purpose of authorizing payment of dividends, without first fully and properly disclosing to all the members of the company the true state of the capital and other accounts of the company, and without disclosing the fact that no dividends could be paid except out of assets which ought to be retained to represent capital. . . .

JESSEL, M.R. :—

The articles of association, which are binding on the directors and on the company, are very plain.

The 107th Article is this : " No dividend shall be declared except out of the profits of the company." A general meeting cannot get over that. The dividend can never be declared but out of profits ; and the allegation on the part of the Plaintiffs is that this dividend is not declared out of profits at all—that there are no profits available. The right to declare a dividend depends on the facts. The word "profits," by itself, is a word which is certainly susceptible of more than one meaning, and one must ascertain what it means in these articles. The 103rd Article says, " The directors shall, with the sanction of the company in general meeting, declare annual dividends, to be payable to the members out of the profits of the company, not exceeding the rate of 6 per centum per annum for each year, on the paid-up capital for the time being of the company, and of one-half the profits of the company above that amount, and they shall declare the other half of such surplus profits to be payable to the scripholders." Scripholders are another class who are not shareholders, who have subscribed moneys and are to be entitled to half the surplus profits. It is quite clear that, whatever these profits are, they are profits of the same kind : half the surplus is to go to the shareholders and the other half to the scripholders.

Then the next article is this : " The directors shall, before recommending any dividend, set aside out of the profits of the company, but subject to the sanction of the company in general meeting, such sum as they think proper as a reserve fund for maintenance, repairs, depreciation, and renewals." It is plain that these "profits" mean something after payment of the expenses ; because you do not get a reserve fund at all until you have paid your current expenses. It is obvious that the word "profits" means net profits.

Then the next article is this : " The directors shall also, before recommending any dividend, set aside out of the profits of the company, a sum equivalent to one per centum per annum on the amount of the paid-up capital for

the time being as a contingencies fund."
There again " profits " obviously mean
net profits. The result, therefore, of
the articles, as I read them, is that a
dividend shall only be declared out of
net profits.

Then I have to consider the question,
What are net profits? A tramway
company lay down a new tramway.
Of course the ordinary wear and tear
of the rails and sleepers, and so on,
causes a sum of money to be required
from year to year in repairs. It may
or may not be desirable to do the repairs all at once; but if at the end of
the first year the line of tramway is
still in so good a state of repair that it
requires nothing to be laid out on it for
repairs in that year, still, before you
can ascertain the net profits, a sum of
money ought to be set aside as representing the amount in which the wear
and tear of the line has, I may say, so
far depreciated it in value as that that
sum will be required for the next year
or next two years.

Take the case of a warehouse. Supposing a warehouse-keeper, having a
new warehouse, should find at the end
of the year that he had no occasion
to expend money in repairs, but
thought that, by reason of the usual
wear and tear of the warehouse, it
was a thousand pounds worse than it
was at the beginning of the year, he
would set aside £1000 for a repair or
renewal or depreciation fund before he
estimated any profits; because, although that sum is not required to be
paid in that year, still it is the sum of
money which is lost, so to say, out of
capital, and which must be replaced.
I should think no commercial man
would doubt that this is the right
course—that he must not calculate net
profits until he has provided for all the
ordinary repairs and wear and tear
occasioned by his business. In many
businesses there is a regular sum or
proportion of some kind set aside for
this purpose. Shipowners, I believe,

generally reckon so much a year for
depreciation of a ship as it gets older.
Experience tells them how much they
ought to set aside; and whether the
ship is repaired in one year or another
makes no difference in estimating the
profits, because they know a certain
sum must be set aside each year to
meet the extra repairs of the ship as it
becomes older. There are very many
other businesses in which the same
thing is done.

That being so, it appears to me that
you can have no net profits unless this
sum has been set aside. When you
come to the next year, or the third or
fourth year, what happens is this: as
the line gets older the amount required
for repairs increases. If you had done
what you ought to have done, that is,
set aside every year the sum necessary
to make good the wear and tear in that
year, then in the following years you
would have a fund sufficient to meet
the extra cost. Now, when I come to
look at these articles, I think that is
what is intended, and that that is the
meaning of the reserve fund. What
the company intended to do was this:
inasmuch as they knew that maintenance, repairs, depreciation and renewals would be wanted, and inasmuch
as they knew that according to the
ordinary commercial rules they ought
not to calculate the net profits until
they had provided for this which was
sure to happen, they said, " We will
set aside a sum of money which we will
call a reserve fund for this purpose."
Although not expended during the
year, it is a reserve fund set aside for
expenditure in the following years,
taken out of profits before a dividend
is made. It appears to me, therefore,
that these articles do recognise what
seem to me sound commercial principles. That being so, from year to
year, as the line got older it would get
worse, and would, no doubt, require a
larger expenditure every year for
repairs and renewals, as a general rule

—I say as a general rule, because sometimes the repairs may be so extensive as to make the renewal of a large portion of the line required in one year, and then the next year there might be a falling off in the amount required: but, as a general rule, as the line got older it would require more money.

Now, the line having been established seven years, I find an eminent engineer telling me in his affidavit in support of the motion that to put the line in a good state of repair will require £30,000: in other words, if you take the deterioration of the line from want of repair from its commencement, it is worth £80,000 less than it was at starting: that is the summary of that gentleman's evidence. He then thinks that those repairs, or the greater part of them, should be done at once. That is a matter of opinion on which engineers may fairly differ, and do differ. The Defendants' engineer, who, I am told, is also an eminent engineer, says he thinks they should not be done at once, but should be done gradually. But still, as I said before, they are to be done. That sum of money is required, or something like it. I cannot ascertain from the affidavit of the Defendants' engineer what sum he considers sufficient: I have no doubt he would fix a much smaller sum. However, for the purpose of my judgment I am willing to take a very large discount off the £80,000, because it is a very much larger sum indeed than is required to wipe away the whole of the dividend the company have declared. Therefore one need not consider whether it is £80,000 or £10,000: either sum would do that; but a very large sum it is, and the Defendants' engineer does not tell me how much.

I do not wish to prejudice any future application the company make under the leave I am going to reserve to them, but I will say that unless they give me something a great deal more definite as to the amount actually required for putting the line into repair than I have at present, I should certainly not be of opinion that the amount they propose to divide among the shareholders is fairly divisible.

[His Lordship then commented on the accounts for the half-year ending the 31st of December, 1878, observing that the existing "reserve fund" was altogether inadequate for the purposes of ordinary maintenance, &c., and that the "contingency fund" was not applicable to such purposes. His Lordship then continued:—] That being so, on the present evidence I am satisfied that there are no profits at present available for division. It may happen that there would have been profits if the company had properly applied the surplus of former years. I must say, looking at the accounts of the company, it appears to be a flourishing company, and I hope nothing I say will damage its future success: but still, I am bound by the articles to say that no dividend is to be paid except out of profits; that there are no profits available, and therefore I grant the injunction asked. At the same time I wish to give the Defendants every possible opportunity of shewing that there are profits available, and I also feel that my intervention is likely to be injurious to the company. If the Defendants can shew me at any time that there are profits available for the purpose of this dividend, I will give them an opportunity of doing so, and therefore I give them leave to move to dissolve the injunction I now grant.

The injunction granted restrained the Defendants from authorizing or making any payment out of the assets of the company in respect of the dividend declared in February, 1879, on the ordinary shares.

By consent the motion was afterwards treated as the trial of the action, and thereupon the injunction was made perpetual.

16 L.R. Ch. 344 (1881)
Master of the Rolls - Chancery

THE Defendants, the *London Tramways Company, Limited*, were incorporated in 1870, under the *Companies Acts*, 1862 and 1867, with a capital of £250,000, in 25,000 shares of £10 each. The whole of the capital had been issued and was fully paid up.

In 1874, in pursuance of a power contained in their articles of association, the company passed a special resolution increasing their capital "by the issue of 8000 shares of £10 each, bearing a preferential dividend of 6 per cent. per annum over the present shares of the company dependent upon the profits of the particular year only."

In accordance with that resolution 8000 preference shares of £10 each were duly issued and became fully paid up. The Plaintiff was the registered holder of 100 of such shares. . . .

The Plaintiff claimed (amongst other things) a declaration that he and all the other preference shareholders were entitled to a dividend on their shares at the rate of 3 per cent. per annum for the year ending the 31st of December, 1878, and a dividend on their shares at the rate of 6 per cent. per annum for the year ending the 31st of December, 1879; payment to the Plaintiff of the sums of £30 and £60, being the amounts due to him in respect of such dividend for the years ending the 31st of December, 1878, and the 31st of December, 1879, respectively; an account of the profits made by the company during the same years respectively, and payment to the Plaintiff of such dividend on his preference shares as upon taking such account the Court should consider him entitled to.

In their statement of defence the company alleged that they had only recently ascertained that from the year 1871 down to the end of the year 1878 their accounts, which were rendered half yearly, had been kept in an improper and misleading manner, no proper or sufficient sums ever having been expended and proper allowance made for the maintenance, repairs, depreciation, and renewals of the tramways, rolling-stock, and other property of the company, and that the amounts from time to time actually charged against revenue in respect of such maintenance, repairs, depreciation, and renewals were grossly inadequate, and far below what ought properly to have been so charged.

The defence then proceeded to state that from the year 1871 to the year 1877 inclusive, the company had, in ignorance of their true financial position, paid large sums to the shareholders by way of dividend, without charging, as they should have done, in each year a proper proportional amount against revenue for maintenance, repairs, depreciation, and renewals; and it appeared that if this proportional yearly charge had been made the balance of revenue or "net profit" in each year available for a dividend would have been comparatively small. . . .

The company then stated in their defence in the present action, that the total sum which ought to have been charged against revenue for maintenance, &c., during the eight years from 1871 to 1878 instead of being paid away in dividends, amounted to £114,460 18s. 8d., and that that sum, having been in fact paid out of capital, represented the amount by which the capital of the company had become diminished in value.

Under these circumstances the company insisted that the preference shareholders were not entitled to be paid any dividend until the company had, by means of the sums earned by them since the 30th of June, 1878, and to be earned, increased the small existing reserve fund applicable for maintenance, &c., to the sum of £114,460 18s. 8d., or, in any case, until the preference shareholders had accounted for and repaid to the company the sums paid to them in excess of what they ought to have received for dividends had the accounts been properly kept. . . .

A report had been prepared by Messrs. *Waddell & Co.*, accountants, at the request of the directors of the company, shewing the amount of profits available for the preference dividend in the year 1878. This report was produced at the trial, and shewed that the balance of net revenue available for the preference dividend, after providing for current expenses, maintenance, repairs, &c., amounted to the sum of £14,932.

In reply to a question put by his Lordship in the course of the argument, Mr. *Waddell* stated that this £14,932 represented, in fact, the actual surplus receipts for the year 1878, after paying all expenses and reinstating the capital as on the 1st of January in that year. . . .

Chitty, Q.C., and *Romer,* for the Defendants :—

We submit that the company were not in a position to make, and could not make, any " profits " until their undertaking had been put into a money-earning condition. The articles of association, which your Lordship referred to in your judgment in *Davison* v. *Gillies,* expressly state that no dividend shall be declared except out of profits. We contend that when expenditure is required for recouping capital, the preference shareholders should, as regards a dividend, stand in the same position as the ordinary shareholders; for both classes of shareholders can only be paid out of income, that is to say, income remaining after payment of what is required for maintenance and repairs.

JESSEL, M.R. :— ....

However, the present question is, to my mind, a very simple one. There is a bargain made with the company that certain persons will advance their money as preference shareholders; that is, that they shall be entitled to a preferential dividend of 6 per cent. over the ordinary shares of the company, " dependent upon the profits of the particular year only." That means this, that the preference shareholders only take a dividend if there are profits for that year sufficient to pay their dividend. If there are no profits for that year sufficient to pay their dividend they do not get it : they lose it for ever ; and if there are no profits in one year, and 12 per cent. profit the next year, they only get 6 per cent., and the other 6 per cent. goes to the ordinary shareholders. So that they are, so to say, co-adventurers for each particular year, and can only look to the profits of that year.

What happened was this. The company improperly allowed their tramways to get out of repair, and paid away their receipts to the ordinary shareholders in the shape of dividends. The result was that on the 1st of January, 1878, the tramways were very much out of repair, and wanted a large sum to put them in a proper state of efficiency. Notwithstanding that, the company did work, and they earned a good deal of money, the profits for the year 1878 being upwards of £14,000; and the dividend required being only 6 per cent. on £80,000, it is quite clear they earned more than sufficient to pay the preference shareholders, supposing these were fairly-earned profits. To see that they were fairly-earned profits, I must look at the report, which I have before me, of an eminent accountant, Mr. *Waddell*, who says they were. He says, in effect, that, considering the state of the line on the 1st of January and the state of the line on the 31st of December in that year, after setting aside sufficient to make good the wear and tear for that particular year, and paying all expenses, there was a net balance of £14,932. That is admitted by the 20th paragraph of the statement of defence, which says, " If a proper proportionate amount had been charged against the revenue of the year 1878 for such maintenance, &c., as aforesaid, the accounts would have shewn, as the fact is, that there was a balance of revenue, and in that sense a net profit in that year of only £14,932 5s. 4d." Therefore if " profits for the year " have any meaning at all, these were the profits for the year. " Profits for the year " of course mean the surplus in receipts, after paying expenses and restoring the capital to the position it was in on the 1st of January in that year. I have had the advantage of having Mr. *Waddell* present in Court, and ascertaining from him that his report in the sense I have stated is expressed according to his meaning, and that there is no mistake in the admission in the defence; that is to say, there was an actual net profit for that year of upwards of £14,000. Then what is there to argue? The argument for the company amounts to this, that inasmuch as they have improperly paid to their ordinary shareholders very large sums of money which did not belong to them, they, the company, are entitled to make good that deficiency by taking away the fund available for the preference shareholders to an amount required to put the tramway in proper order. When the argument is stated in that way, it is clear that it cannot be sustained. The company either have a right to recover back from the ordinary shareholders any sums over-paid or not. If they have a right, they must recover them ; if they have no right to recover them, *à fortiori* they have no right to recover them from the preference shareholders, and, of course, still less right to take away the dividends from the preference shareholders.

It appears to me that the defence is founded on a misconception, and, I am afraid, a misconception of what I am supposed to have decided on a former occasion ; but I have no hesitation in making the declaration which I am asked to make, and deciding in favour of the Plaintiff in this action.

CITY OF GLASCOW BANK v. MACKINNON

9 Court Session Cases, 4th Series, 535 (1882)
Court of Sessions, Scot.

THE CITY OF GLASGOW BANK was established in 1839 as a public joint stock banking company, the capital amounting, after 1843, to £1,000,000 sterling, divided into 100,000 shares of £10 each. In 1860 the capital was converted into stock, each share being equivalent to £9 of the consolidated stock. The company carried on business from 1839 (except during a temporary suspension from 11th November 1857 to 31st December 1857), till 22d October 1878 when it stopped payment and liquidators were appointed. . . .

LORD PRESIDENT.—The serious and important questions which we are now to determine have arisen in the course of the liquidation of the City of Glasgow Bank.

On the 13th November 1880 the liquidators presented to the Court a note, under the authority of the 165th section of the Companies Act, 1862, in which they claim from Mr William Mackinnon, a director of the bank from 1858 till 1870, the sum of £311,666, 16s. 9d., paid away to the shareholders as dividends between 1858 and 1870, on the recommendation of the directors, including the respondent Mackinnon, on the ground that this sum did not represent profits earned, but was, in effect, paid out of the capital of the bank.

If this charge be proved, it certainly amounts to a breach of the bank's contract by those who were appointed to administer its affairs, and, independently of special contract, it would be at common law a gross breach of trust.

---

* The following sections of the bank's contract of copartnery were founded upon and referred to during the discussion :—(For other sections see *ante*, vol. vi. p. 415).

XII. "At every annual general meeting the ordinary directors shall exhibit a statement or abstract of the preceding yearly balance-sheet, and such farther statement or report of the affairs of the company as the ordinary directors may deem expedient or proper for the interests of the company to be made public, as is provided for in article XLIV. hereof, and the annual dividend of profits shall be then declared, and every such abstract shall be binding and conclusive on all the partners, but without prejudice to the provision hereinafter contained as to the appointment of auditors." . . . .

XLIV. "There shall be regular books kept for the business of the company, and the various departments thereof, and all the transactions, affairs, and obligations of the company shall be duly inserted in said books, which books shall be balanced on the first Wednesday of June in each year, at which period statements or abstracts of the company's affairs shall be made out and regularly examined, docqueted, and subscribed by the said ordinary directors previous to the foresaid annual general meeting, to be held in Glasgow on the first Wednesday of July thereafter, and at the said meeting the said statements or abstracts shall be reported for the satisfaction of all concerned ; and as it is of great importance in conducting the affairs of a bank that the business and transactions of the

It is not a charge of negligence or failure in duty ; the fact alleged is an overt act of misapplication of a large portion of the bank's capital, done knowingly

bank should be kept private, on which account all directors and other persons connected with other banking establishments are disqualified from being directors of this company, and as the same reason applies to the examination of the books or documents of this company by other partners than the ordinary directors, it is hereby declared that the partners other than the said ordinary directors shall, on no account or pretence, have right to examine the books and documents of the company, but shall be bound to rest satisfied with the statements and abstracts above provided for : It is also declared that no transfer or other title to stock shall be admitted or entered into the books of the company for twenty days previous to the period when the said books are directed to be balanced as above mentioned, nor until after the said annual general meeting : But further declaring that it shall be competent to a majority of the partners present, by themselves or proxies, reckoned as aforesaid, at any annual general meeting, to appoint, if they see cause, two partners, qualified to be directors, as auditors, to examine and report upon the said statements and abstracts, and also upon the state of the accounts and affairs of the company generally, said auditors, after binding themselves to secrecy in the same manner as the ordinary directors, to have full and free access to all the books, vouchers, and writings connected with the affairs of the company, and also power to call in the aid of the manager, cashier, accountant, officers, clerks, and servants of the company, or any other person who may be deemed competent by the auditors to give information ; and, in the event of the appointment of such auditors, any annual general meeting at which they shall be appointed may be adjourned to some future day or days to receive their report and dispose thereof."

XLV. " Whereas it is of importance to the permanent welfare and prosperity of any banking establishment, and may tend greatly to raise the value of the stock of this company, that the profits made for a considerable time after commencing the business should not be divided, but should be allowed to accumulate as a reserved or sinking fund to meet future contingencies, and to secure a more permanent and large division of profits in future years than could otherwise safely be made, it is hereby agreed that no dividend of the company shall be made for or during the first year of the company unless the ordinary directors shall, in their discretion, deem it expedient, but such profits, or such part thereof as may not be appropriated by the said directors for a dividend, shall be retained and form part of a fund to be called ' the reserved fund,' and in each succeeding year during the continuance of this company the nett profits which shall arise and accrue to the company shall (after setting apart such proportion of the said nett profits as the ordinary directors shall think requisite for forming and maintaining the said surplus fund) be divided amongst the partners in proportion to their respective shares, and the surplus fund for the time being shall be carried to a separate account in the books of the company, and the said fund is hereby declared to be also a reserved fund of capital to meet any emergencies, losses, or extraordinary demands upon the company, and also to prevent, as far as may be, a fluctuation in the amount of dividends of succeeding years : Declaring that the said surplus fund may be applied for the several purposes aforesaid by the ordinary directors in their discretion ; and it shall be lawful for the ordinary directors, besides and in addition to the dividends annually payable to the partners from time to time, to take not exceeding one-third part of the surplus fund, and to apply the same in the way of bonus amongst the partners in proportion to the number of their shares ; and the said surplus fund shall, on the dissolution of the company, belong to and be divided amongst the partners then entitled to the capital stock in the same proportions as they shall be entitled to such capital."

113

and wilfully.

But an allegation that dividends have been paid out of capital may be either a very simple act of misfeasance, easily proved as matter of fact, or it may be only an inference in fact from complicated and continuous transactions stretching over a long course of years, and capable of being construed and judged of only by the application of commercial and actuarial knowledge and skill. That the present case belongs to the latter, and not the former of these categories, may be presumed from the almost unprecedented bulk and variety of the evidence laid before the Court.

The task of analysing and digesting this evidence has necessarily occupied a long time. But the results of our deliberations may, I think, be stated within a comparatively short space.

In 1856 Mr William Gemmell had acquired from an American Railroad Company, called the Racine and Mississippi Railway Company, a number of bonds for $1000 each, which were a first charge on the line, bearing eight per cent interest, having a currency of about thirty years, with a provision of a sinking fund of 1½ per cent to be set aside annually to reduce the principal.

The bank agreed to make, and did make, advances on the security of these bonds, and certain other stocks belonging to Mr Gemmell, or other parties for whom he acted, in 1856 and 1857.

On the 11th November 1857 the bank stopped payment, and did not resume business till the 31st December thereafter. At this date the advances made by the bank on the securities above-mentioned amounted to £117,608. The railway bonds held in security for this advance were of the nominal value of £134,000. . . .

The bonds already mentioned extended over the part of the railroad which was finished from Racine to Beloit. But in February 1858, after resuming business, the bank made farther advances on the security of bonds of 1000 dollars each, over a farther portion of the line which had then been constructed.

Both sets of bonds were a first charge on the railway, and the bonds, with their coupons, furnished security (such as it was) for the interest as well as for the principal advanced.

As to the estimated value of these securities, it is enough to say at present that the railway company were in great embarrassment, in consequence of the depression caused by the war between the Northern and Southern States, and were not in a condition to pay the interest as it accrued due. But if the line afforded a good ultimate security for the principal and interest of the whole bonds issued by the railway company, which were a first charge, the non-payment of interest was, in practical effect, nothing else than an additional advance by the bank on security.

The bank had agents in New York named Irvin & Company, who seem to have been persons of high character, and who, in their correspondence with the manager, while admitting the impossibility of realising during the war, gave a confident opinion as to the ultimate sufficiency of the securities for both principal and interest.

It was in these circumstances that the respondent became a director of the bank in July 1858; and the first overt act of misfeasance charged against him is, that he, as a director, signed the balance-sheet of 1859, to be submitted to the shareholders at the annual meeting of that year.

The financial year of the bank ended in June 1859, and the interest due on the American railway securities, amounting to £7552 for the year, was added to the amount of the debt in the bank books at that date, and was carried to the credit of the profit and loss account. The result, of course, of the operation was to increase to that extent the balance of profit for the year appearing in the balance-sheet.

The contention of the liquidators is that the interest for the year, £7552, not having been received, was not profit, and the dividend of the year was to that extent paid out of capital.

But if no dividend could be paid except out of cash in hand or in bank, representing profits or interest actually received, it is obvious that the business of such a company could not be practically carried on; and the existing shareholders of the company would have good reason to complain that they were deprived of their just share of the profits of the concern actually earned and well secured, because these profits could not be converted into cash before the balance-sheet of the year was struck.

When profits have been earned and not paid, but invested on undoubted security, and these profits have been carried to the credit of the profit and loss account, and a dividend declared and paid out of the balance of profits thus obtained, it is no doubt true, in a literal sense, that the dividend is to the extent of these unpaid profits paid out of capital; because the company, not having cash to represent these earned and secured profits, must find the money to pay the dividend elsewhere; and they can find it nowhere except by applying to the purpose cash which forms part of the floating balance of capital. But if the unpaid profits are fully secured, they become a part of the capital of the company, as a *surrogatum* for the cash of equal amount taken from the floating capital and paid as dividend; and thus the capital is not diminished, but a certain part of the floating balance of capital becomes invested in the securities which the company hold for the earned but unpaid profits in question.

From this it seems to me to follow that in order to convict the directors of this company of paying a dividend out of capital in 1859, it is necessary to prove not merely (1) that they knew that the interest on the American railway investment, though due, was not paid, and (2) that it was brought to the credit of profit and loss, and so divided as clear profit; but also (3) that they had not reasonable ground for believing that the interest was well secured and would ultimately be recovered.

If they had reasonable ground for so believing, they acted in good faith, and so cannot be said to have committed a breach of trust; for while it is the duty of directors to act very cautiously in estimating the securities which they hold, they are necessarily left, by the very nature of their office, to exercise their own judgment and discretion in making such estimate. They owe to the company an obligation to leave a safe margin in striking the balance of profit and loss, so as not to endanger its financial position. But they are equally bound to have a due regard to the interests of the individuals who for the time are the holders of the stock of the company, and to whom they are under an honourable, if not also a legal obligation, to pay such a dividend as, in their opinion, may fairly be paid out of the profits, consistently with the financial well-being of the company. . . .

I have hitherto confined my attention to the conduct of the directors in 1859 (the first year of the respondent's official responsibility), because it conduces to simplicity and clearness to state the principles on which I think this case must be decided as applicable to one period and one act of alleged misfeasance. But it is of course necessary to have regard to the whole conduct of the directors from that year down to 1870 (when the respondent resigned), to determine whether the considerations which seem to me to justify the recommendation of the dividend of 1859 are equally applicable to the varied condition of the American securities during the subsequent years. . . .

One salient point in the case is, that in progress of time the bank's interest in the railway, and the amount of money that they embarked on the faith of its ultimate prosperity and success, increased from £117,000 to £905,000 (including, however, the unpaid and accumulated interest) during the respondent's connection with the direction; and this, on a superficial consideration of the history of the case, has undoubtedly a good deal of the appearance of what is colloquially called throwing good money after bad. But I am satisfied that would be a rash and unjust conclusion, if it be true, as the respondent contends, that the sum of the company's capital which he left invested in the American railways securities, when he resigned as a director in 1870, was well secured. At that date the figures stood thus:—The total amount of principal and interest due to the bank was £905,166. The nominal amount of the securities held for this debt was £974,866, leaving a margin of £69,700 in favour of the bank. Of course, everything depended on the real value of the securities.

It has not been suggested, on the part of the liquidators, that it would have been prudent to write off the debt secured on the American railways as a bad debt, either in respect of principal or interest, when the respondent entered on his duties as a director; and I do not understand that such a proceeding would, in the view of the liquidators, have been justifiable at any time between 1858 and 1870. If such a course had been adopted, the directors would, as a necessary consequence, have ceased to take any steps for improving their position as creditors in the railway bonds, or even to expend any money in watching over their interests as such creditors. But if this course was not to be followed, then it must be at once apparent that, from the nature of the investment, and the financial condition of the United States at the time, this portion of the bank's assets required the most vigilant attention, and, if necessary, the expenditure of more money, in the hope of tiding over difficult and embarrassing times.

It very soon became clear that, unless the directors were prepared to encounter the loss of their advances of £117,000, with accruing interest, they must make up their minds to " nurse the line," i.e., they must advance more money to enable the railroad to be completed to such an extent as to connect Lake Michigan with the Mississippi, without which it could not ultimately prove a paying concern. They had also to prevent or discourage damaging competition, and to get the management of the line out of incompetent and untrustworthy hands.

In the course of all these complicated proceedings they had the constant advice and assistance of Messrs Irvin of New York, whose correspondence proves them to have been persons of large experience and capacity in dealing with such affairs, and they had a special agent, Mr Thomson, who was on the spot, and who, if a somewhat sanguine, was also a very energetic and able man.

The whole money advanced under this advice was secured on substantially the same kind of securities as the bank held from the beginning, and the securities obtained were always large enough, at least nominally, to cover all the overdue interest for the time.

The directors had been constantly assured by their agents, during the twelve years in question, that their investments were sound, and in the end would certainly prove good both for principal and interest.

Notwithstanding these assurances, the directors were very anxious to realise their investments, because they naturally felt that there was too much of the bank's funds locked up in one class of securities, which were for the time unproductive; and their desire to realise was uniformly pressed on their agents and advisers in America. But here they encountered a great difficulty in consequence of the rate of exchange between the United States and this country. If they had disposed of their interests in the railways, they could not have obtained payment of the price except in United States currency, which could not be converted into gold in London without a great loss. There is no doubt that, but for this embarrassment, they could have obtained a price, on more than one occasion, which would have repaid the whole advances, both principal and interest, and even left a margin of gain.

The liquidators, in argument, make a great deal of this topic, and say that the offers which were made are, as indications of the value of the investments, of little account; for the real value, they contend, must be measured by the amount of gold they could have got, as the produce of the transaction, when the money was brought home to this country. But I think this argument is based on a fallacy. No doubt it was impossible, except at a great loss, to bring home the money to this country, and it would, of course, have been much more convenient to bring it home, if the doing so had not been attended by such loss. But nobody supposed that the very exceptional financial condition of the United States, arising out of the war, was to be permanent, or even of any very long continuance, and still less that the Government would become bankrupt. Now, though it was impossible, without great loss, to bring home the money, it was quite possible to invest it in unexceptionable securities in America without any loss. The Government securities, and particularly what were called the 5/20 United States bonds, might then be purchased at par, and these bonds on maturity were payable in gold. It was a further and most important recommendation of such securities that the directors were, by the contract of copartnery of the bank, specially authorised to invest in the "securities and stocks of the Government of Great Britain and Ireland, or of the United States of America, or of foreign states."

The directors did not accept of any of the offers for the purchase of their entire interest in the railways. The precise character and denomination of the securities varied from time to time, according to the exigencies of the railways, and the judgment the directors formed as to the best way of handling for the time the investments which they held. But in the end, *i.e.*, in 1870, they held, as already mentioned, securities of the nominal value of £974,000 for a debt, principal and interest, amounting to £905,000.

The evidence as to the real value of these securities in 1870 is voluminous and multifarious, and an examination of it has left on my mind a decided impression, that, after many years of anxious and careful treatment of the investment of this portion of the bank's funds, the directors had got into comparatively smooth water, and were possessed of a property or investment of a sound description.

Certainly this impression is very strongly confirmed by the undoubted fact, that in 1870 the investment began to pay interest, and continued to do so down to the stoppage of the bank in 1878. The rate of interest, indeed, varied from time to time, but the average of the eight years was four per cent.

Now, it must be remembered that the investment of £905,000, which was thus yielding interest at four per cent, was composed not only of the money advanced by the bank, but of all the unpaid interest at a high rate which had accrued due since 1856; and thus this £905,000, which formed in 1870 an important part of the capital of the bank well secured, included, as one of its component parts, that £311,000 of the bank's capital which the respondent is charged with having misapplied by paying it away in dividends. For while a portion of the floating capital in the form of cash or money at call, or the like, was used to enable the bank to pay dividends corresponding to the amount of the interest due but unpaid on the American railway securities from 1858 to 1870, there was growing up, in precisely the same proportion, an addition to the capital of the bank in the form of securities for the said interest accumulated with the principal sum of the advances made; the result being that in 1870 the amount of the bank's capital stood undiminished by the operations complained of. . . .

Hitherto I have not made any distinction between the position and conduct of the respondent Mr Mackinnon and those of the other directors. But it is only fair to him to notice some circumstances which are peculiar to his case.

It does not appear that he ever made use of his knowledge or influence as a director to procure any pecuniary or other advantage to himself. It was tacitly admitted, in the course of the arguments, that the greater part of his extensive banking business was done with another establishment; that any discounts which he obtained from the City Bank were in the ordinary course of business; and that the bank would have been much benefited if he had been induced to give them more of his custom. . . .

It is stated in Mr Mackinnon's answers that the system of making large unsecured advances to directors and their friends and partners, which proved the ultimate ruin of the bank, had not begun while he was a director. This has not, so far as I can see, been disputed either in the evidence or in the course of the arguments.

For what took place after 1870 the respondent is of course not answerable. New directors and a new manager came into office between that date and the stoppage of the bank, and in this liquidation we have only too good reason to know that their management of the affairs of the bank was of the worst possible description.

After the liquidation commenced, we are informed that the American railway securities were disposed of by the liquidators at a heavy loss—a loss, if I understand rightly, of more than twenty-five per cent. To this the respondent answers, that he cannot be made responsible for the results. He says truly, that the realising of assets for division among creditors is always a very unfair test of the value of the assets, because it must to some extent be gone about hastily, and in a necessarily unfavourable state of the market.

But the respondent goes further, and contends that the conduct of the liquidators, in realising these securities, has been such as to liberate him from all responsibility, even if he had been otherwise liable.

In considering this part of the case, it is necessary to keep always in view that, when the note was presented, Mr Mackinnon had been for ten years entirely unconnected with the management of the bank; that for six years he had not even been a shareholder, having sold out in 1874; that he was in no way a party in the liquidation; and that the first notice he had of the serious charges and the heavy pecuniary claim made against him, was the service upon him of this note in November 1880, or of the relative summons in June of the same year.

In the interval of more than ten years many important events had taken place. In 1870 the then existing board of directors and the manager took over the railway securities from the retiring director as a good investment, which they thenceforward managed according to their own discretion. As time went on the management of the bank became in the highest degree imprudent and even criminal, and ended in ruin and disaster in October 1878. Meantime the gentleman who was manager of the bank while Mr Mackinnon was a director had died; some of his co-directors had gone out of office like himself; and when the crash came, and the liquidation commenced, the respondent was apparently no more concerned than any other outside member of the public.

When the note is served upon him, he learns for the first time, not only that he is to meet a charge of breach of trust going back for a period of more than twenty years, but also that the securities, in dealing with which the breach of trust is said to have been committed, have been realised by the liquidators at a great sacrifice. . . .

In these very peculiar circumstances, I am of opinion that the present claim, even if it were on its merits well founded (which I think it is not), is barred by what has occurred between July 1870 and November 1880. . . .

LORD DEAS.—

There remains only the shorter, but, as regards amount, the much larger question, viz., the claim of the liquidators against Mr Mackinnon in respect of money paid away as dividends from June 1858 to June 1870, both inclusive, as set forth in articles 27 and 28 of the note, as well as in article 26 of the condescendence in the ordinary action. The money thus applied in payment of dividends is represented by Mr Mackinnon and his co-directors to have consisted of interest duly earned upon two of the American railway accounts, and periodically debited thereto accordingly. So far this is not disputed by the liquidators. But they remark that, while the interest so debited during the twelve years mentioned, and treated as profit, amounted in whole to £315,897, 7s. 8d., the payments actually received to account of that interest amounted only to £4330, 10s. 11d., leaving £311,664, 16s. 9d. of a deficiency for which the liquidators hold Mr Mackinnon personally liable.

It appears to me that the defence against this branch of the claim is, or might have been, in some aspects of it, attended with much more difficulty than the other.

Payment of dividends out of capital (which this is said in substance to have been) may be so palpably contrary to the duty of directors that they shall not be heard to allege *bona fides* as a defence against it. Here the adventurous appropriation of unpaid interest to the payment of dividends went on half-yearly for no less than twelve years. I do not doubt that Mr Mackinnon and his co-directors believed that the interest for all the years in question would be recovered in the end, nor do I doubt that they had reasonable grounds for believing so, but I have great difficulty in seeing why the directors, however much they expected and believed that all the interest would be so recovered in the end, should have done that which they might have left undone—namely, paid the dividends for so many terms, in place of waiting till they had first received the interest out of which they were to pay them. I should be sorry to see the course adopted drawn into a precedent—and I hope it may prevent it from being so—that although it may not lead to personal liability in this case, it must be seen to have been so sufficiently perilous as to make it rather a danger to be avoided than an example to be imitated.

One answer, which undoubtedly deserves serious attention, was made to it by Mr Robertson in his very able address for Mr Mackinnon (as indeed all the addresses were extremely able), viz., that in 1870, when Mr Mackinnon ceased to be a director, there was presented to and in the hands of the bank (securities included) property equal in value to the whole principal and interest advanced; and I do not doubt that this may have been so had that property been realised in prosperous times, and in a favourable market. But all answers of this kind leave the difficult question behind, Who shall bear the burden if times are not prosperous, or the markets are unfavourable?

There is one answer, however, to this branch of the claim of the liquidators which I confess has all along appeared to me to be insuperable. That answer has, amongst others, been stated by your Lordship, and it arises thus :—The shareholders were, of course, the parties who received the dividends in question. The debts of the bank have all been paid ; and the liquidators represent shareholders only ; but in that capacity they have no title to sue for these dividends any more than the shareholders themselves, who have already received them. . . .

LORD MURE.— , , ,

The note as laid, on the other hand, proceeds upon the assumption that the investments in America, on which it is alleged no interest was paid at the time it was taken credit for, were within the power of the directors of the bank to make ;

and the complaint is, that those investments being thus unproductive, and no interest having been remitted to this country or received from them in America beyond a comparatively small amount, the directors, from 1858 to 1870, and among them the respondent, allowed the amount of this interest to be carried to the profit and loss account in framing the balance-sheet for the year, and allowed a dividend to be declared on the footing that the interest had been received. And it is maintained that by so doing the respondent was "guilty of a breach of trust in relation to the company," for which he is liable in repetition, under the 165th section of the statute of 1862, to the extent of about £300,000, being the amount of capital or other funds of the bank alleged to have been so misapplied in payment of dividend from 1858 to 1870.

In answer to this demand the respondent, while he admits that the interest on the American advances had not been remitted to this country at the time the yearly balance-sheets were framed, denies that these interests had not accrued. He, on the contrary, alleges that those interests, in each of the years during which he was a director of the bank, had been earned, and were due at the time the yearly balance-sheets were prepared; and that, although they had not been actually paid and become available as cash in hand at the time, they were all along admitted by the debtors to be due; and that securities in the shape of bonds over the railways, or of railway stocks, were from time to time received more than sufficient to cover the amount of money advanced, and the interest due upon those advances. The respondent also alleges that where interest is due, but is not actually available as cash in hand, it is in accordance with the custom of trade, and with mercantile usage, to carry such interest to the profit and loss account for the year in which it is due, and to calculate the profits on that footing, and he maintains that this is not paying dividend out of capital in the sense of being a breach of trust in relation to the company, provided that interest is believed to be properly secured. And the respondent further alleges that, when he left the board of directors in 1870, he believed the American railway securities belonging to the bank formed a sufficient cover for the advances made in America up to that date, and also for the whole interests due on those advances, and that he had good grounds for that belief. . . .

Mr Wetmore, who was a partner of Mr Irvin's house at the time, and is now treasurer of the International and Great Northern Railway, is asked to state "what were the relations from 1859 to 1866 of the bank and this railway account in regard to the earning and realisation of interest upon the outlay of the bank?" and he says,—"The bank owned the securities, and as interest matured on these securities it was put into other securities," which, "as far as the bank was concerned, were new investments." He is then asked to state "what kind of securities the interest was invested in which was collected in behalf of the bank from 1859 to 1866?" and the answer is, "From 1859 on Racine and Mississippi bonds. As interest matured and the plan of reorganising or issuing Western Union securities for part of the coupons of Racine and Mississippi was adopted, they received Western Union bonds, part Western Union stock, and part Western Union preferred stock, and in some cases they received Northern Illinois bonds, which afterwards went into Western Union bonds; eventually they received Western Union securities for all of that interest;"

and he adds, in answer to another question, that "the whole of the interest which fell due upon the securities from 1859 to 1866 was paid to the bank;" and a similar answer is given with reference to the interest falling due, and collected from 1866 to 1869.

Mr Irvin is examined on the same matter, and he states in answer to a question put to him in cross-examination, "The securities taken for interest were new and fresh securities. When the Western branch of the Racine and Mississippi Railroad and Northern Illinois Railroad were being constructed the amounts received for interest were invested in the new securities on those roads, and were expended on their construction. When the Western Railroad Company was organised it included all the former organisations, and all the securities then held were exchanged in bulk for the securities of that organisation in bulk. After the organisation of the Western Union Company in 1866, until the bank's agent came out in 1869, the proceeds of the interest were invested in preferred stock of the Western Union Company, according to my best memory."

So standing the facts, the question to be disposed of is this—Does the mode in which the bank dealt with the interest on these securities during the period embraced in the note, viz., by carrying it to profit and loss account in this country, while investing it as capital in railway securities in America, amount to a payment of dividend out of capital; or is it, on the other hand, to be looked upon as being substantially an investment on American securities of the interest which had accrued there, but which could not then be made available as cash for transmission to this country?

I am of opinion that it is not, in any just sense, a payment of dividend out of capital, but an investment of the interest in America as part of the capital of the bank.

By so dealing with the matter, the interest which had accrued, but which the railways could not pay in cash at the time it fell due, was, in my opinion, paid in money's worth in the shape of these mortgage bonds and stocks, which were taken in lieu of the payment of it as it accrued; and the interest was in this way secured as part of the bank's capital in America. So that the amount of money carried to profit and loss in this country as interest in each year did not operate as a diminution, either permanent or temporary, of the capital of the bank, which it is essential that it should have done in order to subject a director acting in complete *bona fides* to the serious, even in certain circumstances criminal, charge of paying dividend out of capital; and it did not so operate, for this plain reason, because a sum corresponding in amount to that carried to profit and loss as interest, was invested in America in substitution, and as a *surrogatum* for the money taken from the bank in this country when the dividend was paid. This was substantially, therefore, an investment of capital in America, and if done in the *bona fide* belief that the security was sufficient, constitutes a good defence to the present demand. . . . But this is, in many respects, no ordinary case, and the loss on realisation arose from no fault on the part of the respondent. It has arisen under a liquidation rendered necessary by the culpable and reckless, and in some respects criminal mismanagement of the affairs of the bank, begun after the respondent had ceased to be a director; and a careful examination of the evidence bearing on this part of the case has left a strong impression on my mind, that if the realisation had not been forced on by one of the greatest monetary catastrophies that ever occurred no loss would have been sustained. And I think there are also pretty strong grounds for holding, that if the realisation had to be made now, there would not only be no loss, but a considerable profit in the result. I am not disposed to attach the slightest blame to the liquidators for the way in which the realisation was conducted, and I believe they did the best they could in the difficult position in which they were placed. But they were in the position of parties who required to realise as speedily as possible a very large amount of bankrupt estate. Now, such estate proverbially sells cheap, and there is generally a loss on realisation, owing to the purchasing world being aware that it is the duty of the liquidator, or trustee, as the case may be, to endeavour to realise with despatch. The evidence of Mr Harding, a gentleman of great experience in such matters, is very decided upon this point. He says that, according to his experience, there is in liquidation "always a large per-centage of loss in realising, unless the securities are every-day of marketable value. If they are exceptional securities, in my experience an unusual loss is realised,—liquidation being adverse to favourable realisation." And in such a case as the present, where the securities were in some respects exceptional, he rates the loss at twenty-five per cent, which appears to be just about the loss that was here sustained. . . . The loss, therefore, on realisation is, in my opinion, no evidence in this case that the investments were not sufficient in ordinary circumstances to cover the advances. . . .

LORD SHAND.— . . . .
It has been necessary carefully to consider the effect of the various and important changes which occurred in the extension and development of the railway enterprise in which the bank, by its increasing advances, became so deeply interested ; the result of these changes as affecting the value of the bank's securities from time to time ; the reports and views of the bank's representatives in America communicated to the bank here ; and the opinions which were formed by Mr Mackinnon and the other directors and officials of the bank as to the value, present and prospective, of the securities held for the bank's advances and accruing interest. The course of the inquiry, the evidence of accountants, and the arguments for the parties, have made it necessary to form a judgment as to the position of the bank's account with reference to the value of the securities as a cover for the bank's advances and interest and the views of the officials of the bank and the respondent on that subject on the occasion of each of the several extensions of the Racine and Mississippi Railroad. Only ninety miles in length of this line existed when Mr Mackinnon joined the direction in 1858, and in 1870, when he retired, it had been extended to 180 miles, mainly by the expenditure which the bank was induced to make, adding to the line stage after stage during these twelve years, either because favourable anticipations had not been realised, or because unlooked for opposition from active competitors for traffic had been met with. . . . It has been necessary to look carefully into the evidence as to these various transactions, in order to form an opinion on the question whether, as the liquidators maintain, at the dates when they occurred, and with reference to the nature and particulars of the transactions themselves, the position and value of the bank's securities were such as to make it improper to debit the account with interest, and as to the

question whether this became known to the respondent ; but a general statement only can be given, with reference to each of the important points of time in the history of the railway account, of the grounds which have led to the conclusion that the liquidators have failed to establish the propositions laid down by the Solicitor-General, on the proof of which their success in this application depended.

It does not appear to me that there is any dispute between the parties as to the law applicable to this part of the case, as I think appears clearly enough from the propositions in fact which the counsel for the liquidators seemed to concede must be proved to entitle them to decree. It is clear that it is not necessary that there must be cash realised, and in the coffers of the bank, received expressly on account of interest or profits, in order to justify the payment of a dividend. To enforce such a rule would be to run counter to ordinary and reasonable usage in the case of mercantile companies. In order to ascertain the profits earned and divisible at any given time the balance-sheet must contain a fair statement of the liabilities of the company, including its paid-up capital ; and, on the other hand, a fair or more properly *bona fide* valuation of assets ; the balance, if in favour of the company, being profits. These profits may, and must often to a great extent, be represented by obligations of debtors, often secured, and by direct securities over property. They are not the less profits fairly realised and divisible because they exist in that form and have not been received in cash. If profits have been earned, and are, in the judgment of those in the management of the company, secured, the shareholders of a joint stock company are, in the ordinary case, entitled to have such profits which may properly be called realised profits, declared and divided, except in so far as they may be otherwise appropriated either by the express terms of the contract, or by the exercise of powers conferred on those charged with the management of the company ; and the directors may properly use funds otherwise available to them, and forming part of the floating balances on capital account in payment of the dividend. All this, however, infers a valuation of assets, and it is in this operation that it is represented the respondent was guilty of a breach of duty, in having knowingly and wilfully overvalued the American securities when he treated them from time to time as sufficient to cover interest and principal on the bank's advances.

One thing is abundantly clear with reference to such a charge, and to the duty of valuation of assets, that it involves a matter of judgment or opinion, and eminently so with reference to such a subject as the railroad properties on which the bank's advances in the present case had been laid out. The amounts to be carried into the balance-sheet, and profit and loss accounts respectively for the year, depend on the estimate which has been formed of the value of the company's property and securities. It seems to me that where such accounts have been regularly prepared in the ordinary course of administration of a business, and have been given effect to in the fixing and payment of dividends, and more especially, where the acts are challenged after the lapse of a number of years, the Court ought strongly to presume the correctness of the proceeding, and to require clear evidence of want of *bona fides* where, as here, a case is rested on that ground ; for although the charge has not been in these words I cannot avoid the conclusion that it is made to that effect, when it is maintained, as a result of the proof, " that the respondent knew that the interest was being debited and divided ; that he knew it was not being received by the bank; and that he knew there was no reasonable prospect of its ever being recovered." And if it appears that the person against whom the charge is insisted in has taken pains to make himself acquainted with the various considerations which might affect the value of the subject of valuation, in order to form a correct judgment, all the stronger must be the presumptions in his favour, and against the view that would attach to him the want of good faith. Were the law otherwise, I fear it would only deter men of character and means and standing from taking part in the management of joint stock companies.

I must confess that, in the present case, however, I have felt there are considerations which go very far to weaken, I should perhaps rather say to overcome, the strength of the presumptions I have now mentioned. I refer to the fact, which does not admit of dispute, that although interest was regularly debited to the American account, and the amount carried to profit and loss account, no part of that interest over the whole period of twelve years ever reached the bank in this country ; while, in the meantime, the bank's advances had grown from £117,000 to about £600,000 of capital, and the money so advanced had not been lent in the ordinary course of banking business, but had been advanced to be expended in extensions of an American railroad. It cannot for a moment be disputed that this is a most unusual, probably unprecedented, state of matters in the history of a banking company in this country. The fact being proved or admitted that interest was charged, and to a great extent paid away in dividends over so long a period, and in such circumstances, with the *prima facie* unfavourable impression which a proceeding so unusual was calculated to produce, seems to me to overcome much of the strength of the presumptions I have referred to, and to lay a certain *onus* on the respondent— I mean the *onus* of accounting, by a satisfactory explanation and evidence, for the payment of so long a series of dividends in the circumstances. I have accordingly examined the evidence offered in explanation with scrutinising care, and recognising the *onus* that thus lay on the respondent, in circumstances so peculiar. The result, however, has been to satisfy me (1) that the increasing advances were made from time to time under a complete conviction that they were necessary in order to obtain an ultimate recovery of the large sum at stake when Mr Mackinnon became a director ; (2) that while interest was being debited to the railway account, Mr Mackinnon honestly believed that the bank's securities were sufficient to cover the whole amount of principal and interest due to the bank ; and (3) that he had reasonable grounds for firmly holding that opinion.

Before noticing the general grounds on which I rest this conclusion, I must, in the first instance, refer to a point which has always appeared to me to be of primary importance as affecting the decision of the case—I mean the effect of the high rate of exchange between America and this country which prevailed throughout a great part of the twelve years in question, and particularly during the years from 1862 to 1870, both inclusive. From the table contained in the joint statement for the parties it appears that the American currency was so depreciated, that, in place of five dollars being equivalent to the £1, the rates during the years just specially mentioned varied from five to seven, and eight dollars; and even at one time, in December 1864, the rate of exchange was 10½ dollars in the £1. Now, the liquidators, by the evidence of their accountants, and the pleadings of counsel, have maintained that in valuing the bank's securities the various classes of bonds held from the railway companies, and also in estimating the value of the various offers made from time to time for the purchase of the railways and securities, the directors were bound to take the current rate of exchange with this country at the time, and having first made their estimate in dollars, to convert the amount into money sterling, not at the normal rate of 5 dollars to the £1, but at the much lower rate prevailing at the time. If the liquidators be wrong in this contention, I have never seen, and do not now see, how they could possibly succeed in this application; and I rather think this was virtually conceded before the close of the argument. It cannot be disputed, that if, in place of the conversion of the estimated value of the bank's securities in dollars, at the rate of 8½, or 6 or 6½ dollars to the £1, being the rates taken by the accountants for the liquidators in three valuations made by them in 1864, 1866, and 1869 respectively, the normal rate of 5 dollars to the £1 be applied, a very much larger amount is the result,—and so important is the difference, that in several instances of points of time at which valuations have been made by both parties, either with reference to the securities then held by the bank, or to offers of purchase made to the bank, in the one view there is a large deficit on the amount necessary to meet the balance at the debit of the railway account; while in the other view there is either a clear surplus after paying off principal and interest, or the deficiency is so small,—a matter of £20,000 or thereby, on a total sum of £900,000 of principal and interest,—as to make the figures substantially square each other. It seems to be clear, therefore, that in any view that can be taken of the case, the liquidators could only succeed in this application by shewing that the officials of the bank were bound to adopt the principle of valuing their securities in money sterling, according to the rate of exchange of the day. This, I am clearly of opinion, the officials and directors were not bound to do.

In the opening argument on the evidence it was maintained that not only had the bank invariably looked at each offer made for their securities in the single light of what it would produce in sterling money, if at once remitted home, at the rate of exchange of the day, but that it was very much of an afterthought on the part of the respondent to maintain the view that he regarded the state of matters in America as temporary; that he looked for a speedy termination of the war; that with returning peace a strong Government would give security to traders, and lead to the commercial prosperity of the country; and that with all this, in a short time, a return to the normal rate of exchange might be looked for. The respondent's counsel was able, in reply, to shew by a number of passages in the correspondence between the bank and their agents and representatives in America, and in letters to and from Mr Mackinnon, that, as he himself explains in his evidence, he entertained the opinion that the exchange would ere long right itself and come to par, and that there was every reason for believing that the bank would act on that view; and even if they sold their securities, invest the proceeds in 5/20 Government bonds, or other securities recommended to them, and have these realised, and the proceeds remitted, when the loss on exchange could be avoided. In the concluding argument for the bank it was no longer, I think, maintained that there was not evidence to shew that in the event of a realisation of the bank's securities in American currency it was not in the view of the parties to retain the money invested in America till the loss on the exchange could be avoided. The argument finally, and at least mainly pressed, was that a purchase of other securities would have been a speculation into which the bank was not entitled to enter, any more than if they had realised securities at home, and sent out the proceeds to get the benefit of a favourable exchange for remittance, and in the expectation of gaining by exchange afterwards coming to par.

It seems to me that the contention of the bank on this question—a contention which is vital to their case—is unsound. To begin with, the effect of the rate of exchange, entering as it does into the principle of valuation, involves a matter of opinion or judgment, and it would be necessary to shew want of *bona fides* on the part of those who, in making their valuations at the time, or in resolving on the best course to be followed in the event of a sale, acted, or were prepared to act, on the view that they were not called on to give effect to an abnormal rate of exchange which they regarded as temporary. There is no evidence to support a charge of this kind. Again, there is abundant evidence corroborative of what Mr Mackinnon said as a witness, that the subject was presented for consideration, and that if the bank had realised money they would have acted in accordance with his views, which were formed after considerable experience in his mercantile dealings in his own private business. In March 1862 Mr Irvin, the bank's confidential adviser in New York, wrote to the secretary in Glasgow,—" The prospects of the country in connection with our domestic war is much changed. The superior power and resources, as well as determination of the North, is so manifest that the war must soon be closed, or at least be confined during the remainder of its continuance to a small portion of the cotton states, where the revolt may be expected to die out speedily." In November of the following year Messrs Irvin & Company, in another letter to the bank, put their view very plainly. They say, with reference to the prospect of offers for the bank's securities,—" The question of exchange has, to us, presented itself in this aspect—that your property being already on this side, subject to our depreciated currency, if we could, while getting rid of present responsibilities, obtain for you other securities of same amount, of stronger and more available character, the bank would be in a better position for realising their property when exchange became more favourable, and in the meantime be getting interest on the whole." Mr Thomson, the manager of the railways, about the same time wrote to a similar effect. He says in writing to the bank a few days before the letter last referred to,—" The question of exchange would present the separate consideration to the bank, whether the unfortunate crisis in which this country is involved made it advisable to withdraw their money at once at a loss, or whether it was best to allow it to remain in American securities, with confidence that the course of events will restore the amount so held at a par exchange in a few years. · My confidence in the future is strong; and I cannot contemplate the vast resources of the country, the energy and intelligence of the people, without feeling assured that a strong Government will be established, which will succeed the present Government of the Northern States, and take upon itself the responsibilities arising from the acts, or created by the present administration. . . . If other securities could be obtained in exchange for those now held of equal value without responsibilities, or holding so much at risk in one enterprise, would it not be best to make the transaction, and await the restoration of a legitimate mercantile exchange?" It is only necessary to quote further the bank's reply through their secretary on the 5th of December 1863, following on a meeting of the bank directors held two days before, at which Mr Mackinnon was present, when the letters of Irvin & Company, and Mr Thomson, just noticed, were read. The secretary's letter to Irvin & Company is in these terms:—" I wrote you on the 27th ulto., and have since been favoured with yours of the 17th ditto, enclosing Mr Thomson's letter of the 10th, and to both the directors have given their most careful consideration. The suggestion of making an exchange of our interests in the railways for some other securities of a stronger and more available character, free from further outlay, meets with our approval, and would dispose us to hold on, and be content with a moderate interest until the exchange got rectified. The subject will be again taken up after we have a reply from you to our letter of the 20th ulto." The advice of Irvin & Company is what was no doubt given and acted on at that time in the case of many private investors in this country having securities in America. There are other important letters to a similar effect of subsequent dates, and, in particular, a letter from the bank inviting suggestions on the subject, and a reply by Irvin & Company suggesting, amongst suitable securities for investment, U.S. 5/20 bonds, which could be had about par, and one or more letters by Mr Mackinnon, in which he expresses the opinion that exchange will soon be at par. It remains only to be stated that, as appears from the evidence of Mr Guild, the bank, on account of the unfavourable exchange, actually returned to America a sum of £2300, which had been sent home to them in cash, in order that it might be invested in America, and remitted only after the exchange had reached, or nearly reached, par, and farther directed Irvin & Company to retain the interest paid on the Northern Illinois bonds for the same reason.

Again, it seems to me to be quite unsound to represent the proceeding of leaving money in America to be so invested as a speculation of the same kind as the sending out of money for investment. As Mr Irvin observed, property on that side was already subject to the depreciated currency, and it was only an act of fair and reasonable administration on the part of those who thought the depreciation temporary to avoid the loss which would result from their withdrawing it by remittance to this country. And, even if there be an element of speculation in taking that course, which is probably quite true, this cannot affect the question here under consideration, which, after all, relates to the *bona fides* of the valuation or estimate of the bank's assets. I have perhaps dwelt longer on this subject of the rates of exchange than was necessary, but, as I have said, it seems to me to be so important as to be at the root of the case of the liquidators, and it is because of this that I have given my reasons fully for holding that the views maintained on their behalf cannot receive effect. . . .

There has been a considerable controversy on the question whether there was ever any transaction by which the bank received a large amount of securities in name of interest. I think it has been made out that from the time the Northern Illinois Railway was in operation considerable sums were received in cash on account of interest; and although the interest generally falling due on the bonds of the Racine and Mississippi Railway Company, and the certificates for the monies advanced to the Farmers' Loan and Trust Company, was not paid when due, but was expended with the bank's consent in the construction of the extended lines and equipment of the railways, yet the railways were by this expenditure increased in value, and when the amalgamation of the whole lines into one, under the name of "The Western Union Railway Company," was carried out, I think it is clear that securities by the new company in bonds and stock were given to the bank on account of the past-due interest owing to them. I agree, however, in an observation made by the counsel for the respondent, that it is really not very material to the decision of this case whether bonds or other securities were given at any particular time to represent or cover interest expressly *eo nomine*. It was justly observed by the counsel for the liquidators, that shortly after Mr Mackinnon joined the board this railway account became no longer an account in which Gemmell, Watson, and others were the debtors and the parties interested in the railway bonds held by the bank merely as a security. The best arrangement the bank could make was to discharge the debtors, and take over the bonds as their own property. This it was that led the bank into the gradual expenditure of money in extensions of the line; and the result undoubtedly was that the accounts, in place of representing loans to a customer, really represented a speculative enterprise. That being so, the question, what was the bank's position at any particular moment, was really one of valuation of the bank's securities—bonds and stocks—after stock had been acquired—and the amount of any valuation was rather a question of original outlay and profits than of capital and interest, as in the case of a loan to a customer. Accordingly, when interest was being year after year debited to the account, the true question which those in the management of the bank had to solve was whether, on a fair valuation, there was such a profit on what had become really a speculation by the bank as would warrant the carrying of seven or eight per cent to the debit of the account, and so to the profit and loss account. If it be supposed that the bank, under the sale to Mitchell, had got a much larger price, it is obvious this would not have represented interest in any way, but simply so much profit. It thus appears to me that the true question in the case is not did the bank receive regularly the interest on its bonds, although I think that substantially they did so, but rather at the time of balancing of each year was there on a sound valuation a profit to carry to profit and loss account. . . .

I have only to add, on this part of the case, that I cannot doubt that, by the act of amalgamating the lines and consolidating the undertaking into one, the property of the bank was greatly enhanced in value, and, accordingly, the result was immediately seen in the offers which from that time onward were made by different parties for the Western Union Railway. Finally, that railway was sold to Mr Mitchell before Mr Mackinnon left the board, for a certain payment in cash, and bonds and stock, which I think were fairly regarded as sufficient

129

securities for the bank's debt, principal and interest. It is clear that all the parties at the time placed great value on the stock, and had reasonable grounds for doing so. ˙ The investment was thus put in a shape in which the bank were freed from any further call for advances, and they obtained securities on which interest was regularly paid from 1870 till the bank stopped payment. On the merits of the case, therefore, and as the result of a review of the material points in the evidence, I am satisfied that judgment ought to be for the respondent; and, having given the details of the evidence my best consideration, I must add that, so far as I am concerned, I do not think the question one of doubt or difficulty. . . .

FLITCROFT'S CASE

21 L.R. Ch. 519 (1882)
Court of Appeal

In re EXCHANGE BANKING COMPANY.

FLITCROFT'S CASE.

Companies—Directors—Payment of Dividends out of Capital—Set-off—Statute of Limitations.

JESSEL, M.R. :—

This is an appeal from an order of Vice-Chancellor *Bacon*, that certain directors who had improperly paid dividends to the shareholders out of capital should pay to the liquidator the amount of the sums so paid. The question is whether he had authority to make such an order.

The facts are these. The directors had for several years been in the habit of laying before the meetings of shareholders reports and balance-sheets which were substantially untrue, inasmuch as they included among the assets as good debts a number of debts which they knew to be bad. They thus made it appear that the business had produced profits when in fact it had produced none. The meetings acting on these reports declared dividends which the directors paid. The liquidator has taken out a summons to compel the directors to replace the sums so paid, and the Vice-Chancellor, following the decision in *In re National Funds Assurance Company* (1), made the order. . . .

A limited company by its memorandum of association declares that its capital is to be applied for the purposes of the business. It cannot reduce its capital except in the manner and with the safeguards provided by statute, and looking at the Act 40 & 41 Vict. c. 26, it clearly is against the intention of the Legislature that any portion of the capital should be returned to the shareholders without the statutory conditions being complied with. A limited company cannot in any other way make a return of capital, the sanction of a general meeting can give no validity to such a proceeding, and even the sanction of every shareholder cannot bring within the powers of the company an act which is not within its powers. If, therefore, the shareholders had all been

(1) 10 Ch. D. 118.

present at the meetings, and had all known the facts, and had all concurred in declaring the dividends, the payment of the dividends would not be effectually sanctioned. One reason is this—there is a statement that the capital shall be applied for the purposes of the business, and on the faith of that statement, which is sometimes said to be an implied contract with creditors, people dealing with the company give it credit. The creditor has no debtor but that impalpable thing the corporation, which has no property except the assets of the business. The creditor, therefore, I may say, gives credit to that capital, gives credit to the company on the faith of the representation that the capital shall be applied only for the purposes of the business, and he has therefore a right to say that the corporation shall keep its capital and not return it to the shareholders, though it may be a right which he cannot enforce otherwise than by a winding-up order. It follows then that if directors who are *quasi* trustees for the company improperly pay away the assets to the shareholders, they are liable to replace them. It is no answer to say that the shareholders could not compel them to do so. I am of opinion that the company could in its corporate capacity compel them to do so, even if there were no winding-up. They are liable to pay, and none the less liable because the liquidator represents, not only shareholders, but creditors. The body of the shareholders no doubt voted for a declaration of dividend on the faith of the misrepresentation of the directors, so that there really was no ratification at all. It is impossible to say to what extent the company and the share-holders may have been injured by these proceedings. It may be that this reduction of capital has been the cause of the ruin of the company, in which case the shareholders as such may have a right to complain of what has been done. It is not necessary, therefore, to refer to previous decisions to shew the principle on which the directors are held liable. If it be necessary to resort to the doctrine of implied contract *Evans* v. *Coventry* (1) is in point. The order of the Vice-Chancellor will therefore be affirmed, but with this variation, that the directors in each case are to be declared jointly and severally liable and not only jointly liable.

BRETT, L.J.:—

In this case the directors paid away part of the capital of the

(1) 8 D. M. & G. 835.

company for purposes not authorized by the memorandum or the articles of association. I cannot doubt that their doing so was a breach of trust. It is argued that the shareholders by accepting the dividends which were paid out of capital ratified what the directors had done, so that their acts cannot be treated as breaches of trust. I think that there was no ratification at all, because the assent of the shareholders was procured by improper accounts, the untruthfulness of which the shareholders did not know. But suppose they had known it, I think that what was done was a breach of trust which they could not ratify. If they had with full knowledge assumed to ratify what was done, they could not individually have complained, but the shareholders are not the corporation. In my opinion the corporation could at any time before the winding-up have compelled the directors to replace the moneys thus improperly expended, and the liquidator now can do so. Even if the shareholders had all sanctioned what was done, and had remained the same throughout, still the company could have sued the directors for a breach of trust. They are trustees for the company not for the individual shareholders. The liquidator represents the company, and is bound to discharge towards the creditors all the duties which the company owes them. It is therefore his duty when such a breach of trust as this is discovered to get a return of the assets improperly expended that they may be applied in payment of debts. . . .

IN RE ALEXANDRA PALACE COMPANY

21 L.R. Ch.149 (1882)
Chancery

Company—Winding-up—Director—Misfeasance—Payment of Dividend out of Capital—Money borrowed to pay Dividend—Measure of Damages—Shareholders and Creditors Parties to Breach of Trust—Indemnity--Delay—Stale Demand—Companies Act, 1862 (25 & 26 *Vict. c.* 89), *s.* 165 [*Revised Ed. Statutes, vol. xiv. p.* 238.]

The articles of association of a company provided that all dividends on shares should be made only out of the clear profits of the company, and that all moneys borrowed by the company and all moneys received under insurances of the company's property against destruction or damage by fire should be deemed capital.

A building of the company having been destroyed by fire, the company resolved to increase the capital by £150,000 for the purpose of reconstructing the building, and to issue for this purpose 15,000 preference shares. These shares were issued, and during the reconstruction of the building, no profits having been earned by the company, the directors paid four dividends on the shares. The first dividend was paid out of moneys received from an insurance company in respect of the loss occasioned by the fire. The other three dividends were paid by means of moneys borrowed expressly for the purpose from the contractors of the company and a financial company, both of whom had notice of the purpose for which the money was borrowed, and both of whom held a large number of the preference shares:— ....

This was a summons by the official liquidator of the *Alexandra Palace Company*, under sect. 165 of the *Companies Act*, 1862, asking that *James Goodson, M. J. Power, Henry Grüning, Charles Magnay*, Major *J. A. C. Gore*, and *James Murray*, formerly directors of the company, might be ordered to pay to the applicant jointly and severally the sum of £12,671 19s. 8d., being the aggregate amount of the several sums paid by them as directors of the company out of capital to the holders of 6 per cent. first preference shares of the company by way of interest upon the amounts paid up or credited thereon respectively, together with interest on the said sum of £12,671 19s. 8d., at the rate of 5 per cent. per annum, from the times at which the said several sums were respectively paid by way of interest. ...

The company was registered on the 13th of September, 1866. ...

liability of the members was limited, and the nominal capital of the company was fixed at £400,000, divided into 20,000 shares of £20 each.

The articles of association contained the following clauses :- ....

20. "The amount of all calls and moneys paid to the company in respect of shares, and all moneys borrowed, and all moneys raised or produced by sale, conversion, or realizing of the property or any part thereof, and all premiums on leases of the property or any part thereof; and all payments and considerations in money, shares, or securities for the concession of any rights, easements, or privileges in or over the property or any part thereof; and all moneys received under insurance of the property against destruction or damage by fire, or wreck, or perils of the sea, shall be deemed capital.

52. "All dividends and bonuses on shares shall be declared at the ordinary general meetings, and shall be made only out of the clear profits of the company; and no dividend or bonus shall exceed the sum recommended to the meeting by the board."

In December, 1866, the nominal capital of the company was increased to £550,000.

The company constructed on their land at *Muswell Hill* a large building known as the *Alexandra Palace*, which was opened to the public on the 24th of May, 1873. It was destroyed by fire on the 9th of June, 1873. The directors considered that it was necessary to raise £150,000 new capital for the purpose of rebuilding the Palace. A general meeting of the company was held on the 14th of July, 1873, when a special resolution was passed, which was confirmed on the 5th of August, 1873, to increase the capital from £550,000 to £700,000. And it was resolved that the £150,000 by which the capital was thus increased should be issued in 15,000 shares of £10 each, which should bear a preferential dividend of 6 per cent. per annum, and should rank in all respects in priority to the preference and ordinary shares theretofore issued. A prospectus was issued inviting applications for the new shares, which stated that £1 per share was to be paid on application, £1 10s. on allotment, £2 10s. on the 15th of October, 1873, £2 10s. on the 15th of January, 1874, and £2 10s. on the 15th of April, 1874, and that "interest will commence from the respective days of payment, but any applicant desirous of paying in full may do so in advance at any of the above dates."....

H. Burton Buckley, for *Magnay* :—

The dividends were not really paid out of capital. It is quite proper to debit to capital account the interest on capital expended on works, such as buildings, so long as they are unproductive during the period of construction. The value of a building is not merely the sums actually expended on it, but the interest which those sums would have produced had they been bearing interest during the period of construction. . . .

FRY, J. (after stating the nature of the application and referring to the above-stated clauses of the company's articles of association), continued :—

According to the view which I take to be the reasonable one of the construction of these articles, I think that the interest which would be payable on the new shares must be either dividend or in the nature of dividend, and that it is payable only out of the profits of the company. [His Lordship then read the resolutions of the meeting of the 14th of July, 1873, and continued :—]

It has been argued that by those resolutions the company undertook to pay the dividends on the new shares out of funds other than profits ; but it appears to me that they bear no such construction. The only right given to the new shareholders is a right to a preferential dividend, but under the articles of association every dividend is payable out of profits, and out of profits only. . . .

In January, 1874, the company borrowed £2050 from Messrs. *Kelk & Lucas,* and a similar sum from the *London Financial Association,* and a portion of those sums was applied legitimately in payment of the debts of the company, but, to the extent of £1436 6s. 8d., the sums so borrowed were applied in paying what was called a dividend upon the preference shares. In no proper sense was it a dividend, because there were no profits out of which to pay it, and it was certainly in substance a payment out of the capital of the company. . . .

Again, in July of the same year another transaction took place of a very analogous description. Sums of £3000 each were borrowed from Messrs. *Kelk & Lucas* and the *London Financial Association,* and warrants were issued for the payment of dividends to the preference shareholders to the extent of £3838 18s. 1d., which were accordingly paid out of the £6000 thus borrowed.. . .

Similar observations apply to the sums of £4462 10s. 0d. and £2934 4s. 11d. which in January and June, 1875, respectively were borrowed and applied in payment of the dividend warrants of the company. . . .

These being the short facts of the case, numerous arguments have been addressed to me. The official liquidator says that this is a clear case of payment of dividend out of the capital of the company. On the other hand it is contended, in the first place, that it is not a payment out of capital at all. Mr. *Buckley* has very ingeniously argued that this was really a payment out of profits (so at least I understood his argument), because, he says, you are entitled to compute interest on the money you lay out before it becomes remunerative, and to treat that interest as profit and divide it accordingly among the shareholders. I cannot yield to that argument. It appears to me that the calculation which is suggested is a mere "paper" transaction, to use a common expression, and to say that a company can pay their shareholders interest, because they can compute interest on the money they choose to lay out in building, and which is for the time being unproductive, is not an argument which can commend itself to the Court.

In the next place, Mr. *Karslake*, with more courage, has argued that it was necessary for the company to raise this money, and that they could not raise it except upon the terms of paying interest on it during the course of the construction of the building, and that, therefore, despite the clear language of the articles of association, they were at liberty so to do. That argument I cannot yield to for one moment. I do know the obligation which rests on directors to be honest, but I know of no obligation to pay dividends unless they have profits out of which to pay them.

That view is one which it appears to me necessary to enforce strongly, considering the nature of the arguments which have been addressed to me, and I cannot enforce it more strongly than by calling attention to the language of Lord *Hatherley* (when Vice-Chancellor *Wood*) in *Macdougall* v. *Jersey Imperial Hotel Company* (1). That case came before the Court on a demurrer, and the Vice-Chancellor said, "The bill avers that there are no profits, and that interest has been paid, or is about to be paid, out of capital; that the shareholders have paid £4 per share, and are discharged to that extent, and that they are now about to

(1) 2 H. & M. 528, 535.

take back sums equal to £5 per cent. of that very capital in the shape of interest" (which is exactly what has been done here) "On grounds of public policy, and on every principle, not only of honesty as regards the public generally, but of the interests of this company itself, I feel bound to prevent this proceeding. This is not in accordance with the contract entered into with the Legislature on behalf of the public, whereby it was determined that the shareholders should be liable to a certain defined amount and no more, to the creditors of the company, and not in accordance with the contract between the parties, whereby each shareholder was protected against creditors to the extent of the contributive liability of all the others." In my view that lays down the law with perfect precision, and I think no subterfuge by which it is attempted to return capital to shareholders, and thereby to diminish their liability, ought to be countenanced for one moment by this Court. I confess it was with some surprise that I heard the argument addressed to me at the Bar, that the directors were at liberty to pay this money out of capital, because otherwise they could not carry on their undertaking. . . .

LAMBERT v. THE NEUCHATEL ASPHALTE COMPANY (LIMITED)

51 L.J. Ch.882 (1882)
Vice Chancellor - Chancery

The company was incorporated in 1873, with a capital of 1,150,000*l.*, divided into 35,000 preferred and 80,000 ordinary shares of 10*l.* each. By article 97, "the net profits of the company shall be applied and divided as follows :—First, a dividend at the rate of seven per cent. per annum shall be paid on the preferred shares, in proportion to the amount for the time being paid up or deemed to have been paid up thereon. And subject to the payment of such dividend as aforesaid, a like dividend shall be paid on the ordinary shares. And after payment of such dividends as aforesaid on all the shares, the surplus of the net profits shall be distributed by way of dividend rateably amongst all the shareholders in such proportion as aforesaid, but without preference or distinction.

" 98. No such distribution of profits shall be made without the consent of a general meeting. It shall, however, be competent to the directors without such sanction, in the interval between two meetings, to declare an interim dividend on the preferred shares, at any rate not exceeding seven per cent., and on the ordinary shares not exceeding four per cent.

" 99. In the case of any dispute as to the amount of net profits, the decision of the company in general meeting shall be final.

" 100. The directors may, before recommending any dividend on any of the shares, set aside out of the net profits of the company such fund as they may think proper as a reserved fund to meet contingencies, or for equalising dividends, or for repairing or maintaining the works connected with the business of the company, or any part thereof, and the directors may invest the sum so set apart as a reserved fund, or any part thereof, upon such securities as they may select, but they shall not be bound to form a fund, or otherwise reserve moneys for the renewal or replacing of any lease, or of the company's interest in any property or concession."

The company worked under a concession from the Neuchatel government, which was originally determinable on the 14th of December, 1887, but was prolonged till 1907. The consideration paid in shares and cash for the purchase of the said concession, and the goodwill and assets of various companies interested therein, and for procuring the prolongation of the said concession, amounted altogether to 1,058,303*l.* 15*s.* 1*d.*, of which 8,000*l.* only was paid in cash.

Up till 1875 the company carried on business at a loss. In 1876 and 1877 a small profit was made. In 1878, 1879, and 1880 profits were made amounting to 7,993*l.* 7*s.* 6*d.*, 8,165*l.* 12*s.* 1*d.*, and 8,793*l.* 4*s.* 5*d.*, respectively.

The directors declared payment of dividends on the preference shares, but had not set apart any reserve fund, except a sum of 2,000*l.* in 1880 and 1881.

This action was brought by the plaintiff on behalf of himself and all ordinary shareholders, claiming a declaration that, for the purpose of ascertaining the "net profits" applicable for payment of dividends to the preference shareholders, the directors ought, in the first instance, to capitalise out of the gross profits a sum sufficient to replace, by means of a sinking fund or otherwise, the capital lost or expended in the purchase of the wasting property of the company, and an injunction. . . .

BACON, V.C.—This case appears to me to depend entirely on the articles of association. The Court never interferes with the internal arrangements made by companies. The case of *Mozley* v. *Alston* (4) established that as a principle of law. The Court will interfere to redress any wrongs, but the Court never interferes to prescribe to companies what they shall do as to their own internal affairs. That is a principle which is clearly established. That principle applies to this case. It is not that principle alone ; it is the very terms of the articles. There are two classes of shareholders, one called emphatically the preferred shareholders, and the other called the ordinary shareholders. Their rights are clearly defined by the articles of association. The right of the preferred shareholders is to have seven per cent. out of the available assets of the company—available, I mean, for the purpose of distribution and division among the shareholders. The net profits, no doubt, in the universal and general sense, are that which was described in the two cases of *Davison* v. *Gillies* (2) and *Dent* v. *The London Tramways Company* (1), before the Master of the Rolls, and the case of *The Coltness Iron Company* v. *Black* (3) in the House of Lords. It is after the payment of all that is due, that which remains, as one may say, in the till of the company. It is not the sense in which the term "net profits" is used in these articles. It does not signify in what order the clauses of the articles are to be found, but reading the 99th article, as the first article we have to deal with, it says, "In case of dispute as to the amount of net profits, the decision of the company in general meeting shall be final." Can I abrogate that provision? Can I say that anything which I think is net profits is to be net profits if the vote at a general meeting decides that something else shall be net profits. That is a contract between the parties. They have themselves put their own interpretation upon it. They say nothing shall be net profits other than that which we have agreed in general meeting are net profits. That being so, there is the 97th article. [His Lordship read it and continued:] Now if at a general meeting it has been determined that the net profits shall be only a certain sum, no matter what it is, that sum, and that sum only, becomes net profits, and those net profits are to be divided so as to give the preference shareholders seven per cent. upon their respective shares. The difficulty is entirely at an end. I have no authority over this. I have no right to say to a general meeting, "You shall not hold so and so to be net profits." They will say, "It is our affair; we have the right to decide." And at a general meeting, if they think it right that a sum of 2,000*l.* should be set aside, as was done on a former occasion, or 10,000*l.*, or any other sum which they may think it right to carry to a reserve fund, what remains after that deduction is net profits applicable for and

divisible to the payments of dividends, and nothing else. I will not go one step beyond these articles. I will not prescribe to the company, or to the directors, or to the shareholders, what one is to do, or what the other is entitled to have done, for they have by their written contract decided that the shareholders in general meeting shall determine what is the amount of net profits—net profits being the thing which is applicable and divisible in the shape of dividends. It seems to me to relieve the case of any difficulty or doubt. The power of the directors in the 100th article, the greater part of which is transcribed from Table A in the Companies Act, 1862, is, first, to authorise them to set out of the net profits such sum as they think proper as a reserve fund to meet contingencies. What they will do with that is for their directors' discretion, and they will exercise it; what they will include in contingencies is not for me to say or to suggest to them—"or for equalising dividends, or for repairing or maintaining the works connected with the business of the company, or any part thereof; and the directors may invest the sum so set apart as a reserved fund, or any part thereof, upon such securities as they may select"—that is a power which the directors have, that and nothing else. Then it provides further, "but they shall not be bound to form a fund, or otherwise reserve moneys for the renewal or replacing of any lease, or of the company's interest in any property or concession." That refers again to the 99th article, which has vested in the shareholders at a general meeting the power of deciding, when they are deciding what are net profits, what other net profits shall be carried to a reserve fund. As they think right to vote, so it is to be. In this case, there is nothing but the articles to go upon. If there is no infraction of the articles, I have no right to interfere with the affairs of the company. The articles appear to me to have been properly followed so far as the matter has gone, and upon the question of net profits all that is necessary is that a meeting shall be called; the votes at that meeting will declare what are net profits, and the net profits so ascertained will become divisible according to the terms of the articles. I am asked to make an order in the terms of the claim, " that it may be declared that for the purpose of ascertaining the net profits of the defendant company applicable to payment of dividends to the preferred shareholders, the directors of the defendant company ought in the first instance to set apart and capitalise out of the gross profits of the defendant company such a sum as shall be necessary to replace, by means of a sinking fund or otherwise, the capital lost or sunk or expended in the purchase of the wasting property of the defendant company." I have no right to make any such order. The articles have declared that the directors shall not be bound. It is not for me to bind the directors to do something which under the terms of the articles they are not bound to do, more especially since I find that the articles expressly provide the means by which disputes between these classes of shareholders may be settled, as they only properly can be settled, by the votes of the general meeting. I have nothing to do therefore but to dismiss this action. It ought never to have been instituted, because if any one had taken the trouble to read the articles, he would have found that the Court had no power to direct the directors to do that which the articles say they shall not be bound to do. Moreover, the articles have provided for the means of ascertaining what are net profits.

If you will all agree to it, I will make no order as to costs. The directors, of course, must have their costs out of the funds of the company. If you will agree to there being no costs, I shall be just as well pleased; but if you will not agree, then I can only dismiss it with the ordinary results.

Marten, Q.C.—The directors were advised not to pay any dividend. That being so, things came to a deadlock until the decision of the Court could be obtained. The action should be dismissed without costs, having been invited by the directors. Before the litigation, they sent round the opinion of counsel, which was their justification for not paying any dividends.

BACON, V.C.—I think under these circumstances the best thing to do will be to dismiss the action without costs.

141

IN RE FRANK MILLS MINING COMPANY

L.R. 23 Ch. 52 (1883)
Court of Appeal

In re FRANK MILLS MINING COMPANY.

Cost-book Mine—Retiring Shareholder—Contribution.

THIS company was formed on the cost-book principle for working a mine in *Devonshire* without any written regulations.

H. W. Clarke had been a holder of shares in the company for many years prior to June, 1877, but on the 21st of that month he retired from the company. On the 4th of January, 1879, he became the holder of 110 shares, and continued to hold them till the 15th of November, 1879, when he gave notice to the purser to relinquish them. The number of shares at this time was 1279. It appeared that the practice of such companies was that when a shareholder retired by relinquishing his shares an account was made out by the purser shewing the assets and liabilities of the mine, and that if the balance was adverse the shareholder retired on paying to the purser his *pro ratâ* share of the balance. *Clarke* wrote to the purser asking for an account, but no account was sent him. On the 6th of March, 1880, an order was made in the Stannaries Court for winding up the company.

The liquidator, in April, 1882, filed an account between the company and *Clarke* for the purpose of shewing what was payable by *Clarke*. In estimating the assets of the company he deducted from £1960 10s., the amount of the arrears of calls made in 1878, the sum of £959 10s. as irrecoverable, and from £7692, the amount of arrears of calls made in 1879, the sum of £4068 as irrecoverable, and he inserted the amount of the valuation of plant at £1714 12s. The excess of liabilities over assets, as shewn by the account, was £8077 11s. 6d. He then excluded 678 shares as being held by insolvent persons, leaving 601 shares. He claimed from *Clarke* the payment of 110 equal 601st parts of the above excess of liabilities over assets. . . .

JESSEL, M.R. :—

This appeal raises a question of great importance. I do not profess to know what the customs relating to mines on the cost-book system are, but they can, to some extent, be gathered from decided cases. It would appear from the case of *In re Prosper United Mining Company* (1) that such a company is in most respects a common partnership, but that there is a power for any partner to retire at any time upon terms. What are those terms? Put broadly they come to this, that if at the date of retirement the concern is insolvent, the retiring partner pays his share of the deficiency as if the concern were being wound up, but if the concern is solvent then he is entitled to receive his share of the surplus left on deducting the liabilities from the value of the assets. In either case, whether the company be solvent or insolvent, the valuation of the assets must be made on the footing of the company being a going concern. As to the retiring partner's share in the liabilities, if the concern were wound up, he would have to pay his share, having regard to the solvency or insolvency of the other shareholders. He would along with the other solvent shareholders have to make good to the creditors of the company what the insolvent shareholders could not pay. He must on retiring pay on the same footing. This is his position according to the case of *In re Prosper United Mining Company* and according to common sense. If this is the ordinary custom of cost-book mines, and if this is a company on the cost-book system, the only question is whether any agreement between the parties is shewn to have existed which takes the case out of the ordinary rule. In most mines under the cost-book system there are written rules which more or less vary the custom, either by way of superseding it or adding to it. But in the absence of written rules there still may be a variation of the custom by agreement, and the question is how the existence of an agreement having that effect is to be ascertained.

I agree that an express contract is not necessary, and that a contract between the partners may be implied from the course of practice. The question then is whether in the present case there is sufficient evidence of an implied contract to vary the custom. It is said that there is, for that when a shareholder relinquished his shares the company being at the time insolvent, the settled

(1) Law Rep. 7 Ch. 286.

143

practice was that the excess of liabilities over assets was divided by the number of shares, and what the retiring shareholder had to pay was ascertained by multiplying this quotient by the number of shares he held, without having any regard to the solvency of the continuing shareholders. It is said that this practice is sufficient evidence (and some evidence it, no doubt, is) that there was an agreement that the liability of a retiring shareholder should be ascertained in this way. On looking at the accounts it does appear that this course was always followed, and it also appears that in every case the arrears of calls were taken at their full amount as assets, which it is contended is evidence of a contract that the liability of the retiring shareholder should be ascertained without making allowance for any of the arrears being bad debts. This appears to me to be an absurd conclusion. The only other conclusion is that the purser blundered in making out his accounts. It must be remembered that the effect of a course of practice in a large company is very different from that of a course of practice in a common partnership, where every partner attends to the business and is privy to all that is done. The inference to be deduced from the mode in which the accounts have been made out is not nearly so strong in the former case as in the latter. It appears to me to be impossible in the case before us to draw from the course followed on former occasions the inference that there was a contract that bad debts should be treated as good, or that shareholders should be allowed to retire on paying a sum manifestly much less than they would have to pay if the concern were wound up. I think the only conclusion to be drawn is that the purser blundered in making out the accounts. The order therefore appears to me to go on a right principle, but it cannot be supported as it stands, because no allowance is made for sums which have been paid by some of the shareholders who were treated in the account as not able to pay anything, and it does not have regard to the fact that the calculation must be made according to the state of affairs at the time when the notice of withdrawal was given, at which time some of the shareholders who are now insolvent may have been perfectly solvent.

It is said that the plan on which the purser made out the account is very convenient and simple, and that this is a reason why the shareholders may be supposed to have agreed to it. It is very convenient and simple, and that is the reason no doubt why the purser adopted it, but I do not think that a sufficient reason for holding that the continuing shareholders agreed that the accounts should be made out in a way so inconsistent with reason and principle. No balance-sheet can ever be made out for any useful purpose without distinguishing good, bad, and doubtful debts. You cannot properly put down a single debt as an asset without some consideration of the circumstances of the debtor.

There is another point to be considered. The Appellant says that he is entitled to have the assets valued as in a going concern, which this was when he gave notice of retirement. I think he is so entitled. The continuing shareholders took it as a going concern, and the assets must be valued on that footing. It has been disputed whether the liquidator has not valued the assets on this principle. I find, however, that he valued the plant at £1714, and that it has since been sold for upwards of £1600 as broken up. This to my mind is conclusive proof that he valued it at breaking-up price, for I never knew plant which was valued at £1700 as part of a going concern realize anything like £1600 when broken up.

I think that the costs should be left to be dealt with by the Vice-Warden, for it may turn out that the Appellant derives a substantial benefit from the appeal. . . .

IN RE OXFORD BENEFIT BUILDING
AND INVESTMENT SOCIETY

35 L.R. Ch. 502 (1886)
Chancery

Company—Winding-up—Directors—Misfeasance—Rate of Interest charged—Payment of Dividends out of Capital — " Realized Profits "—Directors' Remuneration.

The articles of association of a limited company provided that no dividends should be payable except out of " realized profits," and that no remuneration should be paid to the directors until a dividend of 7 per cent. had been paid to the shareholders. The business of the company consisted chiefly in lending money to builders on mortgages payable by instalments, and the directors treated, as part of the profits available for dividends, the value for the time being (upon an estimate made by their surveyor who was also their secretary) of the instalments of principal and interest remaining unpaid by each mortgagor. Upon this footing the directors paid for several years, out of the floating capital from time to time in their hands, (1) dividends of 7½ per cent. and upwards; (2) remuneration to themselves. Upon a summons taken out in the winding-up of the company by a creditor :—

Held, that " realized profits " must be taken in its ordinary commercial sense as meaning at least " profits tangible for the purpose of division," and that the directors having treated estimated profits as realized profits, and having in fact paid dividends out of capital, on the chance that sufficient profits might be made, were jointly and severally liable, as upon a breach of trust, to repay, and must repay, the sums improperly paid as dividends, and also the remuneration they had respectively received, with interest in each case at 4 per cent.

The directors also, without the knowledge of the shareholders, voted and paid themselves out of the funds of the company a commission on certain purchases and sales, and entered such payment in the books of the company, but made no mention of it in their reports or balance-sheets :—

Held, that they were jointly and severally liable to repay, and must repay, this amount with interest at 5 per cent.

THIS was a summons in the winding-up of this company taken out by a creditor under the 165th section of the *Companies Act,* 1862, for the purpose of obtaining from five of the directors repayment of various sums, amounting to upwards of £40,000, alleged to have been misapplied by them out of the funds of the company.

The company was a building and investment company formed in February, 1866, for the purpose of dealing in land and securities, and the principal charges against the directors were, first, that from the commencement they continually paid to the shareholders dividends out of capital; and, secondly, that they paid to themselves remuneration to which they were not entitled.

The articles of association of the company material to the first charge were as follows :—

Article 102 directed that the directors should cause true accounts to be kept in books of account.

Article 104 directed that in every year the directors should lay before the shareholders in general meeting a statement of the income and expenditure of the company.

Articles 105 and 106 provided as follows :—

" 105. The statement so made shall shew arranged under the most convenient heads the amount of gross income, distinguishing the several sources from which it has been derived, and the amount of gross expenditure, distinguishing the expenses of the establishment, salaries, and other like matters. Every item of expenditure fairly chargeable against the year's income shall be brought into account, so that a just balance of profit and loss may be laid before the meeting ; and in cases where any item of expenditure which may in fairness be distributed over one or several years has been incurred in any one year the whole amount of such item shall be stated, with the addition of the reasons why only a portion of such expenditure is charged against the income of the year.

" 106. A balance-sheet shall be made out and laid before each ordinary general meeting of the company, and such balance-sheet shall contain a summary of the property and liabilities of the company, arranged under proper distinguishing heads so as to present an accurate and comprehensive view of the financial position of the company."

Then, after providing for the audit of the accounts, by the 120th article, the directors were empowered with the sanction of the company in general meeting to declare a dividend or bonus to be paid to the shareholders in proportion to their shares, and the 121st and 122nd articles were in these words :—

" 121. No dividend shall be payable except out of the realized profits arising from the business of the company.

"122. Previously to the directors recommending any dividend or bonus they may set aside out of the profits of the company such sum as they may think proper as a reserve fund, and shall invest the sum so set apart upon government securities, parliamentary stocks or funds, or real securities as they may think fit."

Article 61, upon which the second charge against the directors arose, will be found in the judgment of the Court.

The business of the company chiefly consisted in making loans to persons about to build upon mortgage of the buildings to be erected, which loans were repayable by small instalments extending over a period of fourteen years. It was the practice of the directors to estimate the profits of the company available for dividend by making out an account of liabilities and assets and treating the excess of the amount of assets over liabilities as profits. The most important item of assets in the account was "present value of repayments and value of properties in hand." This value was arrived at by calculating from year to year upon a 5 per cent. annuity table the present value of the instalments of principal and interest remaining unpaid by each mortgagor. The only valuation the directors had made and that on which they acted was one made from time to time by a Mr. *Galpin*, who was their surveyor and also their secretary. And it was the practice of the directors after making a loan to treat the accretion due to this calculation, amounting sometimes to 17 per cent., as a realized profit; and they paid dividends on this basis in several years amounting to 10 per cent., but always, except in one year, exceeding 7½ per cent. These payments were in fact made out of the floating capital from time to time in the hands of the directors, and upon the assumption that the mortgage securities they had taken were sufficient to repay the loans they had made with interest and costs, which turned out in very many instances not to be the case.

Three of the Respondents to this summons, viz., Messrs. *Saunders, Cavill,* and *Wheeler,* had been directors from the formation of the company, and the other two, Messrs. *Scroggs* and *Bravington,* were appointed co-directors with them on the 2nd of May, 1876. On the 17th of April, 1883, a resolution was passed for the voluntary winding-up of the company, and on the 11th of May, 1884, an order was made that the voluntary winding-up should be continued under the supervision of the Court.

The remainder of the facts and the evidence in support of the summons sufficiently appear from the judgment of Mr. Justice *Kay*.

The summons was adjourned into Court and now came on for hearing.

Hastings, Q.C., *Ashton Cross*, and *Hamilton*, in support of the summons :—

1. The directors have habitually calculated their assets for the purpose of dividends upon the footing of including as realized profits estimated profits, *i.e.*, payments which had not been, and in very many instances never were made, without making any allowance for bad debts or depreciation of property ; and they have paid the dividends out of the floating capital in their hands. There is no suggestion that they did so fraudulently, but they are trustees, or *quasi* trustees, of the capital of the company, and this course was *ultrà vires* and incapable of ratification by the shareholders, and therefore the *bona fides* and good intentions of the directors can be no defence as against a creditor of the company: *Flitcroft's Case* (1) ; *Salisbury* v. *Metropolitan Railway Company* (2). They had no proper valuation. Their balance-sheet contained no profit and loss account, and it lies on them to shew that the dividend was properly paid out of profits : *Rance's Case* (3). The payment of dividends out of capital is a breach of trust which directors are jointly and severally liable to make good with interest at 4 per cent. at all events : *Evans* v. *Coventry* (4) ; *Salisbury* v. *Metropolitan Railway Company* ; *In re National Funds Assurance Company* (5). Even 5 per cent. has been allowed : *In re Alexandra Palace Company* (6).

2. The 61st article of association provides that " no remuneration shall be paid to the said directors until a dividend at the rate of 7½ per cent. shall have been paid to the shareholders ; " and as no dividend of 7½ per cent. was ever properly paid, the directors never were entitled to any remuneration at all.

(1) 21 Ch. D. 519. (4) 8 D. M. & G. 835, 845.
(2) 22 L. T. (N.S.) 839. (5) 10 Ch. D. 118.
(3) Law Rep. 6 Ch. 104. (6) 21 Ch. D. 149, 163.

Sir *H. Davey*, Q.C., and *Maclean*, Q.C., for the Respondents, Messrs. *Saunders, Cavill, and Wheeler* :—

These directors were large original shareholders and bought further shares at a premium; their interests were identical with those of the other shareholders, and they have not been guilty of any misfeasance from which they have derived advantage. The evidence shews that they honestly valued their assets through their surveyor, that they had not been party to any dividend which they did not consider had been properly earned, and that if the dividends had been paid out of cash profits only the business could not have been carried on.

Where directors acting *bonâ fide* in the discharge of their duty have honestly valued their assets and have paid a dividend in accordance with that valuation, the Court will not, although the valuation subsequently turns out to be over sanguine and erroneous, order them to repay the moneys they have so paid away, even those paid to themselves : *Stringer's Case* (1); *London Financial Association* v. *Kelk* (2); *In re National Funds Assurance Company* (3); *In re Denham & Co.* (4): *Joint Stock Discount Company* v. *Brown* (5); *Pickering* v. *Stephenson* (6); *Studdert* v. *Grosvenor* (7). In *Rance's Case* (8) there was fraud. In *City of Glasgow Bank* v. *Mackinnon* (9), where it was sought to make a director liable for the payment of interest out of capital, the directors who had acted *bonâ fide* were held not to be liable although their estimate was erroneous, and their valuation turned out to be inaccurate. According to Lord *Shand* (10) " it is clear that it is not necessary that there must be cash realized, and in the coffers of the bank, received expressly on account of interest or profits, in order to justify the payment of a dividend. To enforce such a rule would be to run counter to ordinary and reasonable usage in the case of mercantile companies. In order to ascertain the profits earned and divisible at any given time, the balance-sheet

150

(1) Law Rep. 4 Ch. 475, 486.
(2) 26 Ch. D. 107, 143, 144.
(3) 10 Ch. D. 118.
(4) 25 Ch. D. 752.
(5) Law Rep. 3 Eq. 139; 8 Eq. 381.
(6) Law Rep. 14 Eq. 322.
(7) 33 Ch. D. 528.
(8) Law Rep. 6 Ch. 104.
(9) 19 Sc. Law Rep. 278; 9 Court Sess. Cas. 4th Series, 535.
(10) 19 Sc. Law Rep. 316; 9 Court Sess. Cas. 4th Series, 602.

must contain a fair statement of the liabilities of the company, including its paid-up capital; and, on the other hand, a fair or more properly *boná fide* valuation of assets, the balance, if in favour of the company, being profits. These profits may, and must often to a great extent, be represented by obligations of debtors, often secured, and by direct securities over property. They are not the less profits fairly realized and divisible because they exist in that form and have not been received in cash;" and that is applicable to the present case. Here the value of the security should in fairness be taken not at its value now, but at its value at the time of the valuation, when the company was a going concern, and before the great depreciation which has since taken place. The expression "realized profit" only means "real profit honestly earned" or "profit made," and if the security given is sufficient the profit is made.

[KAY, J.:—Surely "realized profit" cannot be the same as "estimated profit," and is used as a word of contrast.]

"Realized profit" need not be cash profit actually in hand. All profit is a matter of estimate—the balance of assets and liabilities. It is only a question of a proper margin. If a banker discounts a bill he rebates it and divides the difference as profit. But whatever be the meaning of "realized profits" the course of dealing has been ratified by the shareholders; and the clause where the expression occurs is one relating to the rights of the shareholders *inter se*, and the prohibition it contains could be and must after the lapse of sixteen years be held, even without express ratification by the shareholders, to have been waived by them, and their ratification, waiver, or acquiescence would be fatal to any claim of the creditors, for whom the directors of a going concern cannot be said to be trustees: "The creditors have certain rights against a company and its members, but they have no greater rights against the directors than against any other members of the company:" *Poole, Jackson, and Whyte's Case* (1); *Phosphate of Lime Company* v. *Green* (2); *Ashbury Railway Carriage and Iron Company* v. *Riche* (3); *Waterhouse* v. *Jamieson* (4); *Eley* v.

(1) 9 Ch. D. 322, 328.　　　　　　(3) Law Rep. 7 H. L. 653.
(2) Law Rep. 7 C. P. 43.　　　　　(4) Ibid. 2 H. L., Sc. 29.

Positive Government Security Life Assurance Company (1); *In re Empress Engineering Company* (2). Moreover, there is no sufficient evidence that any dividend was actually paid out of capital; and the directors, who could not value for themselves, employed *Galpin*, a surveyor, who was competent, and none the less so because he was their secretary, and were justified in relying on his valuation : *Stringer's Case* (3) ; *Parker* v. *McKenna* (4); *City of Glasgow Bank* v. *Mackinnon* (5).

Buckley, for the Respondents *Scroggs* and *Bravington* :—

These directors were not original directors, but joined the board after the company was an established concern ; and they simply continued in perfect good faith what they believed to be a sound and proper course of business. What are "realized profits " cannot be ascertained except by estimate, in which future loss and future profit must be taken into account, and the question is not whether the surveyor of the directors made a mistake in his valuation, but whether they themselves acted with *bona fides*.

Creed, for the Liquidator.

Hastings, in reply :—

" Realized profits " must be profits actually got, and not profits expected to be received ; and the evidence does not shew that profits had been honestly earned. Neither *Salisbury* v. *Metropolitan Railway Company* (6) nor *Evans* v. *Coventry* (7) were cited in *London Financial Association* v. *Kelk* (8), and none of the cases cited shew that in order to render directors liable it is necessary to prove fraud or gross negligence. If they pay dividends out of capital they are liable, whether they have done so in good faith or not.

1886. Nov. 8. KAY, J. :—

The first and most important charge against the directors is, that from the commencement of the company they have continu-

(1) 1 Ex. D. 20, 88.
(2) 16 Ch. D. 125.
(3) Law Rep. 4 Ch. 475, 486.
(4) Law Rep. 10 Ch. 96.

(5) 19 Sc. Law Rep. 1881, 273 ;
9 Court Sess. Cas. 4th Series, 535.
(6) 22 L. T. (N.S.) 839.
(7) 8 D. M. & G. 835.
(8) 26 Ch. D. 107, 144.

ally paid dividends out of capital. It was argued that even if that were so they could not be made liable unless their conduct amounted to fraud. From that proposition I must express my dissent.

It is settled by authorities which I cannot dispute—

1. That directors are *quasi* trustees of the capital of the company.

2. Directors who improperly pay dividends out of capital are liable to repay such dividends personally upon the company being wound up.

3. This liability may be enforced by a creditor or by the liquidator, under sect. 165 of the Act of 1862, or by the incorporated company before a winding-up.

4. The acquiescence of the shareholders does not affect the creditors in such a case.

5. Such an act is a breach of trust, and the remedy is not barred by the *Statute of Limitations.*

These points were determined in *Evans* v. *Coventry* (1), *Salisbury* v. *Metropolitan Railway Company* (2), *In re National Funds Assurance Company* (3), and in *Flitcroft's Case* (4).

A question has been raised and much argued concerning the meaning of the provisions of the articles of this company relating to the payment of dividends.

The company was a building and investment company. Its business consisted in lending money, generally at 8½ per cent., to persons who were building, the security taken being a mortgage of the property to be built on. The terms of such mortgages were, that the principal and interest should be paid by a number of small equal instalments extending over a period of fourteen years.

Three-fourths of these loans, roughly speaking, were to speculative builders, most of whom had only agreements with the landowners.

In such a business it must often be necessary to take possession of and realize the security, and it was essential that the securities should in every case be sufficient to provide for principal, interest, and costs.

The payments made every year by borrowers would consist

(1) 8 D. M. & G. 835.	(3) 10 Ch. D. 118.
(2) 22 L. T. (N.S.) 839.	(4) 21 Ch. D. 519.

partly of interest and partly of principal; and I agree with the expert witnesses who say that it would not be proper to treat the proportion of interest as being invariable. In the case of each loan the first payment would include the full interest to that time. The rest would be principal, and the next payment would include interest only on the balance of the principal, and so on, the interest being thus diminished after every payment which reduced the principal of the loan. [His Lordship then read the articles of association of the company material to the first charge down to the 121st, and continued:—]

Having listened with attention to all the arguments addressed to me on the meaning of the word "realized" in article 121, which provides that "no dividends shall be paid except out of the realized profits arising from the business of the company," I must say that my opinion has never wavered for a moment. If there were nothing else than what I have read I should hold without hesitation that "realized" must there have its ordinary commercial meaning, which, if not equivalent to "reduced to actual cash in hand," must at least be "rendered tangible for the purpose of division." The article is in a negative form. It is a prohibition against payment, and against the payment of dividends except out of realized profits arising from the business of the company. The precise thing intended to be prohibited is the payment of dividends in respect of "estimated" profits as distinguished from "realized." The meaning of the word in this article is the direct converse of the word "estimated." This is my conclusion from the language of art. 121 itself. It is confirmed, I think, by the next article, the 122nd, which is worded thus:—[Here his Lordship read that article, and continued:—]

The reserve fund contemplated is clearly a realized fund which can be invested, and the direction to invest it is imperative, and if there could be any reasonable doubt as to the meaning of art. 121 this would remove it. The dividend is payable out of the residue of the realized profits after setting apart and investing a portion of them.

The suggestion that the word "realized" may be rejected when it is the emphatic word in the article, or that it means no more than "real profits honestly earned," I cannot accede to.

There is no dispute about what the directors did and omitted to do. They never submitted to any general meeting an account of income or expenditure, so that a just balance of profit and loss might be laid before the meeting as directed by art. 105. No profit and loss account was ever made at all.

I have before me the reports and balance-sheets from the commencement of the company which were presented to the general meetings. I believe that there is no substantial difference between them. Taking the first, from the registration of the company to the 12th of March, 1867, the report states that the net profit in the financial year which they had to deal with was £392 11s. The balance-sheet shews how this was arrived at. On the one side there is a single entry: "The present value of repayments on mortgages held by the company for sums advanced to borrowers, £6293 19s. 11d." On the other side are entered the amount of paid-up capital, the amount of money borrowed, certain proportions of the preliminary and management expenses, some of which were spread over several years, a dividend to the shareholders at 7½ per cent., and then a balance which is stated to be carried forward, but was not in fact carried forward, the sum of these amounts being equal to the estimated sum on the other side. And precisely the same operation was repeated every year, there being no attempt to form any reserve fund, no provision for possible bad debts, losses, or expenses, except that they did not in any year divide the whole of the estimated profits, but left an imaginary balance, which, of course, could neither be realized nor invested.

Now the basis of this estimate in every case was an assumption that everyone of the securities on which the company were advancing money was ample to provide for principal, interest and costs in respect of the advance. And for this they had nothing but the assurance of the surveyor and secretary, Mr. *Galpin*. He it was also who estimated, according to the 5 per cent. table, the present value of the instalments which each mortgagor had to pay. The auditors neither checked the valuation of the securities nor the actuarial estimate of the mortgagors' repayments, and yet the directors, who were forbidden by their articles to pay any dividends, except out of realized profits, paid every dividend out of whatever moneys they happened to have in hand, which has been called in the argument the floating capital, and never attempted in any report or balance-sheet to distinguished realized profits from the estimated profits which they thus purported to divide, or to ascertain out of what fund the dividends were actually paid.

It has been argued that this was done *bonâ fide,* and that where directors in good faith have made an error in the computation on which their balance-sheets are founded, the Court will not lightly visit them with the consequences of a *bonâ fide* mistake. I confess I hardly know what is meant by *bona fides* in such an argument. I inquired whether there was any evidence that the directors had considered the meaning of the articles or had taken any advice upon them. There is no suggestion that they ever did so. There is nothing obscure or difficult in the construction, and it seems to me incredible that any man of business could suppose that this course of proceeding was a division of realized profits.

I adopt the language of the late Master of the Rolls in *In re National Funds Assurance Co.* (1): "A man may not intend to commit a fraud, or may not intend to do anything which casuists might call immoral, and he may be told that to misapply money is the right thing to do, but when he has the facts before him —when the plain and patent facts are brought to his knowledge— as I have often said, and I say now again, I will not dive into the recesses of his mind to say whether he believed, when he was doing a dishonest act, that he was doing an honest one. .... It is impossible in a Court of Justice to call a particular act a *bonâ fide* act simply because a man says that he did not intend to commit a fraud. .... When a man misappropriates money with a knowledge of all the facts, I cannot allow him to say that he is not liable simply because somebody or other told him that he was not doing wrong, or that somehow or other he convinced himself that he was not doing wrong."

On this head it is somewhat important to observe that instances have been given of the so-called valuations of *Galpin* on which the directors relied. In many cases they were no more than a simple statement of the amount which he thought might be

(1) 10 Ch. D. 118, 128.

advanced upon the particular security, and when it is remembered that a very large number of these securities were mere builders' agreements, it is very difficult to believe that the directors acted in good faith in relying upon *Galpin*, or in declaring dividends on the theory that every security was of ample value.

Another matter seriously affecting the question of the good faith of the directors occurred thus. In November, 1881, a committee was appointed to consider the cause of the overdraft at the bank. Upon this committee, Messrs. *Cavill* and *Wheeler*, two of the Respondents to this summons, appear to have acted. They reported in February, 1882, that a large quantity of property had fallen into the company's hands, of which they only received the rent, instead of the repayments, in respect of the money originally advanced thereon ; and that a portion of such property was unproductive from being unoccupied, which arose in many cases from the property being unfinished. This property was valued by Messrs. *Wheeler* and *Galpin* separately at £82,900 or thereabouts. I am informed that it stood in the company's books at a much higher figure, and that, after these valuations a dividend for the year was declared and paid, not upon the value of the properties as ascertained by actual valuation, although the directors' attention had been thus pointedly drawn to the matter, but upon the larger value contained in their books. If this was mere carelessness it was carelessness of a description so gross as, in my opinion, to make the good faith of the directors, to say the least of it, extremely questionable.

As they never in any way distinguished income from capital, or realized from estimated profit, and as they used the floating capital of the company for the actual payment of these dividends, in my opinion, even supposing that their estimate of possible profits was in any sense legitimate, they took upon themselves, by a deliberate disregard of the prohibition in the articles, the risk that these estimated profits might never be realized, and that the capital so employed could not be replaced. In short, they have paid all dividends out of capital, on the chance that profits might be realized sufficient to justify such payments, which is precisely what the articles expressly forbid to be done.

I have said enough to shew that the risk that such estimated profits might not be realized would seem to any prudent man of business a most serious one. It might easily have been anticipated that a company like this, having the command of large sums of money which they were eager to lend for the purpose of encouraging building in the city of *Oxford*, would stimulate that branch of industry to such an extent as greatly to depreciate building property, and this was what actually occurred. No provision was made for the periodical depressions in the value of property to which this country has always been subject, and, if this course of proceeding had been justified by the articles, it would have been a most improvident and reckless mode of carrying on the business of such a company. But when I find that instead of being so authorized it was explicitly forbidden, it seems to me that when the company has been brought to ruin the directors must answer for so deliberate a breach of trust.

This summons is dated the 19th of February, 1884. It has been amended by striking out the whole of the original summons except the last line, which asks for costs, and inserting as a rider a new summons, including the original claim modified in amount, and other claims not mentioned in the original summons. It came on in my Chambers on the 21st of June last, and was then adjourned into Court. A great mass of evidence has been accumulated by affidavits and cross-examination on both sides. Much of this relates to matters more or less irrelevant, and little of it has been of any use for the purpose of the question argued before me. But it would be disastrous indeed if, after two and a half years of investigation and all this costly litigation, I should find myself obliged to send the matter to Chambers, and invite further delay and an increase of these costs by directing inquiries.

The evidence stands in this way: An accountant named *Haines*, who has been in practice for eighteen years since completing his articles, eight of which he spent in the office of Messrs. *Cooper Bros.*, of *London*, has been employed by the liquidator since 1883 to prepare what he calls a deficiency account, shewing minutely the items comprising the losses and expenses of the company from the commencement of the operations. Under these instructions he has prepared a very bulky document,

which is the exhibit marked " J. Y. C.," as to which he says that
such of the figures contained therein as are not calculations were
extracted by him from the books of the company, with the
assistance of a clerk named *Hollingsworth*, who worked beside
him. And he says that the said calculations and extracts are
correctly made and are true and correct in every particular. In
a further affidavit, filed on the 13th of April, 1886, he says that
" J. Y. C." is only incomplete in that there has not been an exact
adjustment between the total of the amounts of advances and
repayments, and the balance outstanding at the date of the liquidator's appointment, but that for the purposes of a profit and loss
account it is substantially complete and accurate, and that there
is only a difference of a few hundred pounds in the balance out
of a total of more than £400,000.

159

I am told that no attempt has been made to impeach that
account or the evidence of Mr. *Haines*, as to its accuracy, although
of course the books of the company might be referred to, and
there has been ample time and opportunity to investigate it,
and accountants have been employed, and have given evidence,
on behalf of the directors upon this summons. It is usual for the
Court to act upon evidence of this kind, because of the impossibility of investigating long books of account in open Court.

Mr. *Cooper*, the accountant who has given evidence in this case
on behalf of the Respondents, in the 11th page of his cross-examination seems to admit the substantial accuracy of "J. Y. C.,"
except that it makes the mistake of apportioning the instalments
paid by the mortgagors between principal and interest by attri-
buting to interest the same amount in the case of every instalment. Now, another accountant named *Yeats*, taking the document "J.Y.C.," has compiled from it another document "J. Y. B.,"
and from this he has made a table called " J. Y. A.," in which
he shews the amount of interest in every year received since
the formation of the company, which was applicable to the payment of dividends, after providing for the necessary outgoings;
and that brings out as a result that the total amount of dividends actually paid beyond what such interest would provide
for, was £59,156 4s. 6d. This, however, was inaccurate, because
in his computation he had committed the error which I have

mentioned of treating the interest portion of such repayment as an invariable sum. This error has been corrected in an exhibit marked "J. Y. V.," the result of which is that the overpayments are reduced to £44,433 4s. 6d. This amount is arrived at after crediting all interest received in every year without setting apart any portion of it as a reserve fund to answer contingencies. The computation, therefore, if the principle is right, is as favourable to the directors as possible.

I think I am bound to accept the evidence as sufficient proof of the amount, and the only question remaining is whether it is right to treat the interest portion of the repayments actually received after providing for the current expenses and outgoings, as the only realized profit applicable to payment of dividends.

In my opinion that is right. Taking a single advance of, say of £1000 at 8½ per cent., repayable principal and interest by equal half-yearly instalments extending over fourteen years, if every instalment were punctually paid it would be the duty of the directors to treat a sufficient part of each instalment as the interest on the advance, or the unpaid portion of the advance, to that time. This amount, after providing for all current expenses and outgoings, and setting apart a sufficient sum to meet contingencies, would be properly applicable to pay a dividend; and it would be improper to pay any dividend in respect of an instalment not actually paid, because until paid no part of that instalment could be treated as realized profit.

I must, therefore, declare that the several Respondents who were directors at the time when these dividends were respectively declared, are liable for the amounts improperly paid away, as shewn by "J. Y. V.," in each year of their directorship. The liability as between the directors liable will be joint and several, and as it is founded upon a breach of trust committed by them, it must be with interest at 4 per cent., which is the usual rate in such cases. . . .

MIDLAND LAND AND INVESTMENT
CORPORATION, LIMITED

Unreported (Shorthand Reporter's notes in
Palmer, Company Precedents, 1912, pp.904-906),
(1886), Chancery

In the case of *Midland Land and Investment Corporation, Limited* (which was before Chitty, J., in Nov. 1886), the question arose whether a dividend had been paid out of capital. It appeared that the directors had employed an experienced valuer to value the assets of the corporation, which consisted of building land and ground rents and contracts and options, and had prepared a balance-sheet in which, upon the basis of this valuation, it appeared that the value of the assets exceeded the debts and liabilities by 100,000*l*., and out of the surplus thus shown the directors had carried 20,000*l*. to the dividend fund and been party to its distribution by way of dividend.

The valuer had in many cases valued the assets at more than they cost the company, and much more than they afterwards realized, and it was contended that the dividend ought not to have been paid out of profits which rested on estimate. Chitty, J., however, was of opinion that the directors were not liable, and the following extracts from his judgment (8 Nov. 1886) are of interest:—

"In declaring a dividend, in my opinion, in trading concerns, the directors are entitled to put an estimate on the value of their assets from time to time, in order to ascertain whether there is or is not a surplus remaining after providing for liabilities; and where they make those valuations from time to time on a just and fair basis, and take all the precautions which ordinary prudent men of business engaged in a similar business would do, they are entitled to treat the surplus thus ascertained as profit. But in saying that, regard must, of course, always be had to the nature of the business. I put this illustration during the argument, and I put it again. There are some trading concerns dealing in goods and the like where the turn-over is rapid, and where the goods are brought to market with the greatest facility. With a large business, and supposing the whole stock-in-trade is turned over and converted into money, in the ordinary course of dealing, within a few weeks or a few months, the directors there are entitled to put a valuation upon the goods, and to say that, having regard to the state of the market, seeing that there is no serious apprehension that the sales will not proceed in the ordinary way, they are entitled to treat, for the purpose of profit, their valuation as a basis on which they can say there is a profit shown. . . . That is a simple case. I put now one that requires more caution on the part of the directors, and that is where the turn-over is not rapid, and where the nature of the business, such as the business these directors had to deal with, is an eminently speculative one, and where they cannot bring their commodity, whether it may be ordinary goods or building land, such as in this case, into the market rapidly, and where they must wait before they realize, and where their market is liable to great fluctuations one way or the other. A case of that kind requires more skill, and more judgment, and more caution. Still I refrain from laying down, and I think I should be wrong in laying down, that, that being a trading concern, the directors were not entitled to make a just estimate of what they considered to be the profits, making all reasonable allowances, and all reasonable reductions with regard to the prospects of trade, and the particular trade in which they are engaged, and the general commercial prosperity which may, or may not, of course, have a direct or indirect bearing on their own particular business. Now, when it comes to questions of valuation, it is undoubted that, except in various rare cases, the directors are not the persons who have the skill. Their constituents, the shareholders, are not to suppose that they have the skill to make valuations which require a special knowledge and special consideration, and the directors under those circumstances pursue a right course if they instruct a gentleman of integrity—a gentleman of reputation in the town or district where he lives, a gentleman who is supposed and generally reputed to be a competent and skilled man—to make a valuation. The directors cannot go round, as I have said during the course of the argument, each man individually, and value the properties such as those which formed the staple of the assets of this company. Their valuations would be useless, and they must therefore employ a competent man. In this case the directors did employ a gentleman against whom nothing has been said. Nothing has been said as to his position, as to his skill, or as to his integrity, and the directors received from this gentleman a report and valuation which is dated the 31st January, 1880, and that formed the basis of the balance-sheet in respect of which the dividend for the year ending the 31st of December, 1879, was declared. . . .

"Upon that report he advised the directors that he had carefully surveyed and valued the whole of the properties, and he concluded his report by stating that he estimated the total present value of all the above properties at 824,747*l.*, and he said he had arrived at this valuation without any knowledge of the book debts of the corporation representing such properties. I understood that to be, that he had arrived at his conclusion without reference to the sums to be found in the company's books. . . . He says in his estimate he had not taken credit for any prospective values. Now, there I think he was right; but I think the directors were entitled to rely on what the skilled valuer told them —that he had, as he says in substance, taken the present value, and had not taken credit for any future, and in that sense speculative, value. . . . The substance, therefore, is that the dividend was to be paid out of the fund which was represented by the surplus, which had been ascertained to be 100,000*l.*, of the assets as valued over and above the liabilities. Now, it is obvious that the directors did not advise that the whole of this estimated profit—because I agree that it is an estimate, and it must be an estimate—should be dealt with. . . . I think, under these circumstances, that it would be a terrible thing for all companies, shareholders as well as directors, to say that this was not justified. . . . I think, therefore, . . . that no case is made out against the directors with regard to the dividend paid on the balance-sheet of 31st December, 1879." ·

LEEDS ESTATE, BUILDING AND INVESTMENT COMPANY v. SHEPHERD

36 L.R. Ch. 787 (1887)
Chancery

Company—Winding-up—Directors—Auditor—Payment of Dividends out of Capital—Misfeasance—Delusive Balance-Sheets—Estimated Profits—Duties and Liability of Auditor.

THIS was an action by a company now in liquidation against certain of the former directors, the representatives of a deceased director, the manager and secretary, and the auditor of the company, seeking to render them liable (amongst other things) for breach of duty in making payment of dividends out of capital and in receiving remuneration to which they were not entitled.

The company was formed in 1869 under the *Companies Act* of 1862, for the purpose, among other objects, of lending money on security.

Its articles of association provided :—

Art. 63. That when and so long as the company should pay a dividend of 5 per cent. per annum, each director present should receive 10s. for each weekly meeting of the board, and when and so long as a greater dividend should be paid, a further sum of 2s. 6d. for every additional 1 per cent. of dividend.

Art. 79. That the directors might with the sanction of the company in general meeting declare annual or half-yearly dividends "upon such estimates of accounts as the directors may see proper to recommend."

Art. 80. "No dividends shall be payable except out of the profits arising from the business of the company; but this clause shall not prevent the declaration of a dividend upon any such estimate of account as aforesaid."

Art. 86. "The directors shall cause true accounts to be kept of the estate and property of the company, of the sums of money received and expended by the company, and the matter in respect of which such receipts and expenditure take place, and of the credits and liabilities of the company. . . . ."

163

Art. 87. "Once at least in every year the directors shall lay before the company in general meeting a statement of the income and expenditure for the past year or for the past half-year, made up to a date not more than one month before such meeting."

Art. 88. "The statement so made shall shew, arranged under the most convenient heads, the amount of gross income, distinguishing the several sources from which it has been derived, and the amount of gross expenditure, distinguishing the expenses of the establishment, salaries, and other like matters. Every item of expenditure only chargeable against the year's income shall be brought into account, so that a just balance of profit and loss may be laid before the meeting. . . ."

Art. 89. "A balance-sheet shall be made out in every year and laid before the company in general meeting, and such balance-sheet shall contain a summary of the property and liabilities of the company arranged under the heads appearing in the form annexed to Table B of the *Companies Act*, 1862, or as near thereto as circumstances permit."

And arts. 98 to 101 inclusive were as follows :—

Art. 98. "Once at least in every year the accounts of the company shall be examined, and the correctness of the balance-sheet ascertained by one or more auditor or auditors."

Art. 99. "Every auditor shall be supplied with a copy of the balance-sheet, and it shall be his duty to examine the same with the accounts and vouchers relating thereto."

Art. 100. "Every auditor shall have a list delivered to him of all books kept by the company, and shall at all reasonable times have access to the books and accounts of the company ; he may at the reasonable expense of the company employ accountants and other persons to assist him in investigating such accounts, and he may in relation to such accounts examine the directors or any other officer of the company."

Art. 101. "The auditors shall make a report to the members on the balance-sheet and accounts, and in every such report they shall state whether in their opinion the balance-sheet is a full and fair balance-sheet containing the particulars required by these regulations, and properly drawn up so as to exhibit a true and correct view as to the state of the company's affairs, and, in case they have called for explanation or information from the directors, whether such explanation or information has been given by the directors, and whether it has been satisfactory; and such report shall be read together with the report of the directors at the ordinary meeting."

The capital of the company consisted of £200,000, divided into 40,000 shares of £5 each; and it carried on business from the year 1869 to the 31st of October, 1882. The business of the company consisted, to a very considerable extent, of lending money on mortgage, on the terms that the money lent, together with an addition representing interest, should be repaid by monthly instalments extending over a period of years; and one of the first transactions of the company was the advance of £600 on mortgage to secure £744 payable in six years by monthly instalments of £10 6s. 8d. Advances of this kind were termed "long loans."

The Defendant *Crabtree*, who had been formerly manager of a flax mill in *France*, was originally a director of the company; but in February, 1870, he was appointed secretary and manager of the company at a salary of £200 per annum, and in 1872 a resolution was passed that he should be paid a bonus of £25 in every year in which sufficient profits should be realized to enable the company to pay a dividend exceeding 5 per cent.

With the exception of the year 1876, when the company made a small profit of less than 5 per cent., no profit was ever earned by the company, and its business was carried on at a loss. Nevertheless the directors declared and, with the sanction of the shareholders given on the faith of the balance-sheets, paid in every year until the year 1882 dividends of between 5 and 10 per cent., and in the year 1882 a dividend of 2½ per cent.; they paid themselves the corresponding attendance fees, and they also paid bonuses to *Crabtree* as if profits had been duly realized according to the resolution.

The balance-sheets presented by the directors and laid before the shareholders in general meeting, were all prepared by *Crabtree*, and were all in the same form. They consisted of a "share account," a "cash account," a "stock account," and a "profit and loss account." The first was merely a statement as to the issued and unissued shares; the second was merely an account of receipts and payments in which capital and income were mixed up together; the third, which purported to shew the amount of "moneys lent," did not give the sum total of the advances made to borrowers, but included prospective interest in respect of "long loans" expected to be received by the company, taken at its full numerical value, although the payment of it was in fact spread over five or six years, and this account was in the view of the Court prepared solely with the view to shew a profit which did not exist; and the fourth was not a profit and loss account properly so called, but simply shewed the proposed mode of application of the balance appearing by the stock account; and in the view of the Court it must have been obvious to men of business that there was nowhere any such statement of income and expenditure as was required by the articles.

The balance-sheets for the years 1871 to 1874 contained similar items, and the amounts were arrived at in the same way. In the balance-sheet for 1874–5 an item of deferred interest was introduced, which did not however comprise the whole of the deferred or prospective interest, and from 1876 to 1880 the item of "deferred interest" fell out of the accounts, and in the item of "moneys lent" a deduction in respect of prospective interest was made, which however fell short of the full amount, and according to the evidence of the expert witnesses, was purely arbitrary. Beyond the deductions so made no allowance or provision was made for bad debts, losses, or contingencies, and all the securities of the company were taken as sufficient. It was admitted by *Crabtree* that in framing the stock account it was the practice first to take ascertained items on both sides, and then to calculate the amount required for a dividend, and to fill in the amount of moneys lent so as to make both sides balance. The balance-sheets so prepared were entered in the books and from them the accounts submitted to the shareholders were copied.

The accounts from 1870 to 1880 were audited by the Defendant *Locking*, who at the time of his original appointment was a clerk in a bank. For the performance of the duties of auditor he received at first a fee of five guineas, afterwards a fee of seven guineas, and ultimately a fee of twelve guineas. The form of certificate given by *Locking* was from 1874 to 1880 as follows:—

"I certify that I have examined the above accounts and find them to be a true copy of those shewn in the books of the company."

In the year 1870 *Locking* gave a similar certificate with the following addition : " The vouchers and receipts correspond in all cases with the payments debited. I have gone carefully into the items as shewn in the stock account, and consider the dividend which it is proposed to declare a just and fair division."

In 1871 *Locking* wrote to the directors a letter with reference to the accounts of that year, containing the following passage : " Stock account ; the making of this account devolves more particularly on yourselves and the manager than the auditors. At the same time the items were fully explained by Mr. *Crabtree*, and I do not consider the estimate overdrawn or likely to give any shareholder cause to object. Of course, it would have been better if the parties had agreed to divide nothing for a few years till a good accumulation had taken place, but a dividend is no doubt a necessity."

The company went into voluntary liquidation on the 31st of October, 1882. It was insolvent to a large extent, and this action was brought by the liquidator in the month of January, 1885, for the benefit of the creditors. The Defendants were *John Shepherd* and *John Scott*, who had been directors from the commencement of the company, the legal personal representatives of *Wm. Bilborough*, who had been a director throughout, but had died since the liquidation, *James Crabtree*, the secretary and manager, *J. B. Barry* who had been a director from May, 1875 to February, 1881, *G. H. Locking*, the auditor, and *W. Whitaker*, who was a director during a portion of the years 1881–1882.

By his statement of claim the Plaintiff sought (*inter alia*) a declaration that the Defendants were jointly and severally liable to make good sums amounting to £3394 18s. 10d. in respect of dividends paid out of capital, £540 2s. 6d. in respect of directors' fees, and £900 in respect of bonuses paid to *Crabtree*, so far as such sums were paid whilst the Defendants were officers of the company. . . .

Decimus Sturges (with him *Tindal Atkinson*, Q.C.), for *Locking*, the auditor :—

The case of Mr. *Locking* is altogether different from that of the other Defendants, and this is the first time that an auditor has ever been made a Defendant to an action of this character.

Locking was a mere servant of the directors, employed at an annual fee, which at first was only 5 guineas, and never was more than £12, and was given for the performance of work of a particular character. It was not his duty to keep the accounts, and according to the judgment of Lord *Chelmsford* in *Spackman* v. *Evans* (1) (the only case in which the duties of auditors are discussed), it is no part of the office of an auditor "to inquire into the validity of any transaction appearing in the accounts of the company." *Locking's* duty was to see that the balance-sheet represented, and was a true result of what appeared in the books of the company; and his certificate goes no further than that. The auditor is a machine for this purpose only, and a true balance-sheet from his point of view is one which shews correctly what appears in the company's books. When he finds in the books that debts are due to the company, all he can do is to ask the directors and manager whether they are good debts, and if he is told that they are, he is justified in making his certificate. He cannot go behind the books of the company. The inconvenience of requiring more from an auditor is obvious.

No fraud can be proved against *Locking*. There was no negligence on his part. He was simply deceived.

Again, the damage is too remote. It was no part of his duty to shew on what kind of estimate the dividends ought to be declared, and the improper payment of dividends was not the natural result of his acts.

Having regard to the amount of an auditor's remuneration, it would be one of the most alarming and ill-paid of occupations if he were to be liable for the remote consequences of the admission of particular items appearing, as he is correctly told in the company's books. The declaration of the dividends was not the result of anything that this auditor did, but was in fact, in the words of art. 79 of the articles of association, the directors' "estimate" of the result of the account, and of what ought to be done, having regard to the state of the books. At all events, the auditor can only be liable for the period not covered by the *Statute of Limitations*, and this being so, the Court should dismiss the earlier balance-sheets from its mind. . . .

Sir *Horace Davey*, in reply:—

Locking, the auditor, was not the servant of the directors, but of the company. According to his own admission he never looked at the articles of association of the company to see what the duties were which he was paid by the company to perform. But this is no excuse; he must be taken to have known what such duties were, and it is quite clear that he did not discharge them, and that his certificates were untrue. It is for the precise purpose of protecting a company from errors, innocent or otherwise, that an auditor is appointed. His duty is not merely to see that the balance-sheet correctly represents what appears in the books. His duty is to check the directors and manager. *Spackman* v. *Evans* (1) only shews that auditors are not the agents of the shareholders, "so as to conclude the shareholders by their knowledge of any unauthorized acts of the directors." From Mr. *Locking's* point of view a true balance-sheet was one which shewed a dividend. But here it was impossible truly to frame a balance-sheet so as to shew a profit. . . .

1887. Aug. 9. STIRLING, J. (after partially stating the facts of the case, continued) :—

There appears to me to be a fundamental difference between the two classes of acts in respect of which it is sought to fix the Defendants with liability. It is now settled by decisions of the House of Lords and Court of Appeal that the capital of a company formed under the Act of 1862 can be legally applied only for the purposes specified in the articles of association. The capital may be lost in the course of such application, and creditors or other persons dealing with the company must take that risk; but they are entitled to act on the faith that no part of the capital will be applied to any other purpose, and in particular that no part of the capital will be returned to the shareholders except in the cases and under the safeguards in and under which a reduction of capital is permitted by the various Acts of Parliament. . . .

It has now been decided that directors are trustees or *quasi* trustees of the capital of the company, and are liable as trustees for any breach of duty as regards the application of it, but when such liability is sought to be enforced it has to be determined on the facts of each particular case whether a breach of duty has been committed.

Now it is obvious that the duties of the directors of a trading company with reference to advances on security made in the course of conducting the business of a company formed for the

(1) Law Rep. 3 H. L. 171.

purpose of making such advances are totally different from those (for example) of the trustees of a settlement. The funds which form the subject of a settlement are intended to be preserved for the benefit of those who may successively become entitled to them, and it is the duty of trustees making advances out of such funds to take care that the securities they obtain are such as will expose the beneficiaries to as little risk of loss as may be. The funds embarked in a trading company, on the other hand, are placed under the control of the directors in order that they may be employed for the acquisition of gain, and risk (greater or less, according to circumstances) is of the very essence of such employment. When the advance of money on security is one of the objects of such a company the acts of directors with reference to the advances are to be judged not by the rules which have been laid down as to the investment of settled funds but (more nearly at all events) by those which regulate the duties of the managing partners of an ordinary trading firm as between themselves and those partners who do not take an active part in the conduct of the firm's business....

The case as regards the payment of dividends out of capital stands in a very different position, and the law as regards it is perhaps not yet completely settled. It follows from the decisions in *In re National Funds Assurance Company* (3) and *Flitcroft's Case* (4) that directors who make such payments either with actual knowledge that the capital of the company is being misappropriated or with knowledge of the facts which establish the misappropriation are liable as for a breach of trust. The present case does not fall within those which I have just mentioned, for I am unable on the evidence before me to arrive at the conclusion that the directors had actual knowledge of the real state of the company's affairs. I have, however, the guidance of the recent judgment of Mr. Justice *Kay* in *In re Oxford Benefit Building and Investment Society* (5), a case which was much—I may almost say exclusively—relied on by the counsel for the Plaintiff, and which, although it is not precisely identical with the present, nevertheless closely resembles it in many of its features. The judgment was given after an elaborate argument by very eminent counsel, and after full consideration by the learned Judge who

(3) 10 Ch. D. 118.
(4) 21 Ch. D. 519. (5) 35 Ch. D. 502.

decided it, and it is certainly an authority not to be departed from by a Judge of co-ordinate jurisdiction except on the clearest ground.

In that case as in the present it was contended that directors who had continually paid dividends out of capital could not be made liable unless their conduct amounted to fraud. "From that proposition," says the learned Judge, "I must express my dissent," and he accordingly held that directors who had omitted to lay before the shareholders proper accounts of income and expenditure and balance-sheets, and who acted negligently or carelessly as regards the ascertaining of the profits which they professed to divide, were jointly and severally liable to repay the sums improperly paid out of capital by way of dividends....

I now proceed to consider the facts of the present case. [His Lordship then read article 63 as to the remuneration of the directors, and articles 79 and 80 as to the declaration and payment of dividends, and continued:—] It was contended on behalf of the Defendants—and I think rightly—that upon the true construction of articles 79 and 80 dividends were payable, not (as in *In re Oxford Benefit Building and Investment Society*) out of "realized profits," or "profits tangible for the purpose of division," but (as in *Stringer's Case* (3)) out of estimated profits. In the words of Lord Justice *Giffard*, in the last-mentioned case, the dividends were to be paid "out of profits, although those profits were not profits in hand."

[His Lordship then read the other articles referred to above as to the accounts, statement and balance-sheet, and the duties of the auditor, and resumed :—]

It was in my opinion the duty of the auditor not to confine himself merely to the task of verifying the arithmetical accuracy of the balance-sheet, but to inquire into its substantial accuracy, and to ascertain that it contained the particulars specified in the articles of association (and consequently a proper income and expenditure account), and was properly drawn up, so as to contain a true and correct representation of the state of the company's affairs.

[His Lordship then stated and commented on the evidence as to the manner in which the books of the company were kept, the

(3) Law Rep. 4 Ch. 475.

statement of income and expenditure rendered, and the balance-sheets prepared, and observed :—]

In my judgment these balance-sheets were prepared by *Crabtree* simply and solely with a view to the declaration of a dividend, and not with the object of exhibiting " a true and correct view of the state of the company's affairs." It is to be observed that throughout no statement of income and expenditure, such as prescribed by arts. 87 and 88 was ever submitted to the directors or shareholders, though the accounts prepared under *Crabtree's* direction in 1880 and 1882 shew that the preparation of such statements was perfectly feasible. The reason why they were not submitted to the shareholders is not, in my judgment, far to seek. The accounts prepared for 1880 and 1882 shew a loss, and the researches of the official liquidator prove that every such statement, except that for the year 1876, must, according to the system of bookkeeping adopted by *Crabtree*, have shewn a like result.

[His Lordship then referred to the certificates of Mr. *Locking* and the letter addressed by him to the directors in 1871, and resumed :—]

Mr. *Locking* stated in his evidence that he did not during the period of his auditorship see the articles of association of the company. This statement, if true, appears to me to afford no excuse for him, for he admitted that he knew of their existence; but it would afford some evidence as to the degree of care which the directors bestowed upon the instructions given to him.

Mr. *Locking* stated in his evidence that he did not consider it part of his duty to ascertain whether the deductions made by *Crabtree* were sufficient, or on what principle they were made: and he admitted them to be arbitrary deductions which *Crabtree* considered sufficient. As regards the securities on which the moneys were lent, he appears to have simply asked whether they were considered to be fully equal to the amount stated, and to have accepted the statement that they were not only equal to, but worth more than the amount placed against them. It appears, therefore, from his own evidence that the duties of the auditor as defined by the articles of association were not in reality discharged by him.

Now the directors were all men of business, and appear to have regularly attended all the board meetings and the general meetings of the company. Each one of them says that he was ignorant of the mode in which the balance-sheets were prepared and of the inaccuracies contained in them, and that he trusted entirely to the secretary and manager and the auditor. I see no reason to doubt these statements, still the fact remains that they did not require either that *Crabtree* should present the accounts, or that *Locking* should report on them in the form and manner prescribed by the articles of association ; and I cannot but attach considerable importance to this, for if the annual accounts of income and expenditure had year after year shewn, in accordance with the fact, that no profit was earned, it is impossible to suppose that the attention of members, probably of creditors of the company, would not have been directed to the question whether or not dividends could under those circumstances be properly paid, and the crisis in the company which occurred in 1882 would in all likelihood have arisen at a much earlier period, with the probable result that either a sounder mode of carrying on business would have been adopted, or else that the company would have been wound up before great loss was incurred. . . .

Now I do not say that a trading company formed, as this was, for the purpose of carrying on speculative dealings in land, may not from time to time have valuations made of the properties which it has acquired in the course of its operations ; and I do not stop to inquire whether the permanent office of the company stands in any different position from other property. Neither do I say that where the articles of association authorize (as in the present case) the payment of dividends upon an estimate of accounts, the directors may not, in proposing or recommending a dividend, act upon the valuations so made from time to time.

The present case appears to me to be widely different. No real estimate of the value of the property was made, and I cannot think that the directors acted as prudent men of business, or as they would have done in conducting their own private affairs, in acting on the unsupported statement of their secretary as to the existence of a valuation which he never saw, and thus converting accounts which would otherwise have shewn a loss into accounts shewing a profit available for the payment of a dividend of 5 per cent.

The conclusion at which I have arrived, upon a consideration of the whole evidence, is, that the directors never exercised any judgment at all with reference to these accounts, but accepted without inquiry or verification whatever *Crabtree* and *Locking* told them. In this respect they failed, as I think, to perform the duty cast upon them by the articles of association. That duty was to cause estimates of account to be prepared, and upon those estimates to recommend a dividend. In the performance of that duty they were no doubt entitled to avail themselves of the advice and assistance of their secretary and manager, and to obtain by that advice and assistance such materials as were proper for the purpose of enabling them to decide upon the questions they had to consider; and having so done they were bound to exercise their judgment as mercantile men on the materials which they had obtained. This, in my opinion, they never did; but in truth they delegated to *Crabtree* the exercise of that judgment and discretion which it was their duty to take upon themselves. Upon the whole, although the directors were, I believe, ignorant of the true state of the company's affairs, and although I find no trace of their having acted with the view of obtaining any improper benefit for themselves, I feel compelled to hold that they have fallen short of that standard of care which, having regard to the *Oxford Case* (1), they ought to have applied to the affairs of the company in the following respects:—(1.) They never required the statement and balance-sheets to be made out in the manner prescribed by the articles; (2.) They failed properly to instruct the auditor, or, at all events, to require him to report on the accounts and balance-sheets in the mode prescribed by the articles; and (3.) they were content throughout to act on the statements of *Crabtree* without inquiry or verification of any kind other than the imperfect audit of the accounts by *Locking*. Those accounts and balance-sheets did not truly represent the state of the company's affairs; and that being so, I think that according to what is laid down in *Rance's Case* (2), the onus is laid upon them to shew that the dividends they paid were paid out of profits. This upon the evidence before me they fail to do.

The liquidator has made out a series of balance-sheets, and profit and loss accounts, such as ought to have been prepared by the directors in accordance with the articles of association. In these accounts the figures (with the exception of those relating to long loans) are in all cases taken from the books and accounts

174

(1) 35 Ch. D. 502.　　　　(2) Law Rep. 6 Ch. 104.

of the company. The instalments received in respect of long loans have been dealt with in the same way as similar payments were dealt with in the *Oxford Case*; that is, the first instalment is treated as applied in payment in the first place of the interest up to the time of payment on the whole principal sum advanced, and next in payment of part of the principal. The second instalment is treated as applied in payment in the first place of the interest on the reduced principal; and so on. The rate of interest has been ascertained in each case by an actuarial calculation, in which the principal sum lent by the company is taken to be the present value of the monthly or other instalments agreed to be paid by the borrower for a term of years. In this way according to the expert evidence on behalf of the Plaintiff (which has not been met by any expert evidence whatever on behalf of the Defendants), the very utmost sum which could in each year be properly treated as income has been ascertained. The result is that in every year a loss appears to have been incurred, and consequently in every year the dividend has been paid out of capital. It was admitted by the Plaintiff's expert witnesses that those calculations were of considerable difficulty, and required actuarial skill which the directors of the company did not and could not be expected to possess: and it was contended on their behalf that the making of an estimate of accounts for the purpose of declaring a dividend was a piece of work which could not be done by themselves, but could only be done upon the advice of skilled persons; that they took and accepted in good faith the advice of such skilled persons, viz., *Crabtree* and *Locking*, and that even if it turned out that such advice was erroneous, the directors ought not to be held liable.

In order that this argument might prevail, it would seem to me necessary that stronger evidence than that adduced by the Defendants should have been given of the fitness of *Crabtree* and *Locking* for the task assigned to them; but in truth it does not appear to me that there was any such difficulty in dealing with the accounts from a business point of view.

It possibly may have been a task of some difficulty to ascertain with mathematical accuracy the precise sums which in any year could be treated as profits, just as (to recur to an illustration which I have already made use of) it might be difficult in working a mine underground to ascertain with precision the exact boundary which corresponded to that defined on the surface, nevertheless it might be easy in the case of the mine to make sure practically that the mining operations were confined within proper limits, and possibly this result might be attained in more ways that one. In the present case the evidence convinces me that there was no difficulty at all in forming (possibly in various ways) estimates of those profits which would have been perfectly sufficient for the purposes of business men, and would have prevented the payment of dividends out of capital. Not one of the directors ever applied his mind to the formation of any such estimate. Everything was left in the hands of *Crabtree*, with the result that, according to the balance-sheets prepared by the liquidator, in a manner most favourable to the directors, a sum of £3394 18*s*. 10*d*. has been paid out of the capital of the company in the shape of dividends. The several Defendants who were directors at the time when these dividends were respectively paid are in my judgment jointly and severally liable for the amounts improperly paid away in each year of their directorship, and must (as in the *Oxford Case* (1)) be ordered to repay such amounts with interest at 4 per cent. . . .

Locking, the auditor, also appears to me to have been guilty of a breach of duty to the company. He has, however, pleaded the *Statute of Limitations* by way of defence, and the Plaintiff, without arguing the question, has admitted the validity of the plea, which will cover all the accounts except those for the years 1878–1879, and 1879–1880. In each of those years *Locking* certified that the accounts were a true copy of those shewn in the books of the company. That certificate would naturally be understood to mean that the books of the company shewed (taking for example the certificate for the year 1879) that on the 30th of April, 1879, the company were entitled to "moneys lent" to the amount of £29,515 15*s*. This was not in accordance with the fact; the accounts in this respect did not truly represent the state of the company's affairs, and it was a breach of duty on *Locking's* part to certify as he did with reference to them. The payment of the dividends, directors' fees, and bonuses to the manager actually paid in those years appears to be the natural and immediate consequence of such breach of duty; and I hold *Locking* liable for damages to the amount of the moneys so paid..

(1) 35 Ch. D. 502.

KEHOE v. THE WATERFORD AND LIMERICK RAILWAY COMPANY

L.R. 21 (Ire.) Ch. 221 (1888)
Master of the Rolls - Chancery

By the writ the plaintiff claimed, on behalf of himself and all other the preference and ordinary stockholders and shareholders of the Waterford and Limerick Railway Company :—

1. An injunction to restrain the defendant Company and the Directors thereof from paying to the preference stockholders or shareholders of said Company, or any of them, the dividends declared and passed at the General Meeting of the said Company, held on the 28th February, 1888 ;

2. An injunction to restrain the said defendant Company and the Directors thereof from applying, towards the payment of the said dividends, any portion of the earnings or revenue of the said Company during the year 1887, which ought to have been applied or set aside for the purpose of making good the wear and tear of the railway, lines, buildings, bridges, rolling stock, and other the property and capital of the undertaking, which occurred during the year 1887, and for replacing so much of same as had, during the said year, been destroyed or lost ; . . . .

THE MASTER OF THE ROLLS (after reading the notice of motion) :—

The case has been, in its discussion, narrowed to the question as it affects rolling stock, including locomotives ; and the application is founded on the statements in the affidavits of Mr. Laurence Kehoe the plaintiff, who is a shareholder, Mr. John Stevenson M'Intyre, an engineer, and Mr. Robert K. Clay, a solicitor.

Mr. Kehoe states that he has been for a number of years a shareholder in the Waterford and Limerick Railway Company, but does not say when he first became one. His affidavit says, " I at present hold in my own name 180 ordinary and £2000 4 per cent. preference shares in said Company." These ordinary shares represent £9000, so that his interest as an ordinary shareholder very considerably exceeds his interest as a preference shareholder.

. . The short case presented by the plaintiff was this :—He says that there are 119 wagons not accounted for, and that it is the duty of the Directors to replace them before they pay any dividends to the holders of preference stock.

Mr. Walker presented the case to the Court in the only way a lawyer could present it, not as a case of imprudence in the exercise of the discretion of the Directors, or unfair conduct to the shareholders; but he argued that payment of dividend under the circumstances is an act wholly *ultra vires*, and of such a character that the Court ought to grant an injunction.

Foss v. *Harbottle* (1) and many other cases have decided that the Court will not interfere with the internal management of a Company. If the shareholders are dissatisfied with the conduct of the Directors, their remedy is to take steps to appoint others in their place. The case, therefore, is reduced to the question, whether the proposed payment of the dividend is *ultra vires?* If it be illegal it is *ultra vires*, and the Court will restrain it; but if not, the Court has no jurisdiction to interfere, even though it thought the act complained of an imprudent one.

It is said that the proposed payment of a dividend is a payment not out of profits but out of capital. It cannot in strictness be said to be a payment out of capital; but if it were proposed to be made out of profits without deducting from such profits an adequate provision for the maintenance of capital, and without providing for the prior charge of replacing the rolling stock, to the extent to which it was the duty of the Directors to replace it before a dividend was paid, the question would, in my opinion, be the same.

That Directors have no right to pay a dividend out of anything but profits is clearly settled. By the Act of 1867 (30 & 31 Vict. c. 127), section 30, it is enacted that "no dividend shall be declared by a Company until the auditors have certified that the half-yearly accounts proposed to be issued contain a true statement of the financial condition of the Company, and that the dividend proposed to be declared on any shares is *bona fide* due thereon after charging the revenue of the half-year with all expenses which ought to be paid thereout in the judgment of the auditors; but if the Directors differ from the judgment of the auditors with respect to the payment of any such expenses out of the revenue of the half-year, such difference shall, if the Directors desire it, be stated in the report to the shareholders, and the Com-

(1) 2 Hare, 461.

pany, in general meeting, may decide thereon, subject to all the provisions of the law then existing ; and such decision shall, for the purposes of the dividend, be final and binding; but if no such difference is stated, and if no decision is given on any such difference, the judgment of the auditors shall be final and binding; and the auditors may examine the books of the Company at all reasonable times, and may call for such further accounts, and such vouchers, papers, and information as they think fit; and the Directors and officers of the Company shall produce and give the same so far as they can ; and the auditors may refuse to certify, as aforesaid, until they have received the same ; and the auditors may at any time add to their certificate, or issue to the shareholders, independently, at the cost of the Company, any statement respecting the financial condition of the Company which they think material for the information of the shareholders." All this was, in the present case, regularly done, and it is most important on the question of *bona fides;* but, as was decided in *Bloxam* v. *Metropolitan Railway Co.* (1), the certificate of the auditors is not conclusive. . . .

The present case however is, as I have said, not one of paying dividends out of capital. If the plaintiff's contention be correct, the Directors and Company are paying dividends out of revenue. But he says that revenue should be applied to replace capital, which was represented by wagons now worn out. I ask can such a question be a question of law, *i.e.* of *ultra vires ?* If it be, there is no room for any discretion on the part of the Directors. If a hundred wagons must be replaced, then so must fifty, or one. I am not aware of any rule of law which prevents Directors, if a part of the ordinary stock is worn out, from replacing it gradually, instead of all at once. Can there be a rule of law which excludes the discretion of Directors in such a case ? They must supply adequate rolling stock : they must repair the permanent way : they must supply wagons, trucks, engines. These are all things *quæ ipso usu consumuntur.* They may have to rebuild stations. In the time and mode of doing all these things there must be a discretion in the Directors. Of course they could not legally sell carriages to pay dividend out of the proceeds. But as to the time and extent of the execution of repairs and replacements there must be a discretion. What consequences would it lead to if they were to have no discretion in such matters ? Take, for instance, the London and North-Western

(1) L. R. 3 Ch. 337.

Railway Company. In such an immense undertaking there must necessarily always be a number of engines, wagons, and other rolling stock temporarily out of repair or entirely worn out. It is the duty of the Directors to keep up the rolling stock to a sufficient strength: it is not only a matter of prudence, but their duty. But is no dividend to be paid to the shareholders, if it can be shown that one truck has been worn out and has not been replaced by another? If the shareholders are dissatisfied with the Directors, let them take steps to remove them. The case was not presented to me as a matter of prudence; and when it is presented as a matter of law, it leads to results which I am not prepared to adopt. In reality this is an attempt by the ordinary shareholders to throw on the preference shareholders all the expense of replacing exhausted rolling stock, thus inverting their respective positions. There is no proof in the case made before me on this motion to show that capital, *as a whole*, has been lost, or that capital, even as represented by rolling stock, has been diminished in value. The evidence before me is, that since 1883 the engines are better and the wagons are better. There is no proof that inconvenience has been experienced on any single occasion from a short stock of wagons. The evidence is that of some classes of rolling stock there is a larger supply than there was in 1883. There is nothing before me to show that if you take the money value of it as a whole it is less now than it was then. On the contrary, Mr. Appleby's evidence is that it is greater. There is not a statement by any person that the traffic has been impeded or interfered with, or repressed by the want of rolling stock. There has been shown to have been considerable expenditure out of revenue to replace and renovate it.

The cases which superficially bear the nearest resemblance to the present are *Davison* v. *Gillies* (1) and *Dent* v. *London Tramway Company* (2). In *Davison* v. *Gillies* (1) the articles of association of a Limited Tramway Company provided that no dividend should be declared except out of profits; that the Directors should, with the sanction of the Company, declare annual dividends "out of profits," and that the Directors "shall set apart," before recommending a dividend, such sums as they may think proper for maintenance, repairs, depreciation, and renewals. And in *Dent* v. *The London Tramway Co.* (2), it appeared that the Company had for many years carried on their business; that there

(1) 16 Ch. Div. 347 *n*.   (2) *Ibid*. 344.

had been payments of dividends half-yearly on the ordinary shares;
but the Directors failed to set apart a reserve fund for the maintenance of their tramway, which eventually became worn out. The
Company having again declared a half-yearly dividend on their
ordinary shares, and the total sum appropriated for the dividend
being as it appeared much less than the sum required to reinstate
the tramway, it was held that the Company could only declare a
dividend out of the net profits, and that the net profits could not
be ascertained without first restoring the tramway to an efficient
condition, or making due provision for the purpose out of the
Company's assets.   An injunction was accordingly granted restraining the Company from paying the half-yearly dividend that
they had declared, but leave was given to move to dissolve the
injunction in the event of their being able to satisfy the Court
that there were profits available for the dividend.   But it was
held in *Dent* v. *The London Tramway Company* (1), which was
decided on the same facts, and in relation to the same Company, that the holders of preference shares, the dividends of which
were " dependent on the profits of a particular year only," were
entitled to a dividend out of the profits of any year after setting
aside a proportionate amount sufficient for the maintenance of the
tramway for that year only, and were not to be deprived of that
dividend in order to make good the sums which in previous
years should have been set apart by the Company for maintenance,
but which had been improperly applied in paying dividends.
Sir George Jessel said :—" I have no doubt what ought to be the
decision on this question.   What would have become of the other
action (*Davison* v. *Gillies* (2)) if it had gone to trial, and had been
fully argued out, I do not know ; but the order made on the motion
for injunction seems to have been the right order on the then
state of facts, although I think it has been assumed that I then
decided a good deal more than I did really decide.   However, the
present question is to my mind a very simple one.   There is a
bargain made with the Company that certain persons will advance their money as preference shareholders : that is, that they
should be entitled to a preferential dividend of 6 per cent. over the
ordinary shares of the Company, ' dependent on the profits of the
particular year only '—that means this, that the preference shareholders only take a dividend if there are profits for that year suffi-

(1) 16 Ch. Div. 353.   (2) *Ibid.* 347 *n.*

cient to pay their dividend. If there are no profits for that year sufficient to pay their dividend they do not get it: they lose it for ever; and if there be no profits in one year, and 12 per cent. profits the next year, they only get 6 per cent., and the other 6 per cent. goes to the ordinary shareholders. So that they are, so to say, co-adventurers for each particular year, and can only look to the profits of that year." That case is, in my opinion, on the ground on which it was decided no authority in favour of the plaintiff here, but in reality, and when taken in connexion with *Davison* v. *Gillies* (1), is distinctly favourable to the defendants' contention.

There can I think be no doubt that *Davison* v. *Gillies* (1) was well decided. The articles provided that before stating a dividend an adequate sum for maintenance and repairs should be set apart, and this was not done. To pay a dividend under these circumstances is to violate the articles. As to *Dent's Case* (2), I am by no means so clear that the decision is right; and I guard myself from appearing to decide that anything can be profits for payment of dividend to preference shareholders which would not be profits available for ordinary shareholders, if there were no preference shares. The point may be well worthy of careful consideration when it next arises. I find great difficulty in spelling out, in *Dent's Case* (2), the contract which the Master of the Rolls was able to discern there; but the question does not arise in this case. Here the clause which *Dent's Case* (2) turned on is wholly absent. The Directors of this Company *may* set apart a fund for maintenance, &c. In *Dent's Case* (2) they *must*. In the latter case there was no discretion; in the present there is no legal obligation. If *Dent's Case* (2) was well decided, it is an authority for the defendants here, while, even if not, it would not at all follow that the plaintiff in this case ought to succeed.

I am of opinion that the plaintiff's case fails, and the motion must be refused with costs.

Solicitors for the plaintiff: *Messrs. Casey & Clay.*
Solicitor for the defendants: *Mr. J. O'Connor.*

---

(1) 16 Ch. Div. 347 *n*.   (2) *Ibid.* 344.

Accounting Books Published by Garland

New Books

Ashton, Robert H., ed. *The Evolution of Behavioral Accounting Research: An Overview.* New York, 1984.

Ashton, Robert H., ed. *Some Early Contributions to the Study of Audit Judgment.* New York, 1984.

*Brief, Richard P., ed. *Corporate Financial Reporting and Analysis in the Early 1900s.* New York, 1986.

Brief, Richard P., ed. *Depreciation and Capital Maintenance.* New York, 1984.

*Brief, Richard P., ed. *Estimating the Economic Rate of Return from Accounting Data.* New York, 1986.

Brief, Richard P., ed. *Four Classics on the Theory of Double-Entry Bookkeeping.* New York, 1982.

*Chambers, R. J., and G. W. Dean, eds. *Chambers on Accounting.* New York, 1986.
Volume I: Accounting, Management and Finance.
Volume II: Accounting Practice and Education.
Volume III: Accounting Theory and Research.
Volume IV: Price Variation Accounting.
Volume V: Continuously Contemporary Accounting.

Clarke, F. L. *The Tangled Web of Price Variation Accounting: The Development of Ideas Underlying Professional Prescriptions in Six Countries.* New York, 1982.

Coopers & Lybrand. *The Early History of Coopers & Lybrand.* New York, 1984.

*Included in the Garland series Accounting Thought and Practice Through the Years.

*Craswell, Allen. *Audit Qualifications in Australia 1950 to 1979*. New York, 1986.

Dean, G. W., and M. C. Wells, eds. *The Case for Continuously Contemporary Accounting*. New York, 1984.

Dean, G. W., and M. C. Wells, eds. *Forerunners of Realizable Values Accounting in Financial Reporting*. New York, 1982.

Edey, Harold C. *Accounting Queries*. New York, 1982.

*Edwards, J. R., ed. *Legal Regulation of British Company Accounts 1836–1900*. New York, 1986.

*Edwards, J. R., ed. *Reporting Fixed Assets in Nineteenth-Century Company Accounts*. New York, 1986.

Edwards, J. R., ed. *Studies of Company Records: 1830–1974*. New York, 1984.

Fabricant, Solomon. *Studies in Social and Private Accounting*. New York, 1982.

Gaffikin, Michael, and Michael Aitken, eds. *The Development of Accounting Theory: Significant Contributors to Accounting Thought in the 20th Century*. New York, 1982.

Hawawini, Gabriel A., ed. *Bond Duration and Immunization: Early Developments and Recent Contributions*. New York, 1982.

Hawawini, Gabriel, and Pierre Michel, eds. *European Equity Markets: Risk, Return, and Efficiency*. New York, 1984.

*Hawawini, Gabriel, and Pierre A. Michel. *Mandatory Financial Information and Capital Market Equilibrium in Belgium*. New York, 1986.

*Hawkins, David F. *Corporate Financial Disclosure, 1900–1933: A Study of Management Inertia within a Rapidly Changing Environment*. New York, 1986.

*Johnson, H. Thomas. *A New Approach to Management Accounting History* New York, 1986.

*Kinney, William R., Jr., ed. *Fifty Years of Statistical Auditing*. New York, 1986.

Klemstine, Charles E., and Michael W. Maher. *Management Accounting Research: A Review and Annotated Bibliography.* New York, 1984.

*Lee, T. A., ed. *A Scottish Contribution to Accounting History.* New York, 1986.

*Lee, T. A. *Towards a Theory and Practice of Cash Flow Accounting.* New York, 1986.

Lee, Thomas A., ed. *Transactions of the Chartered Accountants Students' Societies of Edinburgh and Glasgow: A Selection of Writings, 1886–1958.* New York, 1984.

*McKinnon, Jill L. *The Historical Development and Operational Form of Corporate Reporting Regulation in Japan.* New York, 1986.

Nobes, Christopher, ed. *The Development of Double Entry: Selected Essays.* New York, 1984.

*Nobes, Christopher. *Issues in International Accounting.* New York, 1986.

*Parker, Lee D. *Developing Control Concepts in the 20th Century.* New York, 1986.

Parker, R. H. *Papers on Accounting History.* New York, 1984.

*Previts, Gary John, and Alfred R. Roberts, eds. *Federal Securities Law and Accounting 1933–1970; Selected Addresses.* New York, 1986.

*Reid, Jean Margo, ed. *Law and Accounting: Pre-1889 British Legal Cases.* New York, 1986.

Sheldahl, Terry K. *Beta Alpha Psi, from Alpha to Omega: Pursuing a Vision of Professional Education for Accountants, 1919–1945.* New York, 1982.

*Sheldahl, Terry K. *Beta Alpha Psi, from Omega to Zeta Omega: The Making of a Comprehensive Accounting Fraternity, 1946–1984.* New York, 1986.

Solomons, David. *Collected Papers on Accounting and Accounting Education. (in two volumes)* New York, 1984.

Sprague, Charles F. *The General Principles of the Science of Accounts and the Accountancy of Investment.* New York, 1984.

Stamp, Edward. *Selected Papers on Accounting, Auditing, and Professional Problems.* New York, 1984.

*Storrar, Colin, ed. *The Accountant's Magazine—An Anthology.* New York, 1986.

Tantral, Panadda. *Accounting Literature in Non-Accounting Journals: An Annotated Bibliography.* New York, 1984.

*Vangermeersch, Richard, ed. *The Contributions of Alexander Hamilton Church to Accounting and Management.* New York, 1986.

*Vangermeersch, Richard, ed. *Financial Accounting Milestones in the Annual Reports of United States Steel Corporation—The First Seven Decades.* New York, 1986.

Whitmore, John. *Factory Accounts.* New York, 1984.

Yamey, Basil S. *Further Essays on the History of Accounting.* New York, 1982.

Zeff, Stephen A., ed. *The Accounting Postulates and Principles Controversy of the 1960s.* New York, 1982.

Zeff, Stephen A., ed. *Accounting Principles Through the Years: The Views of Professional and Academic Leaders 1938–1954.* New York, 1982.

Zeff, Stephen A., and Maurice Moonitz, eds. *Sourcebook on Accounting Principles and Auditing Procedures: 1917–1953 (in two volumes).* New York, 1984.

Reprinted Titles

American Institute of Accountants. *Fiftieth Anniversary Celebration.* Chicago, 1937 (Garland reprint, 1982).

American Institute of Accountants. *Library Catalogue.* New York, 1919 (Garland reprint, 1982).

Arthur Andersen Company. *The First Fifty Years 1913–1963.* Chicago, 1963 (Garland reprint, 1984).

*Bevis, Herman W. *Corporate Financial Reporting in a Competitive Economy.* New York, 1965 (Garland reprint, 1986).

*Bonini, Charles P., Robert K. Jaedicke, and Harvey M. Wagner, eds. *Management Controls: New Directions in Basic Research.* New York, 1964 (Garland reprint, 1986).

Bray, F. Sewell. *Four Essays in Accounting Theory.* London, 1953. *Bound with* Institute of Chartered Accountants in England and Wales and the National Institute of Economic and Social Research. *Some Accounting Terms and Concepts.* Cambridge, 1951 (Garland reprint, 1982).

Brown, R. Gene, and Kenneth S. Johnston. *Paciolo on Accounting.* New York, 1963 (Garland reprint, 1984).

*Carey, John L., and William O. Doherty, eds. *Ethical Standards of the Accounting Profession.* New York, 1966 (Garland reprint, 1986).

Chambers, R. J. *Accounting in Disarray.* Melbourne, 1973 (Garland reprint, 1982).

Cooper, Ernest. *Fifty-seven Years in an Accountant's Office. See* Sir Russell Kettle.

Couchman, Charles B. *The Balance-Sheet.* New York, 1924 (Garland reprint, 1982).

Couper, Charles Tennant. *Report of the Trial . . . Against the Directors and Manager of the City of Glasgow Bank.* Edinburgh, 1879 (Garland reprint, 1984).

Cutforth, Arthur E. *Audits.* London, 1906 (Garland reprint, 1982).

Cutforth, Arthur E. *Methods of Amalgamation.* London, 1926 (Garland reprint, 1982).

Deinzer, Harvey T. *Development of Accounting Thought.* New York, 1965 (Garland reprint, 1984).

De Paula, F.R.M. *The Principles of Auditing.* London, 1915 (Garland reprint, 1984).

Dickerson, R. W. *Accountants and the Law of Negligence.* Toronto, 1966 (Garland reprint, 1982).

Dodson, James. *The Accountant, or, the Method of Bookkeeping Deduced from Clear Principles, and Illustrated by a Variety of Examples.* London, 1750 (Garland reprint, 1984).

Dyer, S. *A Common Sense Method of Double Entry Bookkeeping, on First Principles, as Suggested by De Morgan. Part I, Theoretical.* London, 1897 (Garland reprint, 1984).

*_The Fifth International Congress on Accounting, 1938 {Kongress-Archiv 1938 des V. Internationalen Prüfungs- und Treuhand-Kongresses}_. Berlin, 1938 (Garland reprint, 1986).

Finney, H. A. _Consolidated Statements_. New York, 1922 (Garland reprint, 1982).

Fisher, Irving. _The Rate of Interest_. New York, 1907 (Garland reprint, 1982).

Florence, P. Sargant. _Economics of Fatigue of Unrest and the Efficiency of Labour in English and American Industry_. London, 1923 (Garland reprint, 1984).

Fourth International Congress on Accounting 1933. London, 1933 (Garland reprint, 1982).

Foye, Arthur B. _Haskins & Sells: Our First Seventy-Five Years_. New York, 1970 (Garland reprint, 1984).

Garnsey, Sir Gilbert. _Holding Companies and Their Published Accounts_. London, 1923. _Bound with_ Sir Gilbert Garnsey. _Limitations of a Balance Sheet_. London, 1928 (Garland reprint, 1982).

Garrett, A. A. _The History of the Society of Incorporated Accountants, 1885–1957_. Oxford, 1961 (Garland reprint, 1984).

Gilman, Stephen. _Accounting Concepts of Profit_. New York, 1939 (Garland reprint, 1982).

*Gordon, William. _The Universal Accountant, and Complete Merchant . . . [Volume II]_. Edinburgh, 1765 (Garland reprint, 1986).

*Green, Wilmer. _History and Survey of Accountancy_. Brooklyn, 1930 (Garland reprint, 1986).

Hamilton, Robert. _An Introduction to Merchandise, Parts IV and V (Italian Bookkeeping and Practical Bookkeeping)_. Edinburgh, 1788 (Garland reprint, 1982).

Hatton, Edward. _The Merchant's Magazine: or, Trades-man's Treasury_. London, 1695 (Garland reprint, 1982).

Hills, George S. _The Law of Accounting and Financial Statements_. Boston, 1957 (Garland reprint, 1982).

*A History of Cooper Brothers & Co. 1854 to 1954. London, 1954 (Garland reprint, 1986).

Hofstede, Geert. The Game of Budget Control. Assen, 1967 (Garland reprint, 1984).

Howitt, Sir Harold. The History of The Institute of Chartered Accountants in England and Wales 1880–1965, and of Its Founder Accountancy Bodies 1870–1880. London, 1966 (Garland reprint, 1984).

Institute of Chartered Accountants in England and Wales and The National Institute of Economic and Social Research. Some Accounting Terms and Concepts. See F. Sewell Bray.

Institute of Chartered Accountants of Scotland. History of the Chartered Accountants of Scotland from the Earliest Times to 1954. Edinburgh, 1954 (Garland reprint, 1984).

International Congress on Accounting 1929. New York, 1930 (Garland reprint, 1982).

*Jaedicke, Robert K., Yuji Ijiri, and Oswald Nielsen, eds. Research in Accounting Measurement. American Accounting Association, 1966 (Garland reprint, 1986).

Keats, Charles. Magnificent Masquerade. New York, 1964 (Garland reprint, 1982).

Kettle, Sir Russell. Deloitte & Co. 1845–1956. Oxford, 1958. Bound with Ernest Cooper. Fifty-seven Years in an Accountant's Office. London, 1921 (Garland reprint, 1982).

Kitchen, J., and R. H. Parker. Accounting Thought and Education: Six English Pioneers. London, 1980 (Garland reprint, 1984).

Lacey, Kenneth. Profit Measurement and Price Changes. London, 1952 (Garland reprint, 1982).

Lee, Chauncey. The American Accomptant. Lansingburgh, 1797 (Garland reprint, 1982).

Lee, T. A., and R. H. Parker. The Evolution of Corporate Financial Reporting. Middlesex, 1979 (Garland reprint, 1984).

*Malcolm, Alexander. A Treatise of Book-Keeping, or, Merchants Accounts; In *the Italian Method of Debtor and Creditor; Wherein the Fundamental Principles of That Curious and Approved Method Are Clearly and Fully Explained and Demonstrated . . . To Which Are Added, Instructions for Gentlemen of Land Estates, and Their Stewards or Factors: With Directions Also for Retailers, and Other More Private Persons.* London, 1731 (Garland reprint, 1986).

*Meij, J. L., ed. *Depreciation and Replacement Policy.* Chicago, 1961 (Garland reprint, 1986).

Newlove, George Hills. *Consolidated Balance Sheets.* New York, 1926 (Garland reprint, 1982).

*North, Roger. *The Gentleman Accomptant; or, An Essay to Unfold the Mystery of Accompts; By Way of Debtor and Creditor, Commonly Called Merchants Accompts, and Applying the Same to the Concerns of the Nobility and Gentry of England.* London, 1714 (Garland reprint, 1986).

Pryce-Jones, Janet E., and R. H. Parker. *Accounting in Scotland: A Historical Bibliography.* Edinburgh, 1976 (Garland reprint, 1984).

Robinson, H. W. *A History of Accountants in Ireland.* Dublin, 1964 (Garland reprint, 1984).

Robson, T. B. *Consolidated and Other Group Accounts.* London, 1950 (Garland reprint, 1982).

Rorem, C. Rufus. *Accounting Method.* Chicago, 1928 (Garland reprint, 1982).

*Saliers, Earl A., ed. *Accountants' Handbook.* New York, 1923 (Garland reprint, 1986).

Samuel, Horace B. *Shareholder's Money.* London, 1933 (Garland reprint, 1982).

The Securities and Exchange Commission in the Matter of McKesson & Robbins, Inc. Report on Investigation. Washington, D.C., 1940 (Garland reprint, 1982).

The Securities and Exchange Commission in the Matter of McKesson & Robbins, Inc. Testimony of Expert Witnesses. Washington, D.C., 1939 (Garland reprint, 1982).

*Shaplen, Robert. *Kreuger: Genius and Swindler.* New York, 1960 (Garland reprint, 1986).

Singer, H. W. *Standardized Accountancy in Germany. (With a new appendix.)* Cambridge, 1943 *(Garland reprint, 1982)*.

The Sixth International Congress on Accounting. London, 1952 (Garland reprint, 1984).

*Stewart, Jas. C. (with a new introductory note by T. A. Lee). *Pioneers of a Profession: Chartered Accountants to 1879.* Edinburgh, 1977 (Garland reprint, 1986).

Thompson, Wardbaugh. *The Accomptant's Oracle: or, Key to Science, Being a Compleat Practical System of Book-keeping.* York, 1777 (Garland reprint, 1984).

*Vatter, William J. *Managerial Accounting.* New York, 1950 (Garland reprint, 1986).

*Woolf, Arthur H. *A Short History of Accountants and Accountancy.* London, 1912 (Garland reprint, 1986).

Yamey, B. S., H. C. Edey, and Hugh W. Thomson. *Accounting in England and Scotland: 1543–1800.* London, 1963 (Garland reprint, 1982).